THE
Screenwriting
life

THE
Screenwriting
life

THE DREAM, THE JOB, AND THE REALITY

RICH WHITESIDE

BERKLEY BOULEVARD BOOKS, New York

THE SCREENWRITING LIFE: THE DREAM, THE JOB, AND THE REALITY

A Berkley Boulevard Book / published by arrangement with the author

PRINTING HISTORY
Berkley Boulevard trade paperback edition / March 1998

The Penguin Putnam Inc. World Wide Web site address is
http://www.penguinputnam.com

ISBN: 0-425-16496-9

BERKLEY BOULEVARD
Berkley Boulevard Books are published by The Berkley Publishing Group,
a member of Penguin Putnam Inc.,
200 Madison Avenue, New York, New York 10016.
BERKLEY BOULEVARD and its logo are trademarks belonging to
Berkley Publishing Corporation.

PRINTED IN THE UNITED STATES OF AMERICA

10 9 8 7 6 5 4 3 2 1

KEPLER'S BOOKS
An Independent Bookseller Since 1955

1010 El Camino Real
Menlo Park, CA 94025
(415) 324-4321

177578 Reg 4 ID 756 10:35 pm 04/11/98

```
S SCREENWRITING LIF   1 @ 13.95   13.95
S 0425164969
DISCOUNT -     35%                 -4.88
SUBTOTAL                            9.07
TAX                                 .75
TOTAL                              9.82
CASH PAYMENT                      10.00
CHANGE                             .18
```

We'd like to hear from you.
You may leave a message for Clark Kepler
at (415) 254-7680 ext. 289.

*Dedicated to my dad, a terrific, unpublished writer
who passed away just as I completed the manuscript,
and equally dedicated to my mother for her endless love
and support and to my sisters, Margo and Letty.*

Contents

Contents

Foreword

Lew Hunter

It was not "a dark and stormy night" that started Rich Whiteside's not-so-circuitous route to the here and now of his book in your very own hands.

It was, factually, at a pleasant UCLA Writer's Block social (almost a party, but we writers are much too anal and/or guilt-ridden to have an out and out "party" since we know we really should be hunched over a keyboard, hence the word "social") that a fresh and impressive Rich Whiteside (a man you'd like your daughter to marry) asked if he could restart our Writer's Block newsletter. This epistle originated with our (my beloved Pamela's) organization of the UCLA Writer's Block at our Burbank home in 1980 with the founding brothers and sisters: David Titcher, Ron Birnbach, Rich Levier, and Diane Saltzberg. As they became wildly successful writers (but never as wild as they would like nor as successful as their parents would like), no one picked up the newsletter baton. You see, it was no longer needed to inform our screenwriting population at UCLA nor needed to stimulate the monthly social's attendance. Two to three hundred people in our modest three-bedroom manse is more than enough congeniality, loneliness alleviation, and laughs.

So, for easily twelve years, the UCLA newsletter lay fallow, extant, and thanks to Rich W., not extinct.

I swiftly replied to Monsieur Whiteside on his "may I" question, "Yes! Absolutely! Wonderful! Please! Oh my God! Fabulous!"

Rich started the phoenix process to complete "huzzas" from all; month after month of screenwriting tidbits, dimensional info, silliness, and interviews with industry heavyweights.

Then one month, I noticed at the end of his (with zero help, you understand) newsletter, a small "copyright by Rich Whiteside" notation. "Ah ha!" said I, "Grander designs are afoot." Being an occasionally taciturn Nebraskan, I dummied up and waited and waited. Two years later, Rich outed. He wanted to compile a screenwriting potpourri out of his applauded, loved, tumultuous, prodigious, terrific, and even good efforts, often known as work and writing.

Rich aggressively (a must for successful screenwriters) got a contract with my very own prestigious publishing group (the selling geniuses of *Lew Hunter's Screenwriting 434*, thank you, John Duff). And I want to add, with zero help from moi. And . . . drumroll please . . . here we are today holding *The Screenwriting Life*.

Life is a banquet and most poor sons-of-bitches are starving to death.
—Auntie Mame via the wonderful mind of playwright Patrick Dennis.

You are probably a film buff, a new or experienced screenwriter, or some dreaming, inquisitive, creative human between buff and writer. You are about to have a banquet. About to sit at a screenwriting smorgasbord table, happily bowed with a spectacular array of delicacies fit for you kings and queens of screenwriting, be ye the curious, the new or the seasoned WGA pro.

Rich Whiteside has creatively, even brilliantly, pulled together a screenwriting feast from A (animation) to S (software) and from C

(Stephen J. Cannell—TV show runner with credits too long to list) to W (Michael Werb—A-list feature screenwriter—*The Mask, Face/Off*), interviews and information about screenwriting that is unique and actually unparalleled in the arena of screenwriting information now available to you.

I once was pejorative about most screenwriting books, having been an in-the-trenches TV and feature writer since 1969. *Now, no longer. I say get them all!*

They've (we've) become like cookbooks. You take a recipe from this one and that one and the recipes/inspirations help you become the best cook or screenwriter you can be.

When I started my teaching career and let it run concurrently with my screenwriting career, I thought it was my job to help turn out Great American Screenplays. After two years, I discovered I was dead wrong! My goal should be, and now is, to push you to discover, then get closer and closer to you maxing out your potential. Get not the best me out of you, but the best you out of you.

Hence, Rich's/this book is a must for your library screenwriting paper pantheon. It's about training and doing. Formatting and the business of the "business." You have a staggering compendium of gems right here in these pages. A truly spiritually interwoven tapestry of writing treasures that will get you far more than one step closer to your own special potential.

In my *Screenwriting 434* book, I quote screenwriter Mitch Hara, who actually shrieked to one of my gathered classes: "The most amazing thing about Lew Hunter is that he *really, really* believes we *all* have talent!" I did and I do. Guilty. *You can do it*, Charlie or Lucy Brown or whatever your name.

If you're pleading/bleating, "I can't write!" I reply in my best Genghis Khan voice: "Write me a letter telling me you can't write." You *can* if you will. Our mantra at UCLA is "Writers write" period, end of statement.

From that energy, later or hopefully sooner, comes art. My beloved Pamela and I have been to *all* of the magnificent art museums in the world: the Hermitage, the Prado, the Louvre, the Metropolitan, Chicago Art Institute, et cetera. Name the name, we've been there and so have all the masters: Rembrandt, Picasso, Monet, Degas, van Gogh, and on and on and on. *They're all there.* Those fuckers were not sipping absinthe on sidewalk café tables. They got out the canvases. Art.

If you choose, you must get out the pages. Art. Some will be "shining with glory, some dripping as damp garbage" (John Steinbeck). Most importantly, some will be art *if* you *get out the pages!*

I've professionally worked with Chayefsky, Simon, Rose, Bochco, Cannell, Oliansky, Bloodworth-Thomason, Spelling, Bradbury, Sowards, Harris, Link, Levinson, and hundreds more who were perhaps less famous but as talented.

In my current professorial career at UCLA, Wilder, Ravetch, and Frank, Jr., Epstein, Nava, Roth, and Gelbart have well spoken to my graduate screenwriting classes. These special moments in time give me total courage to say *"The screenwriter is an artist."* As novelists and playwrights before, now television and, hopefully soon, motion pictures, the writer is the woman or man who starts it all.

I want to gain more respect for *screenwriters* as *artists*. Rich Whiteside's *The Screenwriting Life* gets us many steps closer to us and the public believing the truth. *The sciter is an artist!*

> *The writer is the most important person in Hollywood . . . but we*
> *must never tell the sons-of-bitches.*
> *—Irving Thalberg, 1939*

Brother and sister screenwriters of the now and then, and film buffs, and all in between, join hands and voices and LET'S TELL THEM! *WRITE ON!*

Acknowledgments

Special thanks:

To Jane Dominik, who spent countless hours helping me edit the manuscript before submission. To Lew and Pamela Hunter, who have always encouraged me and opened doors to some of my key interviews. To my sister Margo for putting up with me as a housemate. To my editor Ginjer Buchanan, who helped me pull off this book. And to Marvin Hunter, a mentor and friend who, like my father, was taken by cancer well before his time.

Introduction

As an aspiring screenwriter, my approach to breaking in to Hollywood is to start out by understanding how the system works. Granted, the system is profoundly dynamic, unpredictable, and capricious; nevertheless it has constants. And where there are constants, plans of attack can be made and executed. Here, between the transcribed reams of facts and opinions, there emerge patterns. Recognizing these patterns and understanding the ebb and flow of the business is the essence of a successful writing career.

This book contains interviews with flourishing, young writers, such as David Koepp (*Jurassic Park*, *Carlito's Way*, *The Paper*, *Mission Impossible*, etc.), who have piled major success upon major success; interviews with seasoned veterans such as Joe Gunn, who in a second career has two decades of television screenwriting experience; interviews with producers of features and television series; and interviews with two of the best screenwriting professors in the world. I have powerful, successful writer-producers who talk candidly about the politics and strategy of succeeding in the business—which can have nothing to do with talent or ability. Each person interviewed is asked to point out common flaws in scripts he or she has read, especially in new, aspiring screenwriters. (This information alone is invaluable to new writers.) Agents talk about the marketplace, how they find new clients, how they help build careers. Every interview, every chapter has something significant in it.

A vital part of each interview is that person's path to his or her current position. I found this to be as informative as direct advice on screenwriting and how the system works.

I suggest that you read the interviews several times because there is a tremendous amount of gold subtly laced in the lining.

THE
Screenwriting
life

ONE

The Draw, Drawbacks, and Politics of Hollywood Screenwriting

"*SHOW ME THE* MONEY!" *I know, it's been overused, but without a doubt, one of the biggest draws to Hollywood is the money. Top actors, writers, directors, and producers make big bucks—it's the California gold rush all over again.*

Please bear with me for the next few paragraphs. The facts set forth are to inform and to set up the interview that follows.

Here is an inkling of the money to be made. Under a Writers Guild of America contract, a freelance television writer can make $24,384 for a Firm Story and Teleplay assignment and up to $25,768 for a Story with Optional Teleplay assignment on a one-hour show. Payment is earned in two stages: the first payment is earned for delivery of the story (usually a seven- to ten-page prose story line), and the second payment is for delivery of the teleplay (the script). For half-hour shows (sitcoms) the figures are $16,579 for a

Firm Story and Teleplay, and $17,417 for a Story with Optional Teleplay (see below).

60 Minutes	(Story/Optional Teleplay)*	60 Minutes	(Firm Story & Teleplay)*
Story	$ 9,727.00	Story	$ 7,315.00
1st draft	14,437.00	1st draft	14,630.00
Final draft	1,604.00	Final draft	2,439.00
	$25,768.00		$24,384.00

30 Minutes	(Story/Optional Teleplay)*	30 Minutes	(Firm Story & Teleplay)*
Story	$ 5,526.00	Story	$ 4,974.00
1st draft	10,702.00	1st draft	9,947.00
Final draft	1,189.00	Final draft	1,658.00
	$17,417.00		$16,579.00

* This table is based on WGA rates for 5/2/97 – 5/1/98.

An Optional Teleplay simply means that the production company has the option to give the writer the teleplay assignment. They can, for example, assign the teleplay to be written internally (within the writing staff), or assign it to another freelance writer, or even stop developing it and never produce it. (See the chapter "Writing for a Dramatic Series: Star Trek.*" In that chapter, the subject is addressed by Jeri Taylor [co-creator/executive producer of* Star Trek: Voyager*] and freelance writer Jean Louise Matthias.)*

A staff writer on a series typically has a base salary per week applied against script assignments. Some writer/producers will actually get the salary plus the above script assignment money. On top of this, there are residuals; if a produced script is re-aired, there are residuals. If it's shown in foreign markets, there are even more residuals. This can add up to a lot of money. As you will discover later in this chapter, a mid-level writer-producer on a successful series can potentially make a half-million dollars a year. So, if income motivates you, you have come to the right source. But Hollywood is not a wonderland where all dreams come true, as you will read.

To get deep into the details of the WGA pay structure is not within the scope of this book. Besides, the big pay is outside of these minimums. It's complicated. I know this firsthand. I worked at Paramount Pictures in Network Television Business Affairs and turned out more contracts than I care to count. The formulas for writer-producers creating a pilot are detailed and often complicated, typically tied to whether the pilot is picked up, how many seasons the series runs, what markets it hits, foreign sales, and the person's involvement—sometimes a writer can create a pilot but not be a part of the ongoing series. IT'S COMPLICATED! That's why there are agents and literary attorneys—they are paid to know these details.

To get a better sense of the money and the politics of Hollywood, I interviewed Carleton Eastlake. He spoke to one of my UCLA screenwriting classes, and he wrote an article on this subject that hit home with me. Carl is a lawyer by trade who changed careers to pursue his lifetime desire to write. Now, he's one of those upper-level writer-producers. At the time of this interview, he was the co–executive producer of The Burning Zone.

As I always do in my interviews, I started by exploring his background.

Carleton Eastlake

What are your screenwriting background, training, and career path to date?

"I really have no formal screenwriting schooling except during the time I was a lawyer in Washington, DC, at the Federal Trade Commission. I used to go to American Film Institute (AFI) classes, which were open to the public. Anyone could sign up for them, and I have the feeling AFI did it because they hoped all these government people would take the courses and love the film industry. Anyway, I was a lawyer for eleven years, took classes at AFI, and wrote short stories, but I never had any formal training.

"The first short story I can remember writing was when I was in sixth grade. Then in seventh and eight grades in the Torrance public schools [just outside LA], I was really encouraged to write. In high school, I turned in a freshman English book report, and the teacher was so impressed he took me aside and said, 'I'm introducing you to the creative writing teacher. This book report is like a short story—you're a writer.' My high school teachers encouraged me to write, and I was published all four years in the high school literary journal—which apparently was unprecedented. However, after high school, my college teachers, for the most part, discouraged me.

"My first contact with film school came during my freshman year at Columbia. The film school had advertised for students. I was interested, so, one night, I went down to sign up. It was a block or two off campus at a rundown building. I went to the front desk, but no one answered the bell, and I thought, 'My parents are right, you can't make a living in the film industry. These people are flakes.' They put an ad in the student newspaper and couldn't even be bothered to man the sign-up desk. I turned around and walked out and never went back to film school.

"After freshman year, I transferred to UCLA because I was following a girl . . . and for other reasons. I was an English major and applied to the undergraduate fiction writing program but didn't get admitted, although I continued to write short stories for myself. At the same time, through a friend of mine who was the editor of *The Loyolan* at Loyola, I began to write film reviews for him.

"I graduated from UCLA with a B.A. in political science and went on to Harvard Law School. There I did cartoons and wrote the student newspaper for the dormitory association. I also produced the mixers, which were really nightclub events. We had a beer and wine license, and they were massive—the biggest nightclub in Boston—so, that was the beginning of my producing background.

"After Harvard, I was an attorney at the Federal Trade Commission for four years until my commissioner quit. I then decided to come back to LA and went into private practice for a year. I also flirted with going to psychology school and actually took an undergraduate major in psychology at UCLA Extension as well as applying to the professional psychology schools. But I started going to interviews and decided I didn't want to be a starving student again. I realized that I was really running away from writing. I wanted to deal with human material, and the direct way of doing that, for me, was to sit down and write—which is where my passion has been all my life.

"When I came back to LA as an attorney, I was still writing poetry and short stories for myself but didn't have a clue about how professional writers actually wrote—the process, that is. I believed these terribly fraudulent plays and movies, such as *Amadeus* or Walt Disney's *Biography of Beethoven*, that portrayed creativity as this great, shining bolt of lightning that strikes you and you suddenly write in one brilliant first draft.

"When I met my wife, [Loraine Despres], I learned the truth— that professional writing is hard work. She was just breaking into screenwriting, and I discovered that she and the writers she knew turned out a page, two pages, maybe five pages a day. And then they had to rewrite. It's a slow, very difficult process. I have since learned that the same was true for Beethoven and Mozart. Mozart would let things sit for years and then go back and do draft after draft. You also hear stories about Fitzgerald writing two famous short stories in one week. Of course, Fitzgerald in his entire life wrote, I don't know how many, thirty or forty, he certainly didn't write a thousand. As soon as I learned that professional writing is a lot of work, I started writing relatively freely.

"The more I watched Loraine write, the more enthusiastic I got about it, and I started really doing it myself by first reading screenplays and watching shows, then analyzing and breaking them down. As it turned out, William Morris represented my first spec script."

Did that sell?

"It didn't sell, nor did the agent there take me on as a client. What happened was, someone there read it and because it was a teen love story, he wanted to try and package it with Valerie Bertinelli. When that didn't work, he dropped it. But, all the same, that was very encouraging."

What was your first sale?

"I was officially represented by Gary Salt at the Paul Kohner Agency, but I was actually represented by his assistant, Mike Margules, who had just come out from New York. I remember seeing Mike for the first time. He was sitting on Gary's couch (because he didn't have an office yet) surrounded by thousands of Post-it notes— his life was organized by Post-it notes: calls, meetings, thoughts . . . Mike introduced me to a video director who had raised the money to get a script written for an independent feature film. I wrote a first draft of this rock-and-roll thriller, which the director hoped Boz Scaggs would star in. It didn't happen, but I had made a sale. On the strength of that, Mike got me a TV pitch at *V*, the science fiction series. I greatly overprepared for it, but that's what it took, and I made my first professional sale to a television show."

And was that the helicopter episode you spoke about in class, that opened up your career?

"That was the famous helicopter episode. Since the *V* script was all about a helicopter, it turned me into a helicopter writer, which landed me work on *Air Wolf*. Then I was at Universal, and after *Air Wolf* I wrote, I'm not sure in what order, but I wrote a *Murder, She Wrote* (the all-woman episode), an episode for *Dalton* (a series that never actually got on the air) and an episode for *The Equalizer*. On the strength of all this, the next year, I got a staff job on *The Equalizer*."

Were you a staff writer on *Air Wolf*?

"No. I was a freelance writer. And *Murder, She Wrote* was freelance. I did two *Murder, She Wrote*'s, and they asked me to do a third, although they never produced the second. But by that time I was on *The Equalizer*."

How did you get from staff writer to co–executive producer on *The Burning Zone*?

"I was on *The Equalizer* (a CBS show) and got kind of hot with the people at CBS—they loved my scripts. Harvy Sheppard [a senior executive at CBS], a supporter of my writing, left CBS to run Warner Bros. television. Once there, he offered me an overall deal, so I went to Warner Bros., where Harvy promptly discovered that CBS was the only network that even knew who I was. And the only people there who knew who I was were Harvy and his staff, and he'd left. He couldn't sell me anywhere.

"So I ended up as a writer-producer for Warner Bros.' *A Man Called Hawk*. After that I went on to *Midnight Caller*, which I lasted only a few weeks on. They hated me; I hated the experience and was desperately unhappy. Fortunately, I got an offer to be supervising producer on *Booker* at Cannell. So I went and did that and then did a bunch of Cannell shows and started rising in the ranks. At some point, Stephen [Cannell] talked me into going on a show called *The Exile* as the co–executive producer, and I actually ran the show. After that I sort of bounced around in the upper ranks of staff writer–producers.

"Suddenly, hour shows collapsed in the early nineties, and people were losing their houses and not making money in the business. I slipped back to being a producer at Universal Studios on the second season of *seaQuest*, for the first five episodes, and then they retroactively gave me the supervising producer title. Then the next season, I was co–executive producer of the show. I then went on to *The Burning Zone*, also for Universal. And that brings us to today."

As an attorney, were you working in entertainment law?

"No, I was at the Federal Trade Commission, vaguely connected to the media because we regulated advertising."

You mentioned that Harvy couldn't sell you because nobody knew you. Is that essential to get work in this business, to be well known?

"The industry goes much more on reputation and spin and perception and perception and personality and contacts than it does on genuine talent. You constantly see some of the biggest names in the industry writing so badly that objectively they would never be hired as a freelancer on a show—if they weren't running the show! It's actually that bad. Typically these are people who probably wrote better at some point in their career. But above a minimum level of writing skill (which is still a very high level of skill, because there is still a difference between professional and nonprofessional writing) there's almost no correlation between quality and success."

What are your thoughts on the financial draw to Hollywood?

"My experience is with the hour drama shows. I'm not familiar with half-hour sitcoms. But the industry pays an extraordinary amount of money. People running shows as executive producers often get thirty, fifty, seventy-five thousand dollars per one-hour episode or even more. And that is often guaranteed over a number of episodes, so even if not all episodes are produced, they still get paid. I have worked for executive producers who, because of that amortization, ended up getting well over one hundred thousand dollars per produced episode.

"But even freelancers for a network prime-time script get between $22,985 and $24,289 for a story and teleplay, depending on how it's ordered. And with that, they get health insurance from the Guild. You sell an hour script, and it's enough money to earn a year's health insurance from one of the best health insurance plans in the country. So, you can make a middle-class living from one sale a year, if you're lucky. Think about it. You get a contribution to a pension. You get a health plan. You get the initial $22,985 or $24,289, and, if it reruns, you get a residual payment, and then there are two further residuals from foreign sales.

"So, if you write an episode of a popular one-hour show, you may make $40,000 or $50,000 out of it. Therefore, people, in theory, can make a living off of one or two freelance script sales per year. Though, of course, those assignments are almost impossible to get."

Why is that? I mean, the perception is that the market is open.

"It's because there are so few shows. The universe of shows is pretty small. Last week, maybe there were thirty hour-rated shows in prime-time, and so it works out to some six or seven hundred episodes that are written per year. Most of these will be written by staff writers. Outside of that, perhaps, there are fifty or a hundred freelance scripts available, and the people that compete for those scripts and get them are usually staff writers who are out of work."

Who have friends who are on staff . . .

"Yeah, and helping them survive. So, it's a really tiny universe. In the course of a year, the universe I work in, including syndication, including cable, will produce forty or fifty hour-drama series, some with orders of only six episodes, though others will have orders of twenty-two or more episodes. As I said, there are only forty or fifty of them, and there are between two and five staff positions on them. That's the universe."

How about the burgeoning universe outside of prime-time television? Like cable . . .

"There's not much. Cable is really part of mainstream television. It's the same people, the same production companies. Sometimes the same budgets, but usually lower budgets. In all of cable combined, there are not many original hours produced. But the lure of Hollywood is, for those few people that actually get those jobs on those shows as producers, they're making $10,000, $20,000 or more an episode. That's a lot of money."

On top of script payments.

"That's right. On top of script assignments. A mid-level writer-producer on a network show may well make a half million dollars or more a year. They're writing four, five, or six scripts, plus they're getting $10,000, $15,000, or $20,000 for every episode of the series. And with most established shows running twenty-two or more episodes a season, it's just enormous amounts of money.

"Because of this, the talent is being sucked into Hollywood. That's what's happened to theater in America, and that's probably what has happened to novels in America. The audiences have been drawn away and the writers have been drawn away."

What about the money to be made in rewriting? It's fairly substantial, isn't it?

"In feature films, the really top writers, which at any one time are ten, twenty, or thirty total, get enormous fees to rewrite movies that are about to shoot. These movies have budgets of forty million dollars or more. And they are going to shoot in a couple of weeks, but they still have problems. Those writers will get a hundred thousand dollars a week or more to rewrite. They will sit down with some movie starring, say, Arnold Schwarzenegger that must start shooting in two weeks and they will get paid one to three hundred thousand dollars for a couple weeks' work. Now, that doesn't mean they work every week, but you don't have to work too many weeks to have a pretty good life. Of course, I don't know any of this firsthand. This comes from reading the trades and talking to agents and other writers."

Tell me about the power of writers, directors, and producers.

"Writers tend to have a lot of power in hour shows. The hour industry was really run by writers for a while. And I think it's still largely run by writers. But I think there's been a bit of a trend back to physical producers having the power as the money becomes squeezed. The people who get creative control are the people who control the bottleneck. In feature films, the bottleneck is the director.

You only want to go out and make the movie once, and it costs many tens of millions of dollars now. That means the director has the ultimate power. In series television, the bottleneck really has been in scripts. To come up with a script to shoot every seven working days is very difficult. Television shows consume an enormous amount of material really rapidly, and the bottleneck always is scripts. And because of that, writers have taken over in television.

"More recently, as the budgets have become almost impossible to shoot on, money's becoming a bottleneck; therefore physical producers seem to be getting more power again—nonwriting producers who are experts at line production. But that's not a scientific impression."

Do you mean they are reducing the number of writers they have in favor of pure producers?

"Not reducing. It's just who has the ultimate power. Who actually decides what is shot and by whom and with whom. Television tends to be run by writer-producers. They cast the shows. They hire the directors, and the directors that want to work again follow the instructions of the producer. The writer-producer has the final cut on the show. And the way to get that power is to be a writer and rise through the ranks and run a show. The power is very comparable to the power of a director in features. However, I think that now that the budgets have gotten so tight, and money and financing are becoming the problem again in TV, you see more cases of shows being run by nonwriters, which usually doesn't work very well, I might add. Those shows tend not to be very well written."

I know Don Bellisario. He's an example of a writer turned producer who creates very successful series.

"Yes, he got there as a writer. Bochco got there as a writer. David Kelley got there as a writer."

How about Dick Wolf?

"Dick Wolf absolutely got there as a writer. Aaron Spelling actually got there as a writer but stopped writing a long time ago. However, he approached the business as a writer. Stephen Cannell is the ultimate example."

In your article, you mentioned that the Writers Guild pension is the best gig in town.

"If you work for ten straight years (or satisfy a complicated formula if you don't work continuously), you vest in the pension plan. And the pensions are very high. Of course, you have to wait until you retire to collect. But it's a terrific pension plan. And I think that is, in part, because so few people qualify for a pension that the pension fund gets contributions from a lot of people that it doesn't have to pay a pension to. But, for those who manage to qualify for it, it's a great plan."

All those people who don't get the full vesting, their interest goes to those are fully vested?

"Yes, the people who do vest. And to work continuously as a writer for ten years is hard to do."

What can cause career downturns?

"Career downturns come from all sorts of things. One is when a certain style of genre show you are very successful in disappears. It's just that different people have different voices and are able to write different types of material. I'm sure, right now, life is harder for people who write formal pattern mysteries because there's only one on the air—*Diagnosis Murder*. I am sure a fair number of writers who wrote westerns fell by the wayside when television programming went from thirty westerns a week to none.

"The next thing that causes downturns is the slash-and-burn economy of the jungle that we work in. That is to say, you are so pressed for time and writing is so hard that no one does a great job of it. Ernest Hemingway has plenty of awful novels, and Joseph Eszterhas has plenty of scripts that he's never been able to sell. The point being that, studio after studio, show after show, producers can take a chance on a given writer and hire him or her. But inevitably they are likely to be just a little disappointed, because no writer is perfect. Not so disappointed that it ends the writer's career, but the writer does have to move on to the next studio, the next show. But after you've done that a while, you've burned out all your opportunities. So, you had a career for five or ten years, but you didn't move up to the next level, and people were never that happy with you and then it is over. You're out of the business. That happens.

"Also, if you don't rise to a certain level of power and prominence fast enough when you get older, people wonder why aren't you so successful? Why aren't you a producer or running your own show, if you're gray-haired now? And people become uncomfortable hiring you. I think there's plenty of ageism in the business."

You mean, if you're older, you're not in touch with the younger audiences?

"It's not only that. I'm sure that goes through some executives' heads. But what also goes through their heads is, 'Well, if these people are great writers, why haven't they succeeded by now? Why don't they have their own show or a big established reputation?' So, if you are a junior producer or a freelancer, I think it probably gets harder and harder. Some of it, though, I think, is sort of age cohort related. I think the baby boomers are going to hang on and be hiring other baby boomers for as long as possible. A lot of this age stuff came when the baby boomers had a very loud voice because there were a lot of them, but they were young, so they complained that everyone ahead of them ought to get out of their way, they were too old to do it anyway. Now that they are older, I don't know that baby boomers are going to be saying the same things. It may be a different dynamic.

"Those are reasons why careers stall out. As for restarting careers, people can write on spec. They write new genres on spec or they do a feature film on spec. They dye their hair. They lose weight. They get a new agent. Sometimes they change their names. Novelists particularly change their names. It's very common for novelists to change their names and keep writing under different names until they have a best-seller. Because they are tracked by name in the computers of the bookstores. So that's very common now. If you have a book that didn't move very well, your agent will say you have to change your name so that Crown Books or whatever chain can't tell you are the same person who only sold fifty thousand copies last time. Because they'd rather take a risk on a new writer than on one who has proven to be mid-level last time."

This leads right into my next area of interest. Tell me about the frustration of writing in Hollywood.

"The essence of writing in Hollywood is that projects are rewritten endlessly. To actually have something shot the way you wrote it is difficult. Of course, you may be doing the rewriting yourself, responding to notes from studios and networks in television and studios and directors in feature films, and it really is possible to shoot a script reflecting the writer's original intentions. I have had plenty of scripts shot with few changes, but even there, what you wrote drew on the parameters of the series. The characters and the people playing them are already established, so that confines what you are doing. It's rare that you get true art as a unique product that reflects the emotional, moral, artistic sensibility of an author. You don't get that. And things are so extensively rewritten in feature films, it's silly.

"Also you have the financial constraints. Even if you're running the show or running your own episodes, you're also writing to a budget as well as to the constraints of the cast and series premise. The number of locations and the type of locations and sets can be severely restricted by the budget. That's the reality."

Also you don't have the luxury of getting as artistic as you'd like to get?

"I guarantee that the people who loved *Starship Troopers* are not going to love the film. There's no way the film can capture the amount of didactic, expositional, philosophical discussion Heinlein put in his novel. And if it did, it would be an awful film. Film is not an intellectual medium. It's an externalized, visual medium. It can still be wonderful and powerful, but seeing Hemingway's *For Whom the Bell Tolls* as a movie is not quite the same experience as reading the novel, by far."

You've been on both ends of notes, giving and receiving. Tell me about notes.

"Whenever a script is written for an episodic television show, it goes to the studio, it goes to the network, and, of course, it goes to somebody on the show. It may just be a producer running it, it may be some supervising producer in the story department, it may go to the entire staff of the show, and everybody gives notes. If you are talking about a freelance writer, eventually the writer will get notes, probably conveyed at one time, and he or she may not even know where the notes came from.

"If you're talking about a staff writer, as the notes come in, the staff will probably hear about them. But not always. There are no rules. Every show is a different little government. A different little nation with its own practices.

"Asking for changes in the script may be as simple as just changing a line or as demanding as changing the entire script from page one. If you are running a show and you get notes from the network or the studio, you have to decide if you're going to do them or fight them. And they will decide how hard they will fight back. Ultimately the network can say, 'Do the notes or we'll not accept it for broadcast, and you'll be in breach.' However, networks almost never do that because they can't write the shows and produce them themselves. So they don't get that insistent. It's all a question of negotiation. Also you can talk them out of it; you can fight for your ideas.

"Sometimes you'll get an irrational, badly run network, and they will insist on bad notes and stand by them, and then you have real problems.

"Now one of the strengths of NBC in recent years, which I saw when I was co–executive producer of *seaQuest*, is they gave us good notes. They were smart; they made the scripts, and they edited film better. The weakness of some networks that I've seen in my twelve years is they give dumb notes and they make their shows worse. I've seen it happen."

Can you give me an example of good notes?

"The most striking note I ever got was from Warren Littlefield on a *seaQuest* script in which Littlefield recognized that I was using a Jungian psychological model for the problem in the script. And he said, 'This is the Jungian model of the Shadow and the Self, isn't it?' I said, 'Yes.' He replied, 'Don't be afraid to say it. Have the characters discuss that that is what's happening.' That was incredibly insightful and incredibly brave. And it's an example of good notes because fans loved that episode and because it had great psychological depth. It was a smart note."

Can you give me more insights into the politics of Hollywood?

"The politics of the business is really difficult. Ultimately every show tends to be a struggle for power. At a minimum, people politely try to keep control of their own material and not have the executive producer or senior producers impose their aesthetic on the material, but to do what's important to them in the script. Sometimes it's just like a family where the family members all want the keys to the car, but it's all very polite. At a minimum, you always have those types of maneuverings or aspirations. But much of the life of a television show is politics. Sometimes very bitter and very deadly politics in which people are trying to blow one another out of the water. Because one way to become king is to kill the king. So, people will try to undermine the executive producer, hoping to inherit the job. Or they will try and undermine another producer, like one of the co–

executive producers, hoping to inherit at least his or her title and influence. And people will maneuver for favor with the studio and try to stand out in the studio's eyes so the studio will give them a show or give them a better deal the next year.

"So, the politics can get very bitter in which people are trying to destroy each other's careers. And that has happened, and on some shows it can get very, very bad that way. In any event, on any show, because writing ability is just the threshold to success for everybody on the show, it is vital that they control and influence a favorable spin with their studio and their network and with the media. Because, for the most part, the senior producers are the people who determine the promotions writers get on that show, what deals they get next year, or if they get on a show next year. And sometimes they are not very good at actually reading scripts, but they are very good at sensing whether they can get along with the person while, at the same time, assessing whether the person is tough enough to run a show (in the case of an executive producer). There is a tremendous Eric Fromm sort of 'flight from freedom' on the part of many executives. They want producers who will forcefully take over a show and relieve them of the responsibility and the anxiety of having to deal with it. They like to be shut out of shows. So, they do want a producer who will yell at them and fight with them, actually. They love people to say, 'I know how to do it. Do you want me to walk out of here, or do you want me to run it and you can just leave me alone?' Because, what that translates into is, 'I take full responsibility. You don't even have to worry about it. Don't go home tonight and study a script. Go home tonight and have fun because I'm in charge and I don't want to hear from you.'

"As long as that producer then delivers a show on budget that makes a good [ratings] number, the executives are as happy as they can be. I've actually heard this from network executives in the recent past. A producer that is too eager to please or a producer who says, 'Do you want me to do this or do you want me to do that? What will make you happy? What will make you happy?', they despise those

17

producers. Because the truth is, executives don't know what's going to work. If they did, they'd be producing shows. They wouldn't be network executives, they'd be making more money producing shows and creating their own production companies if they really knew how to do it. They don't want that burden. They want someone with the vision and power and authority to do it for them.

"That's a big, big factor in the success of careers in television. The whole political spin, fad, social interaction, dominant alpha male, alpha female, personality power sort of thing is more important than being a good writer or being a good physical producer, i.e., actually being able to do a good editing job, good casting job, a good job of standing on the set, stopping the waste of money, and getting the money on the screen. All of that's less important than politics. That's the really important thing that you never see discussed. People never discuss the important aspects of reality. They just don't."

TWO

Writing for a Dramatic Series:
Star Trek

The principal distinction *between television and feature film writing is time. Feature scripts can take years to develop and bring to the big screen, whereas television series regularly develop, write, and produce twenty-two episodes or more in a nine-month season.* Star Trek, *in its various forms, is an excellent drama series to examine because (1) at the time of this writing, it's the only series that accepts unsolicited spec scripts, even from writers without agents, (2) it is one of the longest-running series of all time, and (3) because my first passion was science fiction and no show captures that better on a weekly basis than* Star Trek.

To get a comprehensive sense of what it's like to write for Star Trek, *I interviewed Robert Wolfe, story editor on* Star Trek: Deep Space Nine (DS9), *Jean Louise Matthias, a freelance writer for* Star Trek: The Next Generation (TNG), *and writing interns Michael Mack* (TNG) *and Clifford Wong* (DS9).

What are your writing background and screenwriting training?

Robert Wolfe (story editor, Star Trek: Deep Space Nine)

"Well, first off, I wrote as a kid. In college, at UCLA, I started out as an electrical engineering student but decided I didn't like engineering (it took me about two years to discover this) and I finally ended up in the film department. However, after making my first super-8 film, I decided I never wanted to make a film again. Well, that's not entirely true, but, afterwards, I took one of the screenwriting classes and liked it a lot. In fact, it was Lew Hunter's Screenwriting 434 class. I took a couple of them as an undergraduate, and then I took a little time off from school, but not very long, about a year, and came back to get my master's. Then I entered and placed second in the Goldwyn Awards with one of the first scripts I had written. So, that sort of encouraged me to keep on trying."

Jean Louise Matthias (freelance writer)

"My writing partner, Ron Wilkerson, and I come from an advertising background, and we've done all our screenwriting together. One day, we just looked at *Star Trek* and said, 'We could do that, couldn't we?' So, we bought some scripts from the original series and copied the format in a sort of monkey-see-monkey-do kind of thing. We knew nothing about structure or any of the other things you need to know before you start a script, but we forged blithely forward and sent in two spec scripts anyway . . . where they met with utter silence.

"We realized we had some things to learn, so we went to the UCLA Writer's Program and started taking classes—everything from introduction to screenwriting on up. We took different classes and shared our notes. If Ron took a class in writing the suspense thriller,

I'd take a crime writing class. If he took a directing class, I'd take one in production and distribution.

"Then we started writing feature scripts, because that was what we really wanted to do."

Michael Mack (writing intern)

"In the 1970s, I was an actor at the New Playwright's Theater in Washington, DC, which, at that time, was the only theater in the country that survived solely on previously unpublished plays by new playwrights. I was an actor there. In 1979, I entered the one-act play festival at New Playwright's Theater. They received 550 scripts from across the nation. For places one and two, they did full staged productions. I placed third; that got me a staged reading. I was in high school at the time. A year later, I wrote a full-length play. It also got a staged reading, and then I didn't write anything else for a long time."

After putting writing aside for a while, Michael was inspired by the story of Nat Turner, leader of the only successful slave rebellion in America. He then spent two years researching Nat Turner and his rebellion, and he wrote a screenplay about it.

"In 1990, I became fascinated with the story of Nat Turner and his rebellion. I also heard about the Nicholl Fellowship sponsored by the Academy of Motion Picture Arts and Sciences and decided that I wanted to enter that. So, I entered it with my historical drama.

"That year they received 3,813 scripts. For the quarterfinal round, they cut it down to 186. I made that quarterfinal round; however, I didn't make any subsequent cut."

"I learned screenwriting at first by reading screenwriting books (Syd Field's books, the famous book by William Goldman *Adventures in the Screen Trade*, et cetera) and by hanging around playwrights or anybody who had ever written a screenplay. I took an eight-week course at The Writer's Center in Bethesda, Maryland. The instructor of that particular class was a former executive of Columbia Pictures and is currently head of the television writing program at the University of Maryland.

"But, in terms of formal training as in college, as in something that goes on for a year or more, I have no such training. I picked it up all by myself; I'm self-taught."

Clifford Wong (writing intern)

"I actually started off back in '91. However, I've always been interested in writing, ever since junior high English classes and throughout high school, though I never really thought about pursuing it as a career until much later. I went to UCLA and majored in psychology. Then I went back and got a master's and Ph.D. in human factors engineering. While I was a graduate student, I started working at McDonnell Douglas Space Systems Company on the NASA Space Station program. During all this time, I never really thought about a career in writing—I've always heard about how difficult it is to make a living as a writer.

"The only formal writing classes I had were at the UCLA Extension program. I took introduction to screenwriting, I don't remember the number; then I took a second class, advanced screenwriting. Those two courses helped me quite a bit."

HOW THEY GOT TO STAR TREK

Robert Wolfe

"After I got my master's degree [in screenwriting] from UCLA, I sort of floated around trying to sell my spec stuff but didn't have a whole lot of luck with that."

What type of specs did you write?

"They were almost all the assignments that I wrote in school. I think I wrote like six or seven scripts over the course of the undergraduate and graduate school. They were all features. A couple of the scripts were science fiction, a couple were fantasy, and there was a romantic comedy, sort of a family comedy about race relations and a street gang movie that was a modern-day setting of *Macbeth*.

"So, I had those, of which one of the science fiction scripts got the most interest, but I never sold it.

Right after one potential deal fell apart, my agent had me pitch to *The Next Generation*."

Just to pitch ideas or that story?

"Pitch stories because my agent represented one of the other writers. So, it's not what you know but whom you know."

The recurring theme in Hollywood.

"Yeah, but the fact of the matter is everybody knows somebody, and, eventually if you are stubborn enough, you are going to get an opportunity.

"I wrote my first script in 1987, the one that took second place in the Goldwyn, but it took me five years to sell anything. Eventually, if you stick around in this town long enough, you get your opportunity, I think. Then you've got to make the most of it. So, I sold a pitch after about three tries—three different meetings."

Did they buy the idea, or did they let you write the teleplay?

"They let me write it, actually, but it's a more involved process. First they buy the idea, then they let you write the story. Then, if they like the story, they'll let you write the script. It's a three-step process.

"I wrote a first draft; then they took it away from me. But then they asked me to come to pitch for a new show they were doing, *Deep Space Nine*, which I didn't know anything about. They gave me some material, and I pitched to them. I didn't sell anything I pitched, but they gave me an assignment, I guess, based on the work I did for *The Next Generation*. I did that assignment, which they liked, and they hired me as a staff writer."

Jean Louise Matthias

"My writing partner, Ron Wilkerson, and I had two spec scripts completed before we started looking around for an agent. It was difficult to find someone who wanted to represent us. The agents on the Writers Guild agent list didn't seem to be interested in looking at new talent.

"In advertising, sometimes you have to make an end run in order to get the job done. If the door to an agent was blocked by our status (or lack thereof), we decided to contact producers whose work we liked. If we actually got to talk to someone, we'd send them our work and ask if they'd consider referring us to someone they respect. We got lucky. A gentleman who was at Pacific Western Productions (Gale Anne Hurd's company) liked our work and referred us to a lady who was working as a personal manager.

"We gave her a call. She liked our work, especially the first script we had done, and introduced us to the man who eventually became our agent. Since he also represented one of *Star Trek*'s story editors at the time, we decided to continue to pursue the *Trek* connection as far as it would go."

You wrote a *Star Trek* script on spec?
"We'd written two to which Maurice Hurley had said, 'Thanks, but no thanks.' They weren't bad ideas, but they weren't really right for the show.

"While our agent was trying to get some attention for our feature scripts, we pursued the connection at *Trek*. Even after you get an agent, you still have to make the calls. You still have to pursue the connections and put yourself out there. So we kept calling them, saying, 'Meet with us. Meet with us. Meet with us.'

Finally, at the end of the season, Maurice Hurley said he'd meet with us when production resumed in the summer. But, by then, he was gone. So we started bugging Jeri Taylor, the supervising producer who replaced him. She gave us an appointment to pitch, and we were in seventh heaven.

"We knew that a pitch meeting was a presentation of ideas. We worked long and hard on three ideas that we knew were so wonderful, so fresh and revolutionary, they'd probably buy all three. We went in with story outlines that must have been ten pages each, and we had sweat blood over them. In Jeri Taylor's office, we sat down and got three sentences into the first one when Jeri said, 'No, we can't do that. Next.' OK, two sentences into the second one, 'No, I'm sorry, we can't do that. Next.' Then, I think three words into the third idea, 'No, we can never do that. What else do you have?'

"Ron and I looked at each other, 'Um, well, that's it?' She said, 'OK. Thanks for coming in.' The whole meeting took, at most, seven minutes—including introductions and handshakes. We were devastated. We went down to the Columbia Bar & Grill and spent sixty dollars at the bar, trying to figure out if we were having fun yet. We just kept saying, 'Oh, my God! Oh, my God! How could she? . . . But these were . . . Oh, my god!'

"That could have been the end of it, but Ron has this saying, born of years in advertising, that you've got to 'pick yourself up off the tarp.' That's what it came down to: either we believed in ourselves, or we didn't. Just because one person said no doesn't mean that there's no one out there who will say yes. You just have to keep coming back.

"So we did. We called Jeri back and said, 'We have more ideas. Please let us come in,' and bless her, she did."

How long a time period was that before you called back?

"Three or four weeks, if memory serves. In that time, we did our homework. We found out how a pitch should be delivered. They like to hear four or five ideas, summarized like *TV Guide* log lines with a basic concept to get them hooked. If they like that, they'll want to hear more.

"We were much better prepared for our next pitch. We were still rejected, but it was a better class of rejection: we were invited to come back again with any other ideas we had.

"The third time was the charm."

Michael Mack

The Nicholl Foundation sent Michael a letter stating that his script had made it to the quarterfinals.

"I took a shot in the dark. I took the letter from the Academy. Copied it. Wrote a letter to Rick Berman of *Star Trek: The Next Generation* that stated that I wanted to write for their show.

"He wrote back that he was familiar with the competition and congratulated me for doing so well. He suggested that I send my writing sample to Jeri Taylor, who at that time was supervising producer of *The Next Generation*.

"I sent my historical drama and a sci-fi script. (Neither one having anything to do with *The Next Generation* or *Star Trek* in any way.) A year later she wrote and said that she was offering an internship at *The Next Generation*. Her offer was for late August or early September. I was fine on that. Then, months later, she asked me if I could come out sooner, and I told her about my father's condition—he was not expected to make it through the summer and that I had given up my job to help my mother take care of my dad. She told me my priorities were in the right place and that they'd keep the original offer.

"My father died, we buried him, I moved.

"I think this aspect is important because when she said she wanted me to come sooner, I thought that if I had told her about my father, that would have blown it. I thought I was coming to a place where it was all business, and where nobody cares about anybody. Instead, this lady, my boss, said, 'Your priorities are in the right place; this won't cost you anything.' That's why I mentioned it.

"Anyway, that's how I got the internship. And I have spoken with each member of the writing staff about that, and each member of the writing staff told me that I should not have got an internship that way. It was a shot in the dark."

Clifford Wong

"An opportunity came up through my brother. He told me to go put a CD system in my car, and I did, and the person who put in the stereo system knows a lot of people in the entertainment business. He put me in touch with Gene Roddenberry back in '91. It happened this way. I called and left a message for Howard, the owner of the stereo store, because my CD system was skipping. He returned my call, and I answered, 'Space Station, Clifford Wong.' Confused, Howard said, 'Gee, are you really on the Space Station, or are you a Space Cadet?' We joked around, and then he got serious about trying to help me. He said, 'Seriously speaking, Gene Roddenberry is a close customer of mine.' And I said, 'Oh, really? Well, you know, I've been trying to get a tour of the *TNG* sets for the past two years.' He goes, 'Let me see what I can do.' And from there I got in touch with Gene and his assistant, got a tour of *TNG* sets, and found out that *TNG* is the only TV show that will accept spec scripts from non-agented writers.

"Around July '91, I started writing a spec for *The Next Generation* and by October '91, it was finished, and I sent it in with a release form.

"The spec script was read, and I finally heard from the *Star Trek* offices eight or nine months later. One of the executive producers of *DS9* called me up and told me he read my script and was very impressed with it. But, unfortunately, it was written in a way that was too expensive to produce. Also, they were doing a similar story at *The Next Generation*, but they were looking for something at *DS9*; so he said, 'Based on your script, we'd like you to come in and pitch.'

"I pitched to Ira Steven Behr, Peter Allan Fields, and two interns that were with the show at that time. It was a fantastic experience. I pitched them about nine different ideas. Some of the ideas were being used, some of the ideas were already being worked on, and other ideas just couldn't work with the show. But they said, 'You know, you're in the neighborhood, you're in the ballpark. You know what we're looking for. We'd like you to come back again.'

"Since that first time, I've been back four times."

After making contact, Cliff traded tours with the Star Trek *staff. He got to see the set and Gene Roddenberry, some of the visual effects staff, and a handful of producers and writers, as well as Michael Piller, and got a tour of the Space Station mockups. Cliff kept in touch with the* TNG *people, which eventually led to a meeting with Michael Piller in which they discussed the internship.*

"Michael Piller said he would talk with Ira Behr about me interning for *DS9* and see what could be arranged.

"I kept calling *DS9* on a periodic basis to check the status of the internship, and I got positive feedback. Then Paramount's television group sent me a letter. It was written to the Writers Guild, and it basically stated that Paramount was going to hire Mr. Clifford Wong."

GOING FROM PITCH TO TELEPLAY

Robert Wolfe

"First, there are pitch meetings. Then there are story meetings where you sort of give marching orders to people, and then there are the actual story breaks where we sit down and break down, scene by scene, what the script is going to look like. It's a session where we can throw out ideas, no matter how wild they are, and see what works and what doesn't. They're very emotionally sensitive, especially for the writer who's in there. Usually, that's a tough situation for a free-lancer to be in."

ON PITCHING *TNG* & *DS9*

What constitutes a good pitch? What elements do you look for? What elements are bad?

Robert Wolfe

"It's very difficult to say what makes a good pitch. The person has to tell the story in a persuasive way, and it has to be a story that meets our needs. It has to be a story that we're not doing. Ninety percent of the time, it's not the pitch style that gets a pitch shot down; it's the content of the pitch. It either does something we don't want to do, or it's doing something we are already doing in-house. That's it. Ninety percent of the pitches fall into one of those two categories. Basically, somebody has to come up with an idea we've never thought of, and that's what we buy.

" 'Invasive Procedures,' which was like the fourth episode of the season, was a pitch that somebody sold. It was the kidnapping the worm story. 'Battle Lines' was a pitch. That was the episode in which the Kai got killed in the first season.

"So, it's very possible to sell a pitch, it's just extremely difficult. I wish I could give you more specific advice, but, if I knew the secret to giving the perfect pitch, I'd sell a lot more stories myself."

Michael Mack

"At *TNG*, they take pitches two or three days a week from agented writers. The way it works now is, one day, I believe it's Tuesday, is pitch day. At a certain point in the day, everybody, including Jeri Taylor, takes a pitch—all the staff writers in their separate offices.

"In other words, on Tuesday, at least five writers get a shot. That's the way it is right now. Sometimes they'll decide to take a pitch collectively—Jeri and the staff writers will come together and see one person. Other times, it's just catch-as-catch-can: If you want to pitch a specific individual, and if his or her assistant can fit you in, they will."

Jean Louise Matthias

"We went in to pitch with six short ideas that were basically set-ups with resolutions: What if Geordi got into this situation? How could he get out of it? The ideas were set up as teasers that (we hoped) would intrigue them enough to want to hear more. In that pitch, we sold our first episode, 'Imaginary Friend.'

"After that first sale, the door opened perceptibly. It got easier to get appointments, to present ideas, and then talk about why they would or wouldn't work, whereas, the first time was a 'No . . . next . . . No . . . next' situation with no give-and-take at all. Now the pitch sessions were becoming more productive. We learned not only how to present ideas to them, but how to get feedback out of them, such as: What kind of story do you need? What do you want? What did you like? What didn't you like? With answers to those questions, we could come back even stronger the next time."

Once your story makes it through the initial pitch, you get to brave the story break. Prior to the story break, the idea is written out in a seven-to-ten-page treatment for the staff to review ahead of time.

Clifford Wong

"As an intern, story break meetings are where you are at the white board (an erasable marker board that fills the back wall). Gathered in the room is the writing staff plus, if it's an outside writer, he or she may be involved. Here you take the story idea, or premise or treatment, and break it into a teaser and five acts. Then you break down the teaser and each act into their separate scenes. And the writers just go back and forth. And it will be: 'Teaser, beat one, INT. Ops., et cetera'—I'll be writing it down, recording it on the white board. And for each beat, they'll say who's involved, and what's happening."

Michael Mack

"In these story sessions, you tear it apart. You just rip it apart. And you see what works and what doesn't—it's a brainstorming session."

Sometimes the idea is purchased, and, as it moves into the story break session or beyond, it's suddenly dropped.

Jean Louise Matthias

"Of our six ideas sold, four have been produced. Two stories bit the dust between approval and teleplay, and that's a frustrating thing. You're going along, everyone's liking it, then it's killed. Such is life in series television, but it seems a little more abrupt for a freelancer because you're so far outside the loop."

SCRIPT CHANGES ALONG THE WAY

Every writer I talked to mentioned this constant: the story will be changed.

Jean Louise Matthias

"It's such a collaborative effort once they buy the story. For us, it's been a sliding scale as to how long we get to stay with the project.

"With our first script, 'Imaginary Friend,' we did the first draft of the story and were immediately cut off at the knees. We had no further involvement with it, and I'd say it ended up 50 percent ours on screen. As we've since learned, that's not uncommon with *Trek*, because they have a grueling production schedule, and it takes such a long time to get new writers up to speed. It didn't help that we were new and uncharted.

"For our second sale, 'Schisms,' Jeri had intended to let us take it all the way through teleplay, but, again, she ran up against time constraints and didn't feel comfortable giving it to new writers. We'd improved enough on our ability to deliver a story they could use that about 95 percent of our version finally made it to the screen. We wrote the story, but Brannon Braga did a great job with the teleplay.

"With our third sale, 'Lessons,' we went all the way and earned sole writing credit.

"The stories will change. It's inevitable in series television, especially for freelancers. The best you can hope for is to stay with the project as long as you can so you can have some input on that change."

PRODUCTION MEETINGS

All too often, the dreaded bottom line will significantly impact the scripts.

Clifford Wong

"Production meetings are where they hash out the shooting scripts. When they are beginning to shoot, they'll go through the script page by page and discuss with department heads specific requirements. For example, if they're over budget, they'll say, 'OK, we need to come under budget. What can we do?' And they'll go around to the different department heads and say, 'We gotta do this. We gotta do that. Can you make it? Can you reach it? Can you meet this?' And that's where they hash out the different budget and logistic things in order to make it shootable, within the schedule and within budget."

SCRIPT FLAWS

As part of their routine, interns read spec scripts. Typically, they'll read in excess of forty-five Star Trek *scripts in their six-week internship.*

What are the common flaws you find in the spec scripts you read?

Michael Mack

"The biggest script flaw is a writer changing *The Next Generation* characters. For example, having Picard do things that Picard would not do. Another common mistake is they don't have stories. There is a difference between an idea and a story. I would advise that, just because you have a sci-fi idea does not mean that it's a *Star Trek* idea."

Clarify for me, in the terms that you just expressed, what you mean by, they just wrote the idea?

"OK, consider *Star Trek 6: Undiscovered Country*. Praxis, the Klingon moon and main energy center, explodes. As a result the Klingons are going to run out of energy in the future, but in a future that can be calculated. So, Spock says, 'We need to make peace with the Klingons.' He brings Kirk into the situation, and they have a dinner with the Klingon chancellor, who also wants peace. It doesn't go very well, and the Chancellor returns to his ship. As soon as he is back aboard his ship, it is attacked, the Chancellor is killed, and it appears to all that the *Enterprise* did it. Kirk and McCoy are arrested, tried, and sentenced to a Klingon prison. Spock knows they are innocent and knows he has to figure out the mystery of this attack. Spock unravels the mystery (the Klingons can now fire while cloaked), then rescues

Kirk and McCoy, whose lives are in jeopardy. They deal with that, and peace is restored. Now, that's a story. That's a great story.

"Let me tell you what's a bad spec script. A bad spec script is, Praxis blows up and a Klingon survivor shows up on the *Enterprise* and tells his story over and over for sixty pages, and finally the members of the *Enterprise* crew say, 'Well, we feel sorry for you. Go back and rebuild Praxis.' They say that on page sixty-one.

"We get scripts that are little more than ideas, and a lot of the ideas that come are really only a kernel of an idea. It's not fully thought out. There is no story. That's a big mistake.

"I've also seen too many writers intent on using *Star Trek* for their own purposes. For example, scripts by people who have invented a board game. They write an episode around their board game, and the script has little to do with the *Enterprise* crew or their enemies; it's all about the game."

It's obvious that they want to market the game.

"Exactly. Which is ridiculous. You're not going to get anywhere with that.

"*Star Trek* is looking for drama that is driven by the show's characters. If you don't want to come up with an idea for one of the show's characters, don't write a spec. Don't pitch. That's it. They want stories that center around their people. So, if you don't like that, don't waste your time writing a spec."

Clifford Wong

"For *Deep Space Nine*, it could be a lot of location shots. That's one thing."

You mean, like they are setting it on Earth?

"Right. Exterior shots, for example. It's very costly, for example, to go on location to a national park to shoot a planet shot. Also, a lot of visual effects or opticals could become too elaborate. If you have a lot of opticals in the script, such as space shots, spaceship battles, or phaser battles, those are very expensive. If you include a lot of extras, that could be too elaborate. When you're writing, you've got to be aware that all those things will cost money. Production meetings opened my eyes to the practical issues of a television series and how those issues play a major role.

"I would make sure that the script itself focuses on the main characters. My spec script focused on the main *TNG* characters in addition to a guest star. That's one thing I would always keep in mind—make sure the story revolves around the regular characters on the series.

"As an intern, you read a lot of the spec scripts just to see how they are written. Many of the spec scripts don't focus on the main characters. A lot of the writers focus on a guest character and the guest character's problems. And that's not what the show's about.

"As interns, we learn that the stories and scripts written for *TNG* and *DS9* are about their characters: Troi, Picard, Riker, Geordi, Data, Worf, and Beverly, or Sisko, Odo, Dax, Quark, O'Brien, Kira, and Bashir. I mean, those are the characters. Sure, you can have guest characters, but make your main focus on the regular characters.

"Another flaw is that a lot of specs are technology driven. Meaning the writers have focused the story on the technological issues and filled the dialog with technobabble, which doesn't really push the story through on its dramatic line. It's true that there are *Star Trek* scripts with tech-talk in the scenes; in fact, some have quite a bit, but the writers and producers stress that it's not about tech stuff. It's about their characters. Too much tech just clutters up the script.

"Technobabble in some scenes, maybe a couple lines of dialogue, helps give the show its sci-fi feel. But, if technobabble takes up the entire scene, that's not a plus. It's very distracting and detracts from the reading experience. Besides, *Star Trek* has its own technical advisors who'll work out the tech stuff.

"It's also a mistake when a writer fails to get to know the show. You can tell this is the case when they misspell character names or if they mislabel a set. In my case, when I became interested in writing for *The Next Generation*, I started videotaping the shows. Then I bought the *Star Trek: The Next Generation Bible* (the *Writer's Guide*), the *Technical Guide*, and scripts from episodes I really liked. I studied the writing style and made sure I knew the show: how the characters interacted and how they spoke. Then I jumped into my spec script.

"Another common flaw deals with formats: the way they set up scenes and the appearance of the script."

Could you give me some specifics?

"I mean, how you name the set. How you designate opticals and so forth. For example, if I were writing a spec script, I would probably write something like:

EXT. SPACE—DEEP SPACE NINE (OPTICAL)
Establishing shot.

"As simple as that. Those terms used in the show's scripts would make it a lot easier for the reader. If someone has:

EXT. SPACE—DEEP SPACE NINE
DS9 is orbiting the planet, blah, blah, blah, blah, blah, blah, blah, there is this and this and that and that. An ORANGE glow of blah, blah, blah

"It's too much. I've learned that, if it's not important to the story, don't include it, unless, of course, it does have something to do with the story; otherwise, don't use it."

Jean Louise Matthias

"Our spec scripts were masterpieces of imitation. They had all the form of a professional script, including scene numbers, but none of the function.

"We broke down the sample scripts we got and concluded, for example, that the teaser is two pages and Act One is nine to eleven pages, et cetera. We then built our story around this false structure because we didn't know what really should be happening in the story that gives reason to proper structure.

"Of course, the acts are divided around the commercial breaks, but you have to make it work for the story.

"Ultimately, character development is the goal of any story, especially in *Star Trek*, where the characters are clearly defined, and the audience has had such a long, loving relationship with them. The plot is the means to that end, simply the way we make our character go through his or her changes. A plot-heavy story is boring because there's not enough life breathing through our people. You have to do your homework and really know the *Writer's Guide* (the show's bible).

"We also used to have access to *Trek*'s production guides to help us see the direction they were taking for the various characters, so we wouldn't duplicate story lines that were already in the pipeline."

ADDITIONAL THOUGHTS ON WRITING FOR *STAR TREK*

Now that you've been on staff about a year, how has your perception of screenwriting changed from what you were taught in the master's program? What things do you do differently?

Robert Wolfe

"I don't know that I do anything differently, to tell you the truth. You can write longer speeches on TV than what they let you write in class. That's about it. Lew [Hunter] will disagree with that practice, but you can write more than five lines in one speech and they won't get mad at you."

And you can probably write more dinner scenes.

"Yeah, if you watch *Deep Space Nine*, we have more scenes of people eating food. I think we've got four or five very hungry guys on this staff because there's a lot of food in this show. You can write scenes of people eating dinner, but we try not to, although we almost inevitably end up doing it. You can also write scenes of people giving big speeches and, yes, you can occasionally use stage directions or 'wrylys' [parenthetical expressions written in the dialogue to indicate how a line is delivered, e.g., wryly], although, those are things that need to be used with discretion.

"All of those are good things to avoid. I mean, those are things that tend to be used excessively by people when they are starting out, which is why I think Lew says not to use them at all. You learn not to depend on big speeches where people give the entire exposition of the story. And dinner scenes are easy, which is why they're better not to be done. It's difficult to do a dinner scene that's different from any other dinner scene that's been written before. There's an exception to every rule, but I think that's the reason Lew encourages people not to use those things—because they're easy outs."

ON THE APPROACH TO WRITING FOR *STAR TREK*

Jean Louise Matthias

"Gene Roddenberry used to say about the original series that the science fiction aspect of it was a platform for him to tell people-oriented stories that make a point. He put 1966 man in the twenty-third century because he was trying to communicate with a 1960s audience; true science fiction might posit characters that would be too far removed from us here in the twentieth century to be very interesting. But, if we can identify with the crew in that starship, with that man on the bridge, then we'll be interested in tuning in each week to see what happens to him. I try to keep that in mind. How can we make our people go through something that hits home for our audiences now, and then make it more interesting with a science-fiction angle?"

ON WRITING AS A PROFESSION

Jean Louise Matthias

"The only thing I'd like to say about writing is that you have to be persistent. You have to do your homework and learn your craft. You have to believe in yourself because no one else will until you convince them they should. You have to keep learning, you have to keep writing. YES, EVERY DAY! And you have to keep going in there. Get to know your craft, don't waste anyone's time, and eventually you'll nail it. I think it's the 'eventually' part that keeps writers from realizing their goals.

"My partner really helps me with that. We believe in each other and help keep each other's perspective. You have to be able to get support, either by yourself or through your network of friends and colleagues, or you won't be able to stick with it. After all, writers are the only ones in the industry who create something from nothing. Everyone else's job, no matter how spectacularly well they do it, is interpretive rather than creative. So, we need to learn to value ourselves so that we can teach others to value us.

"Don't decide you're going to be a writer because it's easy and glamorous. It's not. Save yourself the pain. Only be a writer if you are driven to write. You have this thing, this story machine, inside you that has absolutely got to come out. You simply must hear the applause, see your name on that screen, or have someone whose opinion you respect say, 'You've done good work.' If those things aren't enough to outweigh all the insults that you have to put up with to be a member of this profession, you won't make it. But, if they do, you'll make it . . . *eventually*. Remember, the key word is 'eventually.' And then the *Hollywood Reporter* will call you an overnight sensation."

A STAND-ALONE INTERVIEW WITH

Jeri Taylor (co-creator/executive producer)

Star Trek: Voyager

The above interviews were done in late 1993 and early 1994. In September 1996, I interviewed Jeri with the intent of integrating her thoughts with the rest. However, Jeri's interview was so well-rounded that I couldn't bring myself to break it up. So here it is as a stand-alone.

When I arrived for my interview, I was immediately ushered into Jeri's office, where she greeted me with a very warm, unassuming smile.

Upon entering, I was momentarily startled by a life-size cutout of Captain Picard and Dr. Crusher just inside her door. As I continued on inside, I was amazed to find nearly all the horizontal and vertical spaces packed with Star Trek *items—well, packed may be too strong, but the room is definitely a Trekker's candy store. Across from her desk is a couch, and the wall above it is filled with framed still photos of her numerous credits as writer, producer, and director of the television shows she has worked on over the years prior to* Star Trek.

I soon discovered that the room is more than Jeri's private office; it's the hub for all the Voyager *writing efforts. It is here that the entire* Voyager *writing staff gathers to tear apart story ideas and shape them into episodes. To that end, the whole back wall is a large white board, which, at the time of my interview, was filled in with a scene-by-scene breakdown of the next story in development.*

Jeri let me take a seat on the comfortable couch, then pulled over one of the low-back, upholstered chairs, and the interview started.

Concerning your writing background, I can see by your wall that you've done quite a bit.

"Yes, I've been in the business for close to twenty years now. I came into it rather late in life. I am of the generation that really planned only to be a homemaker and mother, which I was doing. But a divorce came along, and I was faced with the necessity of finding a way to take care of myself. For various reasons, I thought I'd give writing for television a chance. If I had known any better, I probably would not have selected this profession, but I found good reasons why it would be a good idea, and so ignorance was my friend. Luck played a part as well.

"I had been working in the business for twelve to fifteen years when a friend of mine, who's on staff here, asked if I would do a rewrite of a *Next Generation* script. I said, 'Yes,' because I was un-employed and was happy to get the work, but I didn't know anything about *Star Trek*. Literally, I had never seen an episode. On the basis of that script, which was long on people and short on sci fi, I was asked to be on staff. When I got here and realized what was truly facing me, it was a bit a of a wake-up call. I had to go to *Star Trek* school and watch all of the original series episodes and all the *Next Gen* episodes and read the technical manuals. It was overwhelming. I hadn't realized what a phenomenon *Star Trek* is. I came to realize what a well-written, intelligent, mature, human drama it is, and that was a delightful surprise to me.

"That was seven years ago, and I've been here ever since and consider myself one of the lucky people of this world to be here."

How many seasons did *Next Generation* go?
"Seven."

So, you came in at the end of the third season or . . .
"Fourth season."

Were you part of the development group for *Voyager*?
"I am one of the co-creators of *Voyager*. Rick Berman, Michael

Piller, and I are the creators of *Voyager* and are the original executive producers. Michael Piller has since gone on to do other things, so he is no longer an executive producer on the show."

Concerning spec scripts, I have found a lot of interest in the fact that *Star Trek* accepts unsolicited, nonrepresented [not represented by an agent] spec scripts. That seems like such a nightmare.

"No, it really isn't. We spend some money on readers to do it. And we receive thousands of scripts a season, but it is well worth it. It is increasingly difficult to find good ideas for *Star Trek*. We have done so many episodes now that just finding that freshness and originality becomes a tougher and tougher chore. There are some 330 episodes now that have been produced, so finding a story that works on all levels is extremely difficult. It is more than worthwhile for us to open up the floodgates for people to try and get their ideas on the air. If we get one premise a season that becomes a show, that's very worthwhile for us. I am absolutely a firm fan of the spec scripts. It serves us, it serves our fans.

"I think in the history of *Star Trek*, we've not bought more than maybe two or three complete scripts because most of them are written by inexperienced people, and, it's sad to say this, but experience does make a difference. You can't just sit down and write a script in most instances. It is a craft which takes practice and experience. So, the scripts are, generally, not that good, but contained within that script may be an idea, or maybe even a full story that will work for us. At that point, we take it over and turn it into *Star Trek*, but it is golden to us to get an idea that can become an episode."

How do spec scripts get to you personally?

"They are sent to our script department. They are read by professional readers who do coverage, a write-up on the script which includes a synopsis, comments by the reader, and a recommendation (pass, maybe, yes, very good). Then they come back to all of the staff members, and, as I said, there are thousands of spec scripts, so each of us takes a turn going through a huge stack of coverage. And based on the coverage, we decide what to do. If we read the synopsis and it's a stale, tired story we've heard and done before, we'll probably pass. If the reader recommends that the writer has some talent and may be worth considering, then we may read a portion of it and, on the basis of that, invite that writer to come in and pitch.

"So, even if that script or idea doesn't work, but there is something in that person's imagination or ability which seems worthwhile, then we may call them in to hear other ideas they might have. The third possibility is if the reader feels that there may be even a germ of something in a script that we might want to consider, we will read the script to see if we agree with that assessment. So, one can either be completely turned away (which happens with a great bulk of them), have an idea or a premise from their story bought from them, or be invited to pitch on the basis of some quality or another."

Who ultimately decides on what will be done? Is that your decision alone?

"We all read the coverage. If it is one of the other staff members and they think there is something worthwhile, they bring it to me, and I ultimately make the decision."

You mentioned earlier that a story has to hit on many levels. What do you mean by that?

"If you could categorize it, the ideal story for *Star Trek* has something that's quintessentially sci-fi going on. In other words, if we deal with a subject matter or an issue, it's not good enough for us to do it in the way contemporary series would do it. We have to give it some spin. We have to make it science fiction in some way, and finding those kind of premises or sci-fi nuts is increasingly difficult. The heart and soul of *Star Trek* are stories about people, stories about our characters, stories that reveal them in some further way, that in the course of the episode put them on the horns of a dilemma and reveal something deeper or new or interesting about the characters.

"What the fans like is the action adventure aspect of it. They love phaser fights, they love to see ships flying around and shooting at each other, and they like to see weird aliens. So, we have to have that action component as well. So, there are at least three different things going on, and all of them have to be solid. All of them have to be as fresh as we can make it."

I know that other series after three or four years have to make some major changes to keep the show fresh. How do you do that at *Star Trek*? How do you keep the show fresh?

"Well, with great difficulty. I don't know that it's a hard and fast rule that you have to do something like that or that our audience wants *Star Trek* to change. Certainly *Next Generation* didn't; there was no major disruption that happened in the middle, and they didn't suddenly have characters change or go in new directions. They simply kept telling good stories.

"We have done some discussion this year [1996] about things that we might do that will breathe life into the show. I think that it got a little serious and a little intellectual last year, and I want to bring back some fun; I want to bring back some more action and embrace the adventure a little bit more. But these are not fundamental changes; these are cosmetic changes and, in a sense, returning it to its roots in the original series rather than taking off in some new direction. I think that the reason for its enduring popularity is that they like it the way it is."

Star Trek was always within the Federation space and dealing with this known world. Suddenly *Voyager* is totally removed from this known world. What problems does that give you?

"We made that choice specifically to force ourselves into fresh storytelling. We felt the Alpha quadrant was getting very, very familiar. It certainly had that comfortable feeling of the neighborhood that you know and where you know all the aliens. And we felt we could only repeat ourselves in terms of stories, so by casting us out into a truly unknown part of space, we would recapture the flavor of the original series, truly going where people from the Alpha quadrant hadn't gone before. We knew we would have to populate it with new aliens and come up with stories that don't depend on Star Fleet, Star Bases or aliens we know. So, it was a calculated move to create originality and freshness."

After writing my original article on writing for *Star Trek*, I have gotten into a lot of discussions about *Star Trek,* and often the discussion will get into the fact that *Voyager,* while heading home, seems to keep running into the same aliens. Will that change?

"Yes, it will. I think that was a very bad mistake. The people we kept running into were the Kazon, and the same Kazon, and, yes, it created the impression that we were standing still in space. So, we won't keep alien adversaries around for two seasons anymore; it just violates the principle of the franchise."

Does that create new problems? I mean, one of the nice things about any series is a familiar villain that keeps popping back up. What unique problems does that present you?

"It's a different problem. It forces us to be creative and to come up with interesting adversaries on a more frequent basis. A lot of mileage was mined from the Romulans and the Klingons and other Alpha quadrant aliens. We do not have that luxury. We might be able to do a half season or even a season where we run into the same people two or three times. But I think we simply are not going to be able to hang onto a race of people for more than a season because it fails to make sense."

Let me jump back into writing-staff questions. How do you select a writing staff, whether on this series or any others you've worked on?

"Because *Star Trek* is unique, it proves terribly difficult to write. One can write a contemporary show brilliantly and be utterly unable to grasp what makes *Star Trek* work. I don't know why that is, but my experience over seven years proves that it is simply so. We know this because over the years many writers, even the most senior, experienced writers have crashed and burned at *Star Trek*. I brought a number of them here to try them out. Michael Piller has done the same. We have also taken recommendations from other staff members.

"So, when we find someone who can write *Star Trek*, we do anything we can to bring him or her onboard and hang onto that writer. There is no revolving door; we don't look to change. We look to find them and then make them happy. Our most recent addition is a young woman, Lisa Klink. I'm so delighted to have another female in this galaxy because it's been very lonely. She came to us virtually out of college with no industry writing experience and interned at *Deep Space Nine*. I read the first draft of an episode she wrote for them and immediately put her on staff. She could simply write it. She got it right from the beginning, and that's without experience, without maturity. She is a remarkable young woman who writes well beyond her years and her experience. Why that is so, I don't know. But, as I say, the people who can write this show are few and far between, and there's no relationship between that and their abilities to write other shows."

What was it about her first draft that got your attention?

"It read like *Star Trek*. Can I define that? No, I can't. I know it when I see it. She got the voice of the characters. She didn't fall into all the traps people fall into of either making them hokey and silly, or superficial, or drowning them in technobabble. She just had an innate grasp of what makes this series work."

What are the common flaws you find in spec scripts and stories that you reject?

"Well, those are two different questions. One is about pitching stories and one is about writing; the two are not necessarily the same. In pitching, we tend to hear the same ideas over and over again. People will come in and say, 'I've never seen this on *Star Trek*.' Well, there's probably a reason for that. Occasionally, it's the idea we haven't thought of. More often than not, it is the planet that's actually a living organism, which is a hokey idea.

"Most of the ideas, I would say, are rejected because they are silly at the core, are more like swords and sorcery than like science fiction, or they are simply familiar—nothing more than a cobbled-together plot that has elements of things we've seen and done just too many times. So, I would say, probably familiarity, predictability, and hokeyness are the main drawbacks in pitches. Frequently people come in and want to change a character completely, making him or her something other than what the person is. If we were going to change a character, we would have done it. So, we want stories and our characters to fit within the mold we've established.

"The writing of scripts is almost an ineffable thing. If I read a script that works for us, I will know it. What are the things that get it rejected? I would say, an immaturity of vision. We get a lot of spec scripts written by young people who have had few life experiences and whose idea of a really great script is just to have lots of battles and fights without having any emotional undertone, without any kind of relationship, any kind of probing of a character on a level and depth that takes it above the adolescent.

"People also get wordy. We see scripts that have people speaking in blocks, huge monologues, and if you really pay attention to our scripts, you'll see that people don't go on and on and on and on and on and on like that. Our characters don't speak in a very formal way. For some unknown reason, people impose a formality onto dialogue. Perhaps it's because some alien cultures may have a different voice to them; they think that kind of formality somehow applies to everybody's voice. So, frequently bad scripts sound like people orating or pontificating.

"Many scripts are horribly expositional. We go to great lengths to disguise exposition. In poorly written scripts, you have people just telling you everything you needed to know about Planet X in a long, dull, talky scene. There are tricks and skills of getting exposition out, and some people are not aware of that.

"So, there are many kinds of traps people fall into. They will be overly technical and just drown us in science, which we actually use pretty sparingly, and are even trying to get more spare than that. These are some of the things.''

In the first drafts of scripts, I noticed that you use ''[tech]'' for a lot of scientific/technical dialogue. Tell me about that.

"Our first draft frequently has '[tech]' in it, not because we don't have an idea of what's going on, but more that there is just a word or something that needs to go into it. We don't ask the technical person to come up with the entire thread of what's going on technically. For instance, what kind of particle beam is it? I leave that to the technical consultants. Our first drafts often have just '[tech]' in them. Then that gets discussed and filled in, and we're fine.''

Is that recommended for people writing spec scripts?

"Unless there's some critical reason, or they have some gift or extraordinary knowledge of science, I would say, 'Use it sparingly.' ''

Please tell me about the writing intern program, bringing interns to be part of the writing staff. That's rather unique in the industry.

"They're not actually part of the writing staff. It's very much a learning position. They are here to absorb. They are here to learn what goes into the writing and production of an episodic television series. They do not contribute. They are allowed to pitch, but it is not as though they've become full-blown members of the writing staff. I think some of them arrive here with that impression, and I want to correct it. They stand at the white board and take dictation for us.

"By that process, they are exposed to our method of creating and hammering out a story. They come to all the meetings, they come to the story breaks. That is probably the most valuable aspect because we sit in this room for days on end, lining out a show, scene by scene by scene by scene. And we discuss what goes on in that scene, who's in the scene, what is the goal of the scene, what is the emotional attitude of the participants of the scene, where are they when they begin it, and where are they when they end it. It's an exhausting process, but it provides a very thorough blueprint for the writer. When the writer leaves this room, he or she should have a full understanding of what is going on in that script. For the intern, hearing us come to those choices is probably the most valuable aspect."

How long does it typically take to complete a story break?

"It can range. To begin with, we always have the writer come in with a beat sheet (a short scene-by-scene, prose treatment of the story with act breaks), the kind of thing on the white board behind me so we have a starting point. Someone like Brannon Braga who has been with *Star Trek* many years usually brings in something that we may not need to put much work into. Even then, it may take a couple of long afternoon or morning sessions to make sure that we are all in tandem about what is going on in his script. What happens more with writers from the outside is that they are just way off the mark. Then it gets tough, and we can spend days in here just trying to figure it out, trying to hammer it out, trying to solve the problems. And so it's been as many as four or five days. It's a very lonely and grueling process. It is hard work. It is the most exhausting thing that we do. Your mind is just going at a fevered pitch every minute of that process. We usually don't do a full day because you just burn out after half a day of that kind of intense concentration, focus, and problem solving. So, it's just exhausting. I go home absolutely whipped right after we get out of one of these sessions."

What is the progression of an idea to teleplay?

"The writer writes a draft of the story [a treatment], then gets notes and probably writes another draft that goes to various places for approval; then we ask the writer to do a beat sheet. After we do this [referring to the board again], we write a first draft of the script. Then, if we have time, we give that writer notes and have him or her do a second draft."

How much time do you typically get between a story break session and when you go into production?

"From the time we decide an idea can become a story—we're talking about weeks of development time. A show is shot in seven days. So, clearly production eats them up a lot faster than we can produce them. We don't get much of a hiatus between seasons. When production stops, all the production people and the cast get three months. We only get two weeks, because we have to start the development process very quickly. We try to get some scripts ahead before they start shooting, but that lead time gets eaten up as the season goes on."

Do you ever reach a panic point?

"Absolutely. My metaphor has been that each season it's like starting at the top of a hill in a snowbank and you start walking downhill. Behind you, there's a little snowball forming at the top of the hill, and it starts rolling downhill heading right for you. As the season wears on, it picks up bulk and speed, and you have to move a little faster and then faster yet. By the end of the season, you're running as fast as you can, hoping that it doesn't flatten you in the middle of the road. So, we're always under stress.

"On my desk is a perfect example. I got a first draft of a script today, and it goes into prep tomorrow. Prep means that the various departments (casting, sets, props, hair and makeup, and costume) examine the script for what they will have to get ready to start shooting. Now, this script happened to be written by Joe Menosky, who is one of our staff writers. He's experienced, and the rewriting he will have to do, he'll do in a prep period. Ideally, we would have a final draft before we start to prep for a show. But that just doesn't happen. So we are just barely ahead of the snowball right now and this is show number nine out of twenty-six for the season. So, this is going to be a long season."

What are the outside influences on the writing process? Does the network have control over the scripts or stories?

"The network has no input. Contractually, they are allowed to say nothing whatsoever. It is not the nature of networks to behave like that, so they're always trying to slip in under the door and give us notes. Mostly, though, they're at a distance. The studio, of course, is allowed to have creative input and does so, but we work very congenially with them."

Who at the studio?

"From the very top levels, Kerry McCluggage (chairman, Television Group), Garry Hart (president, Network Television), and Tom Mazza (executive vice president, Current Programs). Kerry takes a very personal interest in *Star Trek*, as he should, and is a valuable friend. He is very close to us and frequently gives input. However, there is a certain frustration level because they see first drafts, and, often, by the time they get around to reading and doing their notes, we have already corrected many of the things they address. So, they often give us notes that are not germane anymore, but that's just because of the lag time. It's usually not creative differences; we are not in conflict with them at all."

Do you deal with many freelance writers who live outside Los Angeles?

"We take pitches from a great many people, but it is not a completely open policy. And we do take pitches from outside LA, which we take by phone. As a result, we've bought stories from people who live out of town. That necessitates that the writer fly to Los Angeles for the story meeting, the script meetings, and that sort of thing. Generally, that proves so cumbersome that we may work with them through the story but not go on and give them the teleplay. We take it over because we simply don't have time to deal with that and travel."

In my interview with freelance writer Jean Matthias, it appears that she and her writing partner went through a training process. This is referring to the steps they went through. For their first sale, you only bought the premise, the next time you bought the premise and they wrote the story and so on up to their fourth try, when they got to do the whole script. Can you tell me about that?

"I know what you're saying. I would say that Ron and Jean are unique in that way. It's not a process that we put new writers through. They had an ability to come up with ideas that were genuinely useful, and, for that reason, we've always been very open to them, and we were willing to give them the opportunity to do more and more. The reason it seems to be a progression is more coincidental than anything else. In other words, there might have been a time when we would have given them a script assignment on one of their earlier stories, but we didn't have time.

"Because of production schedules, we don't always have time to give a script to untried writers. Our experience is that they will likely give us a script that needs a massive rewrite and, therefore, massive changes for the departments, and we'll have only the prep week to rewrite it. That's just not something we would do to production.

"Ron and Jean seemed to go through this gradual process of giving them more and more, but that was not by design; that's just the way it worked out. As I say, I value them highly because they understand

Star Trek, and they come up with good stories for us. I don't think there is anyone else it has ever happened to.

"If somebody outside can come up with stories for us, we like to give him or her an opportunity to try a script at some point. That would be a natural process. If you can think like *Star Trek,* and you can come up with stories we can use, then, yes, we will reward you by giving you an opportunity to do a script. In what order that happens, is almost luck of the draw."

On average, how many pitches do you take in a week? And do you do that all year round?

"We never close down. Sometimes we get booked so far in advance that we just stop booking pitches for a while so we can catch up. The number of pitches varies. The least that we do is five. Every person on the staff takes one at some point during the week. I frequently take several more than that because there are people like Ron and Jean. Whenever they call, because they are tried and true and valuable and may have something to offer, I give them an appointment. We don't make them wait until the end of the line. There are other people, as well, in that category that I will allow to 'cut the line.' All the staff members have people that they have faith in and that they believe in, and they will add their pitches to their regular assignments.

"So, all said, it probably comes out to seven to ten a week. There have been times when we have taken three pitches a day because we're at the beginning of the season when we need ideas and we just say, 'Let's really gang-tackle the pitching process here and see if we can get some things going.'"

How many story ideas in a pitch?

"We put a limit on that. My rule is three pitches or twenty minutes, whichever comes first. In other words, you have twenty minutes to get three pitches out. If you hit your twenty-minute mark and you've only gotten one out, that's it. Of course, we can be flexible if there's genuine value in what someone is saying. I may even say, 'Let's talk about that and work it out.' But, usually, you know pretty quickly if someone's mind is really focused into *Star Trek* and they are going to have something of value. You don't need to listen to someone talk for an hour to find that out."

What makes a good pitch? Is it the same thing that makes a good story?

"Yes. I want a beginning, a middle, an end, an idea of the character arc, and an idea of what the conflict is. It shouldn't take more than five minutes to give me enough information to know whether the story is going to work for the show or not. That's why we say twenty minutes or three ideas. You should easily be able to do it. Some people have tended to come in here and tell us every single beat of every single scene, give us act breaks, give us dialogue—I mean, it's more information than you need at this level. It makes it hard to hear the story. Some people boil it down a little too much and come in with things like, 'What if Nelix gets stuck on an alien planet?' Well, that's maybe the first scene. I need to know more than that, I need to have more than 'What if they have to save a planet that is dying of a terrible plague?' By the way, no plague stories, I hate plague stories. I use that only to illustrate a bad example.

"You need to have a sense of the story which involves a number of elements: it involves conflict, it involves progression, it involves action. All those things have to come to play, and I need to hear enough to know that it does have a beginning, a middle, and a resolution, and not just a setup."

How much does the budget impact on a script or story?

"Budget is very important. We get a large amount of money to make this show and it's never enough. I am constantly having to rein people in because what we do is so expensive. We could make a contemporary show for half of what we spend on *Voyager*. But we have unique problems. We can't go out on Melrose Avenue and shoot a scene because it looks like modern day. If we ever go on location, we have to go someplace where there aren't structures, where it may have some vaguely alien look, and those are few and far between in Southern California. So, anytime we visit a planet, we have to build that planet on our soundstage, and construction is extremely expensive. We automatically have hundreds of thousands of dollars in set construction and set dressing. Once again, we can't put knickknacks and artifacts from today; we have to manufacture all those so they look futuristic.

"We have standard sets like the bridge, shuttle craft, and so on, but we have to limit the building of additional sets to maybe one sizable set for each episode, like a town square, a marketplace, an office or bedroom, et cetera. That's about all we can afford to build, so we structure the planet part of each story around those sets. It's not easy.

"Another extremely big expense is opticals."

What do you mean by 'opticals'?

"Opticals are all those effects people love to see, like *Voyager* flying through space, phaser fire, and dematerializations. They're all very costly. Every time you see *Voyager* flying through space, clearly we don't have an actual, huge spaceship flying around up there, so we have a model. And that is an optical effect created by putting the shot of *Voyager* against a star field or a warp star field. Phaser fire is an animated process that has to be done by our post-production department—it takes hours in an animating bay to achieve. It's extremely time intensive to get the quality that we insist on. We do some computer graphic imaging now, but we don't do it on a level that looks cartooney. It has to look real, and that is costly.

"Another expense most people overlook are aliens. We have to create a costume for each alien; we don't go to Saks and buy clothes. Everything has to be designed and manufactured. If we do a prosthetic, that requires not only creating that prosthetic but a makeup person to put it on. If we have a special hairdo, that requires a hairdresser. And if we want thirty aliens, which doesn't go very far, and we always want more, but every one of those aliens needs a costume, and needs a hair and a makeup person. Just for that one person. So that's sixty people that have to be added to the crew that week because all of them have to be ready at the same time and it takes hours to put on that stuff.

"So, it's monumentally, logistically overwhelming and costly. We often start by cutting back and end up with fifteen instead of thirty. Still, that's fifteen extra people you have to put on for hair and fifteen extra people you have to put on for makeup plus fifteen $3,000 costumes that you have to build. It's just stunning the way costs just mount up."

How does that affect the writing?

"We can't just say with abandon, 'Let's go to a planet and have a battle.' We can't say, 'Let's go to a planet where we run into this person here and then run into that person somewhere else.' We can only build two sets. So we have to make our story fit into two sets."

Is that part of the story break session?

"Absolutely."

How do you handle episodes you've wanted to do, but there isn't the budget for it?

"We handle this by doing under-budget shows. If we go to a planet, we know it's going to be over budget. There's no way to do it without being over budget, so, we say, 'OK, we're over budget by $100,000 or $200,000.' That means we have to make up that shortfall at some point during season. So, we do bottle shows. That is, shows that take place entirely on the ship with minimal opticals and extras."

Any last thoughts for those honing their screenwriting skills?

"To people who want to write, I advise, broaden your experiences, rather than compartmentalizing them or narrowing them. Expose yourself to as many of life's experiences as you can, to as much varied education as you can because the more you take in, the better what you put out will be. So, I say, don't specialize, don't compartmentalize; generalize.

"Fundamentally, I believe that one who wants to write should do several things. I've mentioned a couple of them. I believe firmly in the idea of generalizing your education and your life experiences, and exposing yourself to as much knowledge, information, and living as you possibly can. I was an English major, a liberal arts major in college, and I don't believe in film school. I believe in something much broader. I believe writers get better as they mature because they simply have more life experiences to draw from, and, after all, when you are in front of the blank page, whether at the computer or at the typewriter, whatever medium, you are digging into yourself in order to write. And the more that's in you, the richer your writing will be.

"The second thing is, you have to write. I like to use the analogy of music. If you want to become a professional violinist, you can't expect to achieve that in a few months or even a few years, nor can you expect someone to pay you to play concerts in that short time. The violin requires practice and dedication and commitment. Writing is the same. There are rare exceptions, but, in general, I think too many people believe anyone can write. That anyone can sit down and do just as well as those who are getting paid for it. Largely that's not true. Writing is a craft. There are things to learn about it. I am still learning every day. Every time you write something, you learn more. It needs to be studied, and it needs to be practiced, and I believe that people who want to write should write and not talk about writing."

LAST NOTE

If you want to write and submit a *Star Trek* spec script, the *Writer's Guide* and sample scripts can be ordered through Lincoln Enterprises at (818) 989-4978. Submission guidelines can be obtained through the Paramount Pictures Star Trek hot line at (213) 956-8301. Also, there is a web site at www.roddenberry.com.

THREE

Writing for a Sitcom Series:
Wings

Writing for a sitcom series is a process that lies somewhere between preparing for a stage play and a standard film. Personally, I can't think of any writing job more demanding than having to be funny on a day-in-day-out basis. Wings is an excellent show to examine because it's a very successful, long-running series. That means, as a team, they have done a lot of things right for a long time.

I searched for writers with experience spanning a number of different sitcom series and was extremely fortunate when the executive producers of Wings agreed to be interviewed: Howard Gewirtz, Ian Gurvitz, and Mark Reisman. I didn't realize there was more than one executive producer on the show until Howard informed me, "There are three executive producers on Wings; actually there are six, if you count Peter Casey, David Angell and David Lee (the creators). But the running of the show is left to Mark Reisman, myself, and Ian Gurvitz (whose name, incidentally, is similar to mine *but there's no relation). Casey, Angell and Lee, of course, do* Frasier—*that's where their energies go."*

The interviews paint a clear picture of what it's like to write for Wings, *but they also provide a glimpse into the world of sitcom writing outside of* Wings.

Howard Gewirtz (executive producer)

"I started on a show called *Busting Loose* starring Adam Larken. I also worked on *Bosom Buddies*. But, my *big* break came when I was a story editor and then a writer-producer on *Taxi*. These are the shows most people would know. In '84, I co-created a show with Glen and Les Charles called *All Is Forgiven*. I did a show with Steve Martin and Martin Mull called *Domestic Life*. I've written for the *Tracey Ullman Show* and *The Simpsons*, but *Wings* is the show I've been associated with the longest."

How long have you been with *Wings*?
"This is my fourth season."

So you started out your sitcom writing career as a staff writer, then worked your way through writing-producing to now executive produce?
"That's right."

Did you go to film school?
"Yes, I did. I went to New York University, which was a great experience. It got me thinking professionally. At that time, I was not directed or geared towards writing—I thought I was going to do something a little more technical. An NYU buddy came out to live in LA while I was still at a production assistant level, and was desperately trying to break into sitcoms—trying to write spec scripts. Spec *Barney Miller*, I believe. I was between things then, and he asked me if I wanted to help by partnering up with him and writing

a spec script, and I did. We got that to an agent, who suggested that we write an episode of a show called *Busting Loose*, which was created by Lowell Ganz and Mark Rothman. You'll know the name Lowell Ganz because he's now associated with Babaloo Mandel, and they write every comedy movie out. So our first professional experience was as program consultants, which was a low level of writer at that time. But we learned a lot."

Mark Reisman (executive producer)

"I started on *Saturday Night Live*; that was my first job. Then I wrote a movie for Paramount called *Summer Rental*. John Candy was in it, and Carl Reiner directed. So I did movies for a while, but I missed television. My first writer-producer staff job was on *Dear John*. Then I did a show called *Flying Blind* a few seasons ago. I came to *Wings* as co–executive producer. The following year, I was asked by Grub Street Productions (David Angell, Peter Casey and David Lee, who created *Wings* and are the executive producers) to run the show and become executive producer. I will have done a hundred episodes by the time I'm finished."

Did you attend film school?

"No. I went to Boston University. I purposely stayed away from writing courses. Although I always wanted to work in TV and film, at the time, I wasn't familiar with film schools and didn't want anyone to squash my enthusiasm. My education was on the job.

"I remember my first TV job. My manager said, 'They will pay you to go to school.' Which is basically what writing for television is, if you take advantage of it. You start at the very bottom, and you are paid to go to school. This is one of the few businesses that pays you because they believe you have an innate or raw talent, and then they bring you along. If you're smart, you will learn from some terrific writers."

Ian Gurvitz (executive producer)

Did you go to film school?

"No. I've always written in one form or another. In college, I started writing Russell Baker–style pieces and freelance articles for the school paper."

Where did you go to college?

"Ithaca College in upstate New York. Ithaca had a big TV-radio school. I started out there, but after a year and a half, I transferred to philosophy, for personal reasons."

How did you move from there into television?

"Well, I'll give you the fast track. I finished my B.A. there. I took a year off and went to Colgate University for grad school in religion. Spent a year in Japan after that, long enough to teach English, study Japanese, and bag my master's thesis. I realized I wasn't an academic. I enjoyed making things up too much, and academia has a thing about sticking to the truth. So, I came back to New York facing square one, looking for a job. At the time, my brother had moved to LA and had begun working as a personal manager, managing comedians, so I started writing jokes for his comics, twenty-five bucks a pop. From there, I started doing half-hour spec scripts and spec pilots, all in New York while taking trips out here occasionally to test the waters. Then I started writing spec screenplays in between working in advertising and public relations—things like that. My brother would send my scripts around to the studios, and I ended up getting an agent through these writing samples. About '86, I optioned a screenplay to Zanuck-Brown—my first sale—which added a little reality to the notion that I could possibly make a living at this and allowed me to run screaming from advertising. Not that I hated it, but it wasn't what I ultimately wanted to do."

What were you doing in advertising?

"Copywriting, producing commercials, things like that. But I was also writing TV and movie scripts at night, on weekends, occasionally during work. And every chance I got, I took trips to LA, but I didn't want to just come out with a computer and a pocketful of dreams and say, 'Where's the work?' It's like, the hopeful writer–schmuck line forms to the left.

"There's a great scene in the movie *The World's Greatest Lover*. Gene Wilder is on a train to LA to enter some kind of 'You, too, can be Valentino' talent search. He's wearing a dapper white suit and fedora. His wife asks him why he thinks he'll make it in Hollywood. He says, 'Because I'm unique!' Then he gets off the train, and on the platform are hundreds of guys, literally clones, wearing the same suit and fedora. That's how I feel about Hollywood. In any event, that project eventually went into turnaround, but it led to a movie rewrite at Lorimar, which led to an overall deal there for a year. So my family and I moved to LA. That was about '87."

Have you had any formal screenwriting training?

"No. As far as movie writing, I just read every screenplay I could get my hands on. It was really a matter of just seeing the format and then trying to tell a story, learning more each time I did it. There's something about not knowing the rules at first that helps because you're free to indulge yourself. When you don't have a head full of story structure classes—you're not reined in by the dictate that requires an event by page ten, a crisis by page thirty, a bigger crisis by page sixty, then the hero's eventual trial by fire and personal epiphany. When you're not restrained by that, you can write it the way you want to write it."

Now that you've achieved this level of success and experience, do you still feel that way?

"To start, it doesn't hurt to go on raw energy and determination, but I've worked in TV for the last ten years, and it's really been on-the-job training. To me, that's been vital. In the beginning, your natural abilities and ideas will take you so far. But eventually you need skills—writing skills, producing skills—and it is really learning by doing. You *will* need to know story structure, so classes can be helpful, although nothing replaces experience.

"The first job I got was a one-hour romantic comedy. Up to then, I had been writing a lot of spec multicamera [sitcom] scripts. This was a single camera show, and not as joke heavy. So it opened me up to a different style, which I then began taking onto other shows, but those shows were different. With single-camera film, multicamera film, multicamera tape, the style of writing and knowledge required for producing can vary. Of course, there's overlap. But in time, you need to know the difference."

THE WRITING PROCESS ON A SITCOM

Howard Gewirtz

"There are ways in which shows are done that are fairly similar from series to series, from pitching the story to outlining to writing a first draft. Then the first draft goes through the writing staff, and that becomes the draft the actors read at the table, which they rehearse. Then that draft is rewritten.

"In short, writing on a sitcom is constant rewriting and rewriting and rewriting. Even with the best writers, it's a very, very rare occurrence where most of a writer's first draft is what is ultimately filmed. A very rare occurrence.

"We rewrite based on the process that works for Broadway, in a very concise way. What they often do on Broadway is take a play out of town and then work on it after playing before an audience. When they see it on its feet, they know what works and what doesn't. We don't actually have a live audience for rehearsals, but just hearing it read by the actors, we can tell if what seemed like a funny joke when we proposed it in the room is not working for the actor. It may not be the actor's fault, it's just a joke that's not working. Certain things that work at the table don't quite work when you mount them—when the actors start walking through and blocking the show. You also find scenes that you thought might have worked aren't quite working, and you have to rework those.''

How does an idea get picked up for an episode and make it through the writing process?

"We have to do twenty-four to twenty-six stories a year, and sometimes it works when someone just has a notion. Sometimes it works when someone has an event that has occurred in their life, and it sparks a discussion and you'll say, 'Well, that'd be funny. What if that happened to Joe? What if that happened to Helen?' But, usually, it's a situation where the writers are gathered around, and we know we need a story, and we start just discussing ideas. Sometimes it's as prosaic as, 'We need a Helen story. We need a Helen-Joe story. We need a brother story. We haven't done a Roy story, let's think of a Roy story.' So sometimes we just think of a character and do an episode on that character. Sometimes it's a free-for-all.

"Now, just a little aside, the year Helen and Joe were engaged was our biggest story arc. I think it was our most successful arc because it's such a basic life experience that everyone's gone through. So, A-stories and B-stories came out of the preparation for the big day. Ultimately, it gave us the push for that year.

"Otherwise, we're into what we call free territory where we don't have a big arc going. We just have to come up with another individual story. So, to not be too long-winded, when someone has a notion, we start talking about it, and then we literally take out a white board and start outlining. Once we feel confident that the idea is rich enough to become a story, we start breaking it down into acts. What's the Act One action, what's the Act Two action, what's the Act Three action? Then we become more and more specific, so that ultimately we've told a story in the writers' room that has three acts. Then the writer goes to flesh that out and comes back with an outline, which has suggestions of dialogue, jokes that were pitched in the room, jokes the writer has added. Then we make notes on that outline, and the writer goes off and writes the first draft. Then we'll all look at that first draft.

"When the writer turns in his or her first draft, we give the writer notes, and they do a second draft. After the second draft, the staff takes it, we go over it line by line, and make what we call our table draft from that. This is, by the way, under ideal circumstances, when we have the luxury of time. Usually, that's earlier in the year, before we're in production. Then the actors read that draft at the table, and we make notes. Actually, *Wings* is not typical, in that we read at the table and rehearse and do our rewrite based on a reading and a run-through in one day. More typical is, the actors will come in, read the script, and go home while the writers make changes based on the reading. Then the next day, they'll put it on its feet and do a run-through, and the writers will make changes based on the run-through. We've compacted that two-day process, having the reading and a run-through, into one day."

When you say a run-through, you mean a staged reading?

"Well, not really reading so much at that point. The actors are performing; they have their scripts in their hands, what we call 'holding their books.' But we're seeing some blocking. If there's physical action dictated in the script, we're watching that. We're watching whatever the director has inputted. We're watching now for the actors' input. We're watching a show.

"Obviously, some scenes work, some scenes don't. Some scenes work with the jokes, some scenes don't; we go off and do a rewrite. Usually, after that first run-through is our biggest rewrite, which almost invariably goes into the evening; not very uncommonly into the early morning. By now, *Wings* is working well enough so that at 11:00 P.M. or 11:30 or midnight is about as late as we will go; rarely will we have to go later.

"If you talk to other shows, 3:00 A.M. isn't uncommon, 4:00 A.M. isn't uncommon. I've seen 7:30 A.M. come and go."

Mark Reisman

"The process is that we break the story in the writers' room, and the writer who's responsible for that episode will go off and do a detailed outline. Then the writer comes back and we pitch on it and give notes, and the writer does a first draft. This is in a perfect world when you have time. Then the process is repeated, and the writer goes off and does a second draft. After the second draft the script will be what we call mimeoed—it goes to the room of writers, including the writer who wrote it, and page by page we will go over it. It is made funnier, made clearer, and rewritten from page one.

"The degree of rewriting depends upon each script. When it's done, it will go to the table to be read by the actors on a Wednesday. Most weeks we shoot on Tuesday; it's a five-day schedule. Then there will be a rewrite based upon the reading. Thursday we see a run-through; see the script performed 'up on its feet.' Then it is rewritten again. The same thing happens Friday. Monday is camera blocking day. The cameramen come in and learn their marks, and at the end of that day there's also a run-through.

"Again, the script's rewritten. When we shoot on Tuesday, there's a three o'clock run-through and final notes. There's usually not a lot of rewriting because you want the actors to be able to lock into their performances and memorize the lines. But there are more notes to the actors at that time. That night the show is shot. Between scenes, things sometimes are punched up or rewritten, or the actors are given notes and the director will have some comments, while we shoot the show."

In a nonperfect world, how does that get truncated?

"Actually, what would get truncated would be the number of rewrites the original writer has. In preproduction, when there's time, you do the outline, you do the first draft, you do the second draft. During the season, as time becomes a factor, you might do an outline and a first draft. Then the room rewrites that. When the crunch really comes, you might find that the writer only does a first draft."

Do you get involved with the casting process?

"Absolutely. Usually, in the course of the week on a half-hour sitcom, you are involved with probably four or five episodes in various stages. You're breaking a story on one. You're doing the current one. You're editing a past one and you're casting that one or the next one."

THE SUBJECT OF NOTES

What are your thoughts on notes? What do aspiring writers need to know about notes?

Ian Gurvitz

"You know, it's always a rush when you get your first assignment. The first TV job I got was on a show called *A Fine Romance*, a one-hour romantic comedy. When I did my first script and I turned it in, I sweated bullets (and you're always sweating bullets). Then I got my notes a day or so later, and I felt as if I had been vivisected. It was the most painful experience I ever had—ego crushing. It's like a comic telling a joke and hearing dead silence. Sixty pages' worth of that. Not all silence but, 'No, this is wrong. No, change this.' I walked out of there feeling as if I'd just experienced the death by a thousand cuts.

"Then I did a rewrite in, whatever it was, a week or so, and the executive producer liked the second draft. I felt as if I had been through hell but lived to tell about it. The thing is, that never stops.

What you learn in time is how to handle the process and realize that a first draft is a first draft. The reason there's a room full of people to read it and have opinions is not so they can all carry you on their shoulders and applaud your brilliance and say what a wonderful writer you are, how perfect this is, and let's carve it on two stone tablets. The reason is so they can add their talents to it and it becomes a communal project. The biggest skill is learning how to take notes and not hang onto every word, not lock yourself into the script as you did it, but let people improve it. Ninety percent of the time, they make it better.

"Experientially, the first draft is more fun to write. The second draft is usually painful because you just grit your teeth going, 'Oh, they killed that joke. They don't see the brilliance of this. Now I'm turning it into some pedestrian piece of garbage.' By the time you're done with the second draft, you realize it's a better script."

If you feel strongly about a joke that's been panned, can you stick with it?

"Oh, yeah. The way we work in the room here is very collaborative. If people don't jump all over something, you can say, 'Can I give this a chance? I'd like to hear it.' I remember one run I did in a script where, during the rewrite process, it got changed just enough so that, to me, there was no point in keeping it. So, when we were proofing it, I said, 'I'd like to go back to the way I had this, I think it's better. I don't think it will work at all the way it is.' And they said, 'Sure.' And it worked; it stayed in all week and made it to the final cut. So that was sort of satisfying. But a lot of times, you've just got to let go.

In dramas, it seems that it's scenes that get cut . . .

"Well, in single-camera dramas, one scene could mean another half day of shooting or another location, and the inclination is, 'Do we really need this scene? It will save a whole setup. We don't have to move an entire cast and crew anywhere.' In multicamera, as long as you're in a standing set, you can afford to work and work a scene until it plays."

Do you get a lot of network notes?

Howard Gewirtz

"*Wings* has been in a position for the last few years where network notes [the network involvement] are not very heavy at all. They've been pleased with the show, pleased with the direction. They don't come in and propose to us what to do. So their notes are pretty light. Every now and again, during sweeps period, the network may ask, 'What stories are you doing for sweeps?' Or, 'Are there any actors we can 'stunt'? If you stunt cast a role, it means, for example, 'This week Jean Claude Van Damme is on *Friends*.' That's a big stunt, and that's a favorite around sweeps time because, obviously, it will generate another point or two or three in terms of ratings.

"Anyway, *Wings* has not been a show that's been getting heavy network notes. Newer shows tend to. When a show is respected by the network and it's working, the network doesn't get very heavy. When a show's brand new, they're more involved; or when a show is struggling, they get more involved."

Mark Reisman

"A lot of times with notes, I would say, don't necessarily listen to the lyrics, listen to the music. That is, if the actor can't articulate exactly what they are feeling, and maybe what they're saying doesn't sound right to you, try to listen between the lines and get the feeling of what they're saying. I find many times, especially with a show like *Wings* where the actors have been here so many years, they truly know their characters. They're not trained writers, but if there's a problem they're feeling as actors, I try and tune into that. It's like that at all levels, from studios to networks and on down. A lot of times when they say something, I think some writers are too quick to dismiss a note from an executive; and a lot of times, you can listen to the gist of what they are saying and see if it makes sense. Obviously, it doesn't make sense all the time. If you get the sense of it—maybe it's the sense of truth he or she is trying get to."

Do writers sometimes get notes and dismiss them out of hand?

"Sometimes writers are too adversarial with networks and studios. Of course, people will say things that are wrong—it's a given. But writers also say things that are wrong; that's a given."

What influence do the actors have on their characters? Can they come to the writers and say, "I'd like to see my character move in this direction"?

"Every show is different . . . it all depends on who the actors are. We respect the actors on *Wings*. As I said, they've been with the characters longer than I have. They've been here from the beginning; I haven't. They've grown with the characters. If they say something, I'll ask them why. I ask what their reasoning is. And we definitely listen. It doesn't mean that everything has to be acted upon, but we listen and might go in the direction they suggest. I think, especially when you've been on a show a while, you welcome stimulation, however it comes. I told the actors this year [1997], 'This is our eighth year on *Wings*. It could possibly be our last. Is there anything you've always wanted to do with your character?' Sometimes just the germ of it will kick us off into an area.

"But, again, I have to emphasize, every situation and every show is different. I might not do that on a different show with different actors. It's really on a case-by-case basis."

Howard Gewirtz

"We get plenty of input from the actors. At this point, these actors have been playing these characters for seven years; they may feel a scene isn't quite right, or isn't working. And sometimes they can be quite articulate and helpful, putting on their thinking caps and saying, 'Well, what if we did this?' Sometimes it's not that specific, and they may say, 'I don't know. It's not quite right. It's not ringing true for me. It doesn't seem as if my character would do this.' Then we'll go back and think about it and try to figure out what the problems are and solve them.

"One of the things we've been pleased with since we've been running the show is that we generally do figure it out, and the script is almost always better after we've done our rewrite. One might think, 'Well, of course, it is. Why wouldn't it be?' But I've worked on many shows where it's *worse* after a rewrite! Where there is a certain amount of floundering, and nobody knows quite what to do. So, by this point, I think we've gotten adept enough at doing *Wings*, that there's little panic at any stage, no matter what's going on.

"Let's say we have a reading, and it's just terrible, which doesn't happen often. But it's just a bad reading, and we know we have a lot of work to do. We shrug and say, 'We have a lot of work to do.' But nobody panics, and I think part of that nonpanic is, we know how to do this show. We know who the characters are. We know what we can do, so we know we can help the show.

"I've been on shows where there is panic, 'Now what do we do? We don't have a script. We don't have a show; the actors are balking.' I guess what I'm saying is that *Wings* has been pretty smooth the last few years. I'm not saying it was always smooth, but it's been smooth since I've been here."

Ian Gurvitz

"In television, the characters become set early on, so that doesn't change much—it's the dialogue and story lines each week using those constant characters. In that, everyone has a say, although different writers' rooms have different styles. Some are democratic; others are more autocratic. Ultimately, it's the executive producer's call. Our room is like living in a Robert Altman movie. Do you know the poker game in *M*A*S*H*? That's what it's like. It's just nonstop overlapping talking and occasional screaming until somebody says, 'All right. Wait. Wait. Wait. What's this line? Do we want that? OK, do it like this.' In terms of the actors, after every scene during run-throughs we go face-to-face, and everybody can say whatever they want. There is sort of an unwritten rule where you use tact in doing it. If an actor doesn't think something will work, their job is to give it all they can. If it doesn't work, it will become obvious to all present when they try wholeheartedly. As opposed to actors who will tank material to make sure it doesn't work, which has happened. Not on this stage, but in other places.

"You have a gentlemen's agreement: you try to make it work even though you don't like it, and we'll see that, with your best efforts, it stunk, so we'll change it. It's sort of a code if an actor says, 'I don't know if this is exactly right, or it needs to be set up better. I don't exactly feel right. I feel more as if he should say "X." ' You have to trust their feelings a lot because there tends to be more truth in the actor who's trying to make the character work or the bit work. Because they're inside it. They'll use language like, 'Something feels wrong.' Or, 'I don't feel that he or she would do that.' When they're talking about how they feel about it, chances are that's where the truth lies. Again, they're not always right. Sometimes they just miss it, they just don't see it. But, hopefully, you get a dialogue going.

"That's in an ideal world. There's also the not-so-ideal world where actors come in, throw the script down and say, 'I'm not doing this shit.' Not on this show, but it's happened on others."

OUTSIDE WRITERS

Do you take pitches from outside writers?

Howard Gewirtz

"We occasionally do. Not a lot, as we have a full staff of writers. What happens is a kind of staff chemistry, where the staff really knows the show—knows the innermost workings of the show. And part of that staff process is, we all sit around and talk about stories and story arcs—what might be good over a period of a few shows or just the general shape of the season. We've become familiar with the rhythms of the characters—what works, what doesn't work; which characters work well together, which characters work less well together.

"There are just so many little things you couldn't possibly know by just being a viewer of the show. But we will occasionally take outside pitches and assign outside scripts, maybe a couple of times a year. Although it's no reflection on the writers, it's almost always problematic. It's just a question of . . . there's a certain essence when you're on a show that starts to flow through you. If you're outside of the process, it's difficult for that to happen, and it's almost always the case that, even if it's a great outside writer who has excellent references, who has worked on other shows, some of the characters don't quite sound like the characters ought to. So we have to put it though our filter, so to speak, and make it more like our characters—make it more *Wings*.

Makes sense. The staff has lived with those characters for years.

"Yeah, that's right. I had to learn it, too. While my first script wasn't bad, it wasn't as good as I was ultimately able to do. In my first attempt at *Wings*, I was writing things that didn't quite sound like the characters."

THE POLITICS OF WRITING ON A SITCOM

Any thoughts on the politics in screenwriting?

Mark Reisman

"I think the biggest point, and I'm going to apply this to half-hour, but it also applies to features and playwriting, is that the longer you've been in the business, the more you welcome rewriting. They say writing is rewriting, and I absolutely agree with that."

Ian Gurvitz

"Because this is so collaborative, among the people you work with on staff, the actors, the director, the studio, the network—you really have to learn to listen. That's one of the most important skills you can pick up from being in a room. Some people treat what everyone else says as 'the bullshit between when I talk the first time and when I talk the second time.' There are people who are just enthralled with the sound of their own voices and enchanted with their own opinions. You have to learn to listen to people and actually hear what they say.

"In terms of politics, although there's an exception to every rule, not being a prima donna helps. There are people who, when creating shows, just come in and say, 'Screw you all. I'm doing it my way.' You hear stories of writers who did that on pilots or shows and have since gone on to be very successful. Had they taken the network notes, it would have ruined the pilot or show.

"In this business, people pay homage to somebody with a vision who sticks to that vision—not letting anyone corrupt it. Yet there are compromises that, well, it's hard to say that you have to make them, but they're there. Sometimes people who want a show on the air will tell you, 'Come on, come on. Compromise. Hire such and such an actor, or change such and such a part.' It's hard to know when to say, 'No, I won't do that, I think you're wrong.' Even if it means not getting the show on the air, especially when you're facing a roomful of people who have a large stake in it. Money and reputations are on the line, so there's pressure.

"Ultimately, you have to learn which battles to fight and to trust your instincts and say 'No' in the politest way you can find. Say, 'I hear what you're saying, but I really think you're wrong. I prefer not to do that.' Which, depending on the situation, can be easy or hard. If it's one joke or a story line in an episode, it's not so tough. If it's a pilot where the network's counting on it for next season, and the studio is deficiting a lot of money, and you won't do X to Y, the stakes get a little higher."

Howard Gewirtz

"Politics is kind of general. Every show's different. Some shows are highly political, with stars who are out of their minds, and you've got to cater to them hand and foot—it's just a nightmare. Then there are some shows, and *Wings* is more in this category, where things work sanely. It's as sane and humane a situation as most of the shows I've worked on have been.

"On *Taxi*, we had the most brilliant cast and some of the most brilliant writers: Jim Brooks and the Charles brothers and others. That was just a magisterial thing to watch and cut my teeth on because I was learning from the best craftsmen in the business.

"But politically, I think you're talking about some of these shows that hit the tabloids. I'm not endorsing the tabloids and saying everything they print is true, but there are certain people who are difficult to work for, obviously. That becomes a more political situation.

FINAL THOUGHTS

Howard Gewirtz

"As far as for anything overall, basically, if you're serious about this, you have to keep writing. The best thing for an aspiring writer is when another aspiring writer gives up, obviously, because you have less competition. So, if you're of the mentality, 'Well, I wrote three spec scripts and they didn't like them, and those spec scripts are better than anything they are doing, so the heck with this,' that's the best thing for the remaining spec script writer who's going to write four or five of them until he or she starts getting it.

"So, if you are really serious about it, you just have to keep on producing spec material until someone's willing to pay you. I *would* say there's probably more competition now than when I started. Some very heavy competition because, since the time I started, there are a lot of writers who are Harvard and Yale educated, coming from the best Ivy League schools in the country, who have decided this is a career option. When I started, it wasn't, and some of those people are predictably smart and good at this. So, not to be at all discouraging, there is a lot of competition.

"On the other hand, real, special talent is rarity. Writing is not like a trade where, if you buckle down and work hard, you can do it. You may not be able to do it, no matter how hard you buckle down, because there is that intangible thing: talent. Especially in comedy writing, that instinct, that ear for comedy, that ear for being able to write a joke and know how to write a punch line. I don't believe that can be taught. It can be honed, and you can learn—you can become smarter about it—but if you don't have that gift, nobody can teach it to you."

Ian Gurvitz

"There's one thing that's always gotten to me. There are an awful lot of people trying to write for a living. You get spec scripts by the truckload. Most of them have the proper form down and simultaneously show no writing ability whatsoever. Some are average, others painfully bad. I'm being brutally honest. While not everybody working in film or TV is a genius, many people trying to break in simply can't write. They're just not writers. They aren't funny on paper and probably aren't funny in person.

"My advice would be, find out if you really have talent. Don't give a script to your mother or your brother or your best friend or wife or husband because chances are they're going to tell you, 'Oh, it's wonderful. You're a genius.' Get it to somebody who will really give you critical feedback. Get it to an agent, who's going to be in a position to either take you on as a client or not; someone who will give you a dead-on brutal answer. Of course, you'll get dozens of opinions on the same script, ranging from, 'I loved it' to 'It sucks.' Depending on which you hear more of, that's your answer.

"If you do that, and you think you do have what it takes, don't rush it. Rewrite until it hurts. Eventually you're going to have to get out a few spec scripts, and they're going to be on a pile with a hundred other scripts read by somebody who's not in a mood to read them. Nobody *wants* to read your script. They're way too busy or cranky or tired and just want to get home to their families or out to a bar, and, yet, people are looking for fresh talent. You will get a limited number of chances; make them count.

"Don't send a spec script out until you're positive it's flawless. People do get hired off spec scripts. What you often hear is, 'I picked so-and-so's script off the pile. I wasn't in the mood, but I read three pages, and it just knocked me out. That's how you get your first job.

"So don't rush out a script in your eagerness to have someone read it. I made the mistake early on of sending out first drafts. I realize now, do a second pass and a third pass. Take a couple weeks and don't look at it. Do another pass and another pass. When I did that, I got a job. Whatever you do, never send a spec script to that same show. It's suicide. With few exceptions, as clever as you think it is, you'll never be able to impress the people who think about that show every day of their lives. Find out which shows people want to read. At one point a few years ago, there were more *Seinfeld* specs than people in the country. Ultimately, though, write whatever you have a feeling for—what's in your head.

"My biggest advice, again, would be to find out if you're good. If you think you have talent, don't stop working at it. Most people who write do it because they have to, it's in them—that's what they are. So, when people say, 'I want to write, but I can't find the time,' I don't believe it. If you want to write badly enough—if you *need* to write—you'll find the time, whatever it is you want to write. I think when people say, 'I just don't have the time,' it's an excuse. These are not people who love to write. These are people who 'want to be writers' for the cash, the ego, whatever. Most of them don't succeed. On the other hand, some do, while occasionally more talented people can't catch a break. If you're one of those, you'll spend a lot of time chewing your own liver and pulling your hair out. But keep at it. If it's something you want badly enough, chances are, it will happen."

FOUR

Writing for Television Animation Series

For this chapter, *I interviewed David Titcher (a former Disney animation staff writer), Steve Roberts (story editor–writer with ten years' experience), and Duane Capizzi (writer–story editor–producer). My expectation was that animation writing would be the same as feature writing, but with action way over the top and dialogue slanted for odd voices. I was wrong, very wrong. If I could sum up in one word David and Steve's thoughts on animation writing, it would be* exasperating: *notes from everyone in the food chain; it's very detailed, surgically precise writing; a lot of work for not a lot of pay and no residuals. However, both feel strongly that animation writing has significantly improved their overall writing skills as well as broadened their approach to "live action" screenwriting.*

What's your writing background and how did you get into animation?

David Titcher (writer)

(1991–1994) Staff Writer at Disney
DARKWING DUCK
BONKERS
THE LITTLE MERMAID

WHO'S THE BOSS?, one episode
PUNKY BREWSTER
(1996) optioned feature:
THE ARMY-NAVY GAME

PRINCE CHARMING for United Artists
FIGHT LIKE A GIRL for Goldie Hawn Productions
ADAM GETS EVEN sold to Smart Egg Productions
NICK OF TIME sold to Hollywood Pictures
MORGAN STEWART'S COMING HOME for Kings Road Productions
ACTION JUNKIES sold to Interscope

"My training comes from UCLA, where I got my bachelor's. Then I was in the UCLA master's program for four years but took only writing classes. I didn't take one class toward my degree. Somehow I slipped through the cracks where they didn't notice. I figured out how to do that and finally decided to leave. Then I went into the business, and I've done all sorts of different writing. I've done movies, television, sitcoms, animation, plays."

When you left UCLA, did you leave because you had work?

"I had a script optioned right out of film school, but I think I would have left anyway because I'd been there four years. I loved it there. I could have been there forever—such a great environment. Every quarter you'd be writing a new script. I was able to do that as opposed to what everybody else did, which was one quarter, make a film, then take a film history class. It was probably useful for them, and it probably would have been useful for me, but I just wanted to write, so I was able to do it. I took Lew [Hunter] seven times."

Did you leave because you had learned what you wanted and felt it was time to, as they say, "get off the pot"?

"Yeah, even though in film school you are off the pot and it's even more so now. Everybody has an agent, and people are selling stuff in film school. It was just starting to happen when I was there."

What was the first thing that you got optioned?

"It was something called *Home Front*. It eventually became a movie called *Morgan Stewart's Coming Home*, which starred Jon Cryer and Lynn Redgrave. I'm starting to get residuals again for it, which is nice. But that was a film that, they sort of screwed up my script, so I wasn't real happy with it."

They rewrote it?

"It was rewritten, and the producers alienated everybody. They fired everybody. They fired me, they fired other writers, they fired two directors so the director's credit is Alan Smithee. Are you familiar with Alan Smithee?"

No.

"Alan Smithee is notorious in Hollywood because it's the only pseudonym that a director can use. In most cases, whenever you see Alan Smithee, it means there's a director who refuses to have his name on it. So it's a symbol of something that's theoretically going to be bad. Some people don't know that, and there have been articles written on the work of Alan Smithee; what an eclectic director he is, and all that. As a matter of fact, I think, a film just came out last week with that name in the credits. It's fairly rare. In the last thirty years there have only been about twenty films that have done that.

Don Siegel was the first director to do this. He took his name off of a movie for some reason, I forget why.

"As a matter of fact, when my movie came out, I was interviewed all over the country about it. For some reason, the exposure of the pseudonym came out for the first time around then. Actually, I think, through me, because I have certain journalist friends and somehow it just spread. I was getting calls from all over the country to be interviewed about it."

How did you get into animation?

"I had a friend who was working at Disney on *Darkwing Duck* and he said, 'Why don't you submit?' You have to submit a sitcom script, and I had just done a *Who's the Boss?* episode, so I submitted that, and they liked it. From that I got a story assignment, which they liked, and then they hired me on staff."

For *Darkwing Duck?*

"I did a story for *Darkwing Duck*, but they hired me on staff for *Bonkers.*"

Steve Roberts (writer/story editor)

Writer:
ROBOTECH II: THE SENTINELS, eight episodes
C.O.P.S., ''Break-In''
REAL GHOSTBUSTERS, ''Poultrygeist''
ALF, two episodes
ALFTALES, ''Hansel and Gretel''
NINJA TURTLES, ''Cowabunga Shredhead''
LITTLE NEMO, pilot and series bible
TALE SPIN, four episodes
DARKWING DUCK, three episodes
ALADDIN, seven episodes

OLD MACDONALD'S FARM, D.I.C.
THE MASK
EARTHWORM JIM
TIMON AND PUMBAA
THE SAVAGE DRAGON
ACE VENTURA: PET DETECTIVE
LOGGERHEADS

Story editor:
DARKWING DUCK
BONKERS
DUCK DAZE

"I wrote short stories as a kid and as an undergrad at UCLA, even though I was in critical studies. I wrote scripts for student films and things like that. I got my first paid job as a writer over ten years ago in the usual way—I knew somebody. A friend of mine who worked as an animation artist for many years got a job as a story editor, even though he had no writing experience. He knew I'd written short stories, plays, student films at UCLA, et cetera, and he needed writers, so he invited me to go to this meeting where they were looking for writers. At the end of the meeting, everyone was handed a different three-page premise and had one week to write a script from it for the phenomenal sum of $500 (which was as much as I was making a week as a full-time editor at a small publishing company).

"There were about twelve people at the meeting. Within a couple weeks it was down to six people, and by the end of the show there were only three of us writing all of the episodes. All three of us ended up as story editors for different studios."

Kind of trial by fire.

"It was pretty much trial by fire. The thing is, I was able to get the opportunity because I knew somebody who was in a position to get me into a meeting.

"I didn't get any other writing work right away. I continued to make a living as an editor and pursued writing on the side. I kept in touch with the other writers I'd met to stay on top of what shows were going into production, at which studios, and who was in charge—especially who the story editor was. Then I'd call up the story editor, tell him my credits (and make up others I knew were safe), ask him to send me the series bible, and offer to pitch stories. Knowing who to call when you don't have a reference is essential. Next is knowing how to sound as if you know what you're talking about. After that is persistence. If you keep pitching stories and nagging the story editor until you drive him nuts, he'll give you a script just so you'll go away."

Duane Capizzi (writer/story editor/producer)

EXTREME GHOSTBUSTERS
ACE VENTURA: PET DETECTIVE
THE MASK
THE SAVAGE DRAGON
ALADDIN
THE RETURN OF JAFAR
BONKERS
DARKWING DUCK
TALE SPIN
ALF

"I went to UCLA and graduated in 1985. I was not a film major; however, I wanted to be a filmmaker. I decided that if I were to tackle a career in film, I wanted to approach it from a writing standpoint. I felt that studying literature would give me a good understanding and background, so I opted to go for something more academic than [film] career oriented and majored in English.

"Then I fell into animation writing by accident. I had done some writing on the side and got a lucky break. A good friend of mine was working in animation and when I graduated, he said, 'Why don't you come pitch some stories on the show I'm working on?' I did, and next thing I knew, I was saying good-bye to graduate school. So, it was a mix of having raw talent and a lucky break, and I was sort of thrown into a sink-or-swim situation where I learned on the job."

What kind of writing were you doing on the side?

"Short stories. I had written some animation scripts for a show that never got produced. But it actually enabled me to have an animation writing sample, which got me my first real job."

How do stories start, and what path do ideas take to becoming an animation teleplay?

Steve Roberts

"First you submit story ideas. This is done either verbally by phone, in a meeting, or in writing. A one-line pitch is called a 'springboard' and a more extended idea is called a 'primeline.' I prefer submitting my ideas in writing so I don't have to waste time talking to the story editor. That's because you don't get paid for it, and the ball is in their court.

"If one of your springboards is accepted, the next stage is the 'premise,' where the real writing begins. The premise is a brief description of the story and is usually two to three double-spaced pages. You can pitch a premise verbally, but it's a bad idea. A good premise contains all the broad strokes of an outline; it takes a lot of work. You'll still have to write it up eventually, and your ideas can easily be stolen. A premise pays almost nothing, so even if you can prove your story was stolen, you'll be lucky to get $200, even if you make a big stink out of it.

"From my experience, whether submitting story ideas or premises, it's not quality but quantity that counts. Odds are that one out of every ten story ideas will be accepted, and one out of every three premises will be accepted. Anything above that doesn't seem to work. That is, if you turn in more than ten springboards or three premises, you'll probably still only get one accepted. However, the formula is not idiot-proof. I've frequently thrown in bad story ideas with good ones to play the odds and had the bad ones get approved.

"The third stage is the outline, about ten single-spaced pages. This is the first stage where you make any money. The outline pays one-third of the price of the script, which is usually about $6,000 (i.e., $2,000 for outline). Even if the outline is killed, which is rare, you get paid for it. You usually get one week to write the outline, and a standard animation contract requires you to do one rewrite. Once you turn in the outline, your story editor rewrites it, usually off the top of his head, turns it in, and the producer, studio execs, network execs, Broadcast Standards and Practices, sponsors, et al. give notes on it. This can take several days, so by the time you get the outline, you usually don't have time to do a rewrite and, therefore, have to go directly to script.

"An animation script is about forty pages long for a twenty-two-minute episode, approximately two pages for every minute. That's because an animation script is a shooting script. There are no live actors, no camera operator, no set decorator, et al. in animation. An animation script has to describe every action, every camera shot, angle, and movement, the mise-en-scène, the expressions of the characters, et cetera. You are required to do everything you're not supposed to do in a live-action script.

"By the time you go to script, your outline has been rewritten by your story editor and you have notes from as many as nine different people. You should get two weeks to write the script and are obligated to do one rewrite. You often have less than two weeks and won't have time to do a rewrite because, even though you have a deadline to meet, the execs in charge of the show don't and they have eaten your time with notes."

David Titcher

"In animation, there is a lot of input from all levels—there are a lot of executives. Six executives will often give six different comments, and you have to address them all for some reason. In sitcoms [you're more likely to get feedback from] just one person. Here there was a litany of different people, and you had to figure out whom to please.

"Sitcom work is much more lucrative, but in animation the hours are better. Also, in animation, there's not the pressure because you're just doing your own stuff. On sitcoms you're always working multiple episodes plus that week's episode. So, here you're just sitting in your office working on your one script. A lot of time turns out to be downtime on animation staff writing."

How does the writing differ?

"Animation writing is the hardest writing I've ever had to do. It is very difficult."

What makes it more difficult?

"If you are writing a feature script, it's one page per minute. An animation script is two pages per minute. So you're writing twice as much material for everything. You have to write everything that's going to be on the screen, which means you also have to direct, in terms of camera angles—every camera angle. As a feature writer, I was trained not to do that. So, I had to relearn a whole way of doing things. Plus, since a lot of time it's being animated in different countries, if you don't put it on the page, it won't get drawn. For example, if you have somebody's hand up in the air for two frames, you have to say that their hand goes down. You just can't put down, 'he smiles'; you have to state how his lips curl up. It's detailed to the point where you're spending most of your time on insignificant detail and not on making it funny and making the story work. That stuff was easy. Just trying to think this way drove me nuts.

"My first story editor was cool about all of this, and he could put in a lot of the detail. But my second story editor was just nuts about this stuff, and it was like, 'Well, you had the hand up here and three frames later the hand's going to be up, but you have him doing something else with the gun.' The physics of body language you had to work out."

Since you don't have a director, do you get the chance to see the storyboards and say, "Hey, you got this wrong here, et cetera?"

"They don't really do that, yet everybody is of the opinion that it would be good if the writers and the animators spent more time and focused on this kind of stuff and worked together. There has always been a rivalry between the two. Everybody thought it would be a great idea, but nobody encouraged it. It really didn't happen. As a matter of fact, I rarely knew any of the animators even though they might have the office next to me. The writers socialized together, but you never really knew who the animators were."

If you were really opposed to the notes, did you have to defer to them or could you debate them?

"I had a story editor who was quite combative, and he'd get into big arguments with everybody and eventually got fired as the story editor. But he went in and argued a lot."

With the writers?

"He argued with the producer of the show, whom he knew, and who brought him to the business. They had the kind of relationship where he could do that. He argued a lot, but basically he rarely won an argument, and the producer would just rewrite a lot of the scripts himself. Frequently, after all this writing, you turn in your script, and then the producer would come back with a radically different point of view on it. This was the producer that later got fired. But all of the producers end up rewriting the script themselves."

Who gets the last chop?

"The producer."

So it goes through the story editor to the producer, who puts the final spin on it, and that's what goes to the animators.

"Right. The producer spends a lot of time doing that."

Duane Capizzi

"In animation, the story editor is really more of a show runner. I have a broad scope of responsibility that extends beyond the writing. For example, extending into how the characters are designed and having some say over artwork elements. Because I'm not an artist myself, in those situations, I usually work in tandem with a producer who is an art director–producer or an animation director–producer.

"A story editor has a lot of say over the whole writing process of the show and is the one who reports to the clients. As a story editor I try to have control over all the storytelling elements: the finished scripts, voice recordings and storyboards. Having input to voice recording is important because, sometimes, a line of dialogue is read inappropriately. When it is, it can change the meaning or fail to get across the intended meaning. I prefer to be present at voice recordings and make sure lines are delivered properly. However, I'm always open to actors' interpretations and find that many times an actor can actually plus the material or give you a fresh reading that you didn't quite have in mind. But usually at the point of recording, I've lived with the story and script for four to eight weeks, so I know it fairly intimately. At the storyboard stage, you want to make sure that the story is being told, that the right points are being hit. If you are doing a comedy, you make sure that the gags are playing visually."

Do you make the voice tracks before or after the cells are done?

"Before. Generally we go from script to voice recording, so that even the storyboard artists work with the voice track in mind. A board artist may have an idea how to play something that involves a whisper rather than a scream. Ideally you'd like to leave the door open to go back and do voice pickups. Unfortunately, a lot of Saturday morning budgets don't allow for that. I think Warner Bros. is one of the few studios in town that will openly go back and keep on revisiting an episode until they get it right. They just put a lot of their money right up there on the screen. Most shows tend to have limited budgets and can't afford to do that. So, sometimes we just have to work with what we've got."

Did you, as a producer, get an overwhelming amount of notes impeding the ability to keep a script focused?

"Day in and day out, that really is the most critical challenge that we face (we, the writers, and we, the story editors). I don't know that the process is really different in animation from what it would be on a live-action show. The bottom line is that it is often frustrating, but I think it's just a fact of life that any given show is going to have clients (production companies and networks). And a lot of shows that I have worked on have had more than one client, which then becomes extremely problematic.

"A classic example is when I worked on the animated spin-off of the New Line motion picture *The Mask*. In that case, we had the network, CBS, we had New Line, who had ownership of the movie, we had Dark Horse, who was the creator of the comic book and who had creative say-so in the series, and then we had the animation company, which was Sunbow. However, technically, Sunbow is not an animation company because they don't have a studio with artists and animators employed. So, Sunbow, while they packaged the whole deal, had to subcontract to Film Roman. In this case, there were five entities involved and, as the story editor, I acted as the middleman attempting to maintain the creative vision of the show. On a daily basis, I have to fight battles, or decide which battles to fight and which ones to compromise on.

"A lot of my job is fighting battles. Many days, eight hours will go by, and I will suddenly realize I've been on the phone for eight hours straight. Then it's time to get some writing done."

What kind of battles?

"Everything from schedule battles to creative battles. Sometimes the simplest creative matter, if you've got five clients that have to agree, can be difficult. The process of going to each of them, and, if there is an agreement, at some point stepping back and letting them fight it out. These could be small issues, these could be large issues. Comedy and entertainment are subjective, and when you have five clients, potentially you have five different opinions. Before long, you could have a story pulling in five different directions. It's up to me to keep it all coherent and sane and somehow entertaining.

"On the other hand, I just try to tell myself that it goes with the territory—it's just something to get used to. It can be hard, and it's often frustrating. I try to be a buffer for my writers. I try not to have the writers plugged into what goes on behind the scenes. I don't want to distract them too much with that. I try to get most of the decisions made and hand down to the writer something that makes sense: 'OK, this is what needs to be changed.' Often the writer will have an opinion, and that's great, and then we can work it out from that angle. Sometimes I will go back to the client with what I think is a better idea that the writer and I have come up with—sometimes that new idea flies, and sometimes it doesn't.

"The bottom line on the writing front is that as much goes into writing an animation script, and perhaps even more so, as a live-action sitcom or drama script. All the rules of storytelling apply. At the same time, though, we seem to have the added burden of directing more on the page because we've got to hand this off to storyboard artists who need to be up and running, who are on very tight schedules. So we have to make the written page artist-friendly. All this means there's a greater need to fully break down shots and direct on the page. And some writers I've tried out don't have a knack for doing that. They're only used to writing in the dialogue, block style. Furthermore, you need to have a sense of what works visually or not. We're talking about limited animation. If you're writing for a thirty- to forty-million-dollar Disney feature, it's another thing. Part of the draw of animation features is the magic of how much animation can capture human acting and human emotion. And with most TV animation, limited animation, you don't have that.

"So, I think a writer has to have a sense of what will work well, or, if you can't rely on something as subtle as a facial nuance to get something across, know how to get a similar desired effect. So, there's really a lot that goes into these things. I know that some writers have tried animation, thinking it will be an easy few bucks, but it never is. It's quite an art to get it right. It's a crime we're not WGA yet.

"It's a lot of work and, as has been prefaced here, a lot is demanded of the writer for essentially very little money, in my opinion. The basic script rate for an animated script for Saturday morning network TV hasn't changed in ten years, so we're a little behind. I think the writers deserve to get a lot more. It's frustrating."

Is it true that there are no residuals in animation?

David Titcher

"Absolutely, no residuals in animation. In fact, here's an example that affected friends of mine who worked on *Aladdin*, the series. When the show was about to go on, somebody who was quite smart said, 'Let's take the first four shows of *Aladdin, Return to Jafar*, and turn it into a direct-to-video thing. Rather than show them as the first four episodes, we'll show it as a direct-to-video sequel to *Aladdin*.' And they did. It sold something like fifteen million copies. It was all gravy—like two hundred million in profit right there. I sat down and worked out the potential residuals and I told my friends [the eight writers that had done these four episodes], 'If you were under the Writers Guild rules of residuals, you would have each gotten over a million dollars.' But, because they're not, they got zero. A couple of them still working there when the video came out got one week's salary as a bonus, but most of them weren't, so they didn't get anything."

Steve Roberts

"Once you've written an animation script, you get six thousand dollars, and then they own it. They can rerun it as much as they want, and it's pure profit to them. Six cartoons I know of that I wrote were released on video, and I didn't get a dime."

Did you at least get credit?

"Yeah. I wrote the first *Ninja Turtles* ever to be released on video, and it sold like hotcakes, and I didn't get a dime out of it. If I got residuals on that one video alone, I would be living in a house instead of an apartment."

How do you go about hiring staff writers for a show?

Steve Roberts

"When I became a story editor at Disney, I got to choose from the writers on staff who weren't already tied up on another show. First, I chose a writing team which consisted of two guys in their early twenties who'd only written three scripts. Before they were hired, they'd never written anything. They had a friend at Disney in the art department who arranged for a producer to read one of their writing samples. They wrote a cartoon script in one weekend, sent it in, and got hired. I read their scripts and could tell immediately that these guys were extremely imaginative, although hopelessly undisciplined. Their first script had so many typos in it, it was obvious they'd never read it, let alone rewritten it. I read them the riot act and told them I was their editor, not their proofreader. It ultimately turned out that one of them was a flake and the other was doing all the writing for both of them. The flake is not employed, and the other guy is now a story editor.

"My second choice was a team of women writers. There were few women writers on staff, and a lot of people believed they only got hired because they were women. I chose them because they were much smarter, funnier, and better writers than most of the other writers. The only problem I had with them is that they were much stronger on dialogue than on visuals. You have to write a lot of sight gags in animation, and their background was writing freelance sitcoms. Their first outline was heavy on dialogue. I had them rewrite the outline without any dialogue in it, and they adapted very quickly. When a show we were working on went sour, they were, unfortunately, the first ones scapegoated and were not renewed as writers. They are now making a very lucrative living as staff writers for a network sitcom.

"For my third choice, I decided to bring my own writer on staff and had Disney hire David Titcher. Although I knew David from UCLA, I wanted him because he was a good writer, and I insisted he go through all the necessary steps to get on staff: submitting writing samples, getting the producer's approval, et cetera. He submitted a script for *Who's the Boss?* that I thought was better than any episode of *Who's the Boss?* I'd seen. Although David had no experience writing for animation, I wanted him because I knew he was an intelligent and talented writer who knew how to structure a script, write smart dialogue, grasp characterization, et cetera. You can teach someone how to write an animation script, but you can't teach someone how to write a quality animation script."

What are some of your war stories and other experiences on staff?

David Titcher

"*Bonkers* was the Heaven's Gate of cartoon shows, a notorious show. I mean Disney killed fifty scripts. That's never happened in the history of animation."

What were the reasons for killing the scripts?

"We were doing sixty-five episodes, which is basically what you do with any animation show. For about a year, there were seventeen writers on staff for the show, and, collectively, we completed about sixty-five episodes. Then the first animated episodes started coming back from South Korea, and they came back very badly animated."

Let me understand, from the script they generated cells?

"They do some storyboarding at Disney, and then they sent it to South Korea to do the animation, but when the animation came back, apparently it was very bad. So, the president of the division panicked and rather than blaming the animation and sending the script to be animated in another place, he blamed the writing, and they killed fifty scripts. They couldn't kill them all because they had twenty in the process of animation. So, they had twenty shows they had to keep. Then they stopped everything for three months, with people on staff, and created a whole new *Bonkers*. They kept the character Bonkers, but everybody around him was different now. So, now you have forty-five episodes that are one *Bonkers* and twenty that are the original. So, it's confusing. He's a cartoon cop, but he has a different partner, you know, the whole thing. It's not like the second shows were better, they just sent the second ones to Australia, where the good animation was. So, it seemed as if they were getting better episodes, but, if you analyze them, they're about the same."

What are the pressures on you as a story editor?

Steve Roberts

"You have people who represent Standards and Practices, people that represent the network, and you have the actual executive of the company. On one show I worked as a story editor, I had to take notes from eight people. One of the biggest functions of a story editor is that you're in a position of having a certain amount of creative control, but you quickly find out that it's an illusion of having more authority.

"The first problem I found with being a story editor is that you have to work a hell of a lot more than any individual writer. You might be working on as many as three scripts at a time as well as the outlines for somebody's next script as well as trying to come up with new stories all the time. When I was a staff writer, I had plenty of time to do crossword puzzles. As a story editor, after hours I would go over to one of the writer's houses, or they'd come over to mine, and we'd be working out what the story was going to be."

So you're always on the job.

"Yeah. You're always on the job."

What kind of input did you get from Standards and Practices? Can you cite a couple of examples?

"For instance, you can't show somebody on screen punching somebody else. If there is a physical fight scene, you just can't show the connection between two people. So, there is a lot of stuff that relates to violence. Their notes, as far as I was concerned, were usually valid. The guidelines up front are clear, so you can avoid having any run-ins with Standards and Practices to begin with. To me it was purely pragmatic. It was getting notes from idiots who were totally screwing up your story and who are incapable of understanding the effect the notes would have. That I found far more frustrating."

Did you get conflicting notes?

"Yes. I had plenty of occasions where I got back a full outline that had been rewritten. In one case, it was the second or third draft of an outline when all of a sudden somebody decided he or she hated it, but everybody else loved it. That one person had the authority to kill it. That's happened to me on more than one occasion. Not too long ago I had an entire script, a second draft (basically the final draft of the script), thrown out by somebody who said he didn't like it. Nobody else had any problems with it, whatever. He had plenty of opportunities to decide he didn't like it in the outline stage, but it was the final script he decided he didn't like, and didn't give any reasons, and it was dead. So, basically, you have a lot of people with God-like power who do not have to back up their subjective opinions."

What's the hardest part of animation writing?

Steve Roberts

"I think it's visualization. The main thing about writing an animation script that's unique is that you have to direct it on paper: you don't have actors to emote, you don't have sets—basically you're starting with a tabula rasa. And in animation, absolutely everything originates from the script. There are no designs—unless it's something like *Darkwing Duck* who's got a bat cave set up and that's part of the concept that's already designed. You also might have characters designed for the whole series—but a background will be designed on the basis of where your story is going to be set, the locations. So, if you have a scene set in a department store, only after the fact are they going to start designing a department store. This means you have to specifically call out things that need to be in that scene. You have to actually describe the editing, you have to edit the thing on paper. So, you have to call out every single cut. For example, you have to call out 'long shot,' 'close up,' 'racking shot,' 'following shot'—all camera movements, angles, pans, and so on. You have to understand what all that means in order to apply them properly. You're basically writing a shooting script."

Do you have to tailor your writing for known voices, such as Mel Blanc?

"No, but I've had cases where the villain in the show is a character I have to come up with myself. In those cases, I have to describe the villain and everything, and only then after the script is finalized, might they cast that part. Then I might find that the character has been cast with some guy who has a high-pitched, goofy voice, which is totally antithetical to what I had in mind and totally spoils the way this character comes across.

"I had a case where I wrote a character that was to speak in a totally dry, deadpan way and they cast a guy who speaks in an over-the-top, goofy way. Of course, that meant the lines I wrote, designed to be delivered deadpan, were totally screwed up. I think it's much funnier when a character who is totally over-the-top insane thinks he's completely rational. When they cast somebody who has a Steven Wright–type delivery, it works perfectly. If you can have outrageous lines delivered in this totally deadpan way, they are a lot funnier than they would be if they are read as if the guy knows he's insane or is ranting."

When I started looking into animation writing, I discovered, to my amazement, that it was not officially covered under the Writers Guild of America (WGA). Animation writers are part of the Motion Picture Screen Cartoonists (MPSC) union, which mainly covers the animators. Screen credits for animation do not count toward getting into the WGA.

Why aren't animation writers in the Writers Guild?

David Titcher

"Animation writers would like to be in the Writers Guild, but they're not; they're covered under this animation union, which covers all the animators. But, in my opinion, from a writer's standpoint it's a weak guild. What happened was, in the seventies, the animation guild went on strike. It was like the worst strike ever; they were about to lose the strike so badly that the union wasn't going to exist anymore. They were basically fighting Hanna-Barbera, which pretty much did everything in those days, and the two guys who started the union many years ago were Hanna and Barbera. Well, they didn't want to be a party to destroying the union they had created, so they made some sort of deal. It looked really bad for the animators because they got this horrendous deal, but, in a way, it worked out because now you see an explosion of animation being done in America. And that's probably because that deal made it viable to do animation in America. It worked out that it ended up giving a lot more people in animation work, but nobody knew that at the time. At the time, to many people, it seemed like a disaster."

It made it easier to get started and become profitable in animation?
"Yeah. They still send the scripts overseas to actually be animated—all the TV shows do, that is. I would imagine they still do feature animation films in America.

"They all do blocks of it, then they send it to Korea, France, Australia; they send each episode to a different country. Which, actually, you'd think it might be better if they would send all of the episodes to one place, and then that place would know what the show was about, but they send it to maybe eight or nine different places."

Steve Roberts

"When animation writers were first recognized, they ended up becoming unionized under the umbrella of the animators union. So, that's one of the problems—the animation writers are a very small part of the MPSC. I'm a big believer in unions because, for your dues, you get great health care. Here's the problem: most of the studios are not union shops. In order to continue to get your health insurance, you have to chalk up a certain number of hours per year at a union shop. That's a big problem because typically it's very tough on writers at studios that don't have any union representation. Only the big studios, like Warner Bros. and Disney, are union shops. But the lion's share of the work done is in nonunion shops, and animation writers are not really organized. In the MPSC union, the emphasis is on the artists, not writers, so there's no movement to help the writers gain some clout."

You're talking about the actual animators?

"Yeah, the ones who do artwork—that's how the animation union started in the first place, it was for the artists; the writers became involved later.

"To me, the union is very weak on its representation of writers, and to a great extent that's the fault of the writers for not really being involved in the union. I feel that, if we're ever going to get residuals, we have to get together and go on strike. But nobody wants to do that; it's just too risky because there's also this attitude that writers are always replaceable. They feel the studio will say, 'Oh, we'll just get somebody else to do the work.' And there's a good reason to be worried about that sort of thing."

David mentioned to me that the WGAw (Writers Guild of America, west) was pursuing something to do with animation writers. I contacted the WGAw and discovered that they have formed the Animation Writers Caucus. It is open to Guild members and non-WGA persons who have written at least a one half-hour animation screenplay or teleplay. Guild members can join for free, and non-WGA members pay $75 per year through an associate membership. The AWC will get involved in negotiating some points of animation contracts.

The AWC has a steering committee that also meets about once a month. It puts on seminars and panels of industry professionals to discuss topics of interest to professionals in the animation field. Today, there are 275 members in the AWC. It is estimated that this figure represents over two-thirds of those working as animation writers on a regular basis.

The holdup to bringing animation completely into guild control is getting the key animation companies to become signatories on a per-show basis. But the WGAw is taking a first step. By early May 1995 they expected to have the first company signed. Work under WGA animation signatory contracts will qualify for entry into the WGA, as well as for health benefits. Unfortunately, pay is not going to be leaping up to full-blown Minimum Basic Allowance. As for residuals, Guild animation deals include a reuse fee, but not standard residuals as for live action.

WGA members will still be able to work for nonsignatory animation companies, at least until there are enough animation signatory companies to justify changing this rule.

For more information contact the WGAw at (213) 782-4511.

How does a writer break into animation writing?

Steve has already covered this topic in his comments about hiring staff writers, and David mentioned how he got in. However, below are some additional thoughts I feel are useful.

Steve Roberts

"You need to get some basic inside information of some kind, at least as far as what shows are going into production and who the story editor is. You don't want to call up and get some receptionist on the phone and say, 'Who's the story editor? I want to speak to a story editor.' You need get the name of the story editor on the show and also find out if they need writers. If they are looking, you'll generally be asked for a writing sample. And, if they are willing to use you, then you have to pitch stories."

David Titcher

"General sitcom writing is good training for animation writing. They don't hire people based on animation scripts, at least when I was applying; it was all done on sitcom scripts. The same sort of skills. Then you have to learn an additional skill on top of that, which is this whole, 'Everything you write we draw' thing, and you have to be so careful about it. That's something that you learn when you're there, and I'm not sure I ever really learned it actually. It was just not the way my mind thought. It was so detailed, and I was more of a big picture man."

Do you have any last thoughts?

Steve Roberts

"One point I always like to make with a new writer who hasn't done animation before is to say that in animation you get an opportunity to direct, but you have to do it on paper, and you don't get any screen credit for it, nor do you get paid for it.

"A big problem in animation today is that there's almost no communication whatsoever between the writers and the animation artists. It's almost like the environment, when I was at UCLA, between students in production and critical studies. It's as if there's a rivalry or something. In critical studies, they'll look upon the production students as ignoramuses, and in production they think of the critical studies guys as a bunch of eggheads. I think it all fits together. But in animation as a writer, you have absolutely no communication whatsoever with any of the people who are doing the artwork. There is no coordination. At the very top level, the producer of the show is the only point where these intersect. So, you're not getting any input whatsoever from the artists, who could be extremely valuable in terms of how you could be executing action scenes or sight gags. All you can do is try and describe something and hope they get it or take some initiative and think of a better way to do it. More often than not, though, the storyboard artist is simply going to execute what you've written and not take any initiative. I think it's a big problem that the writers and artists do not communicate. Even at Disney, where they're all working on staff, on the same floor, there aren't any meetings where the writers and artists are together. The story editor won't even be involved at all in what's the art side is doing except maybe reviewing storyboards.

"If you looked at old Warner Bros. cartoons, *Bugs Bunny* and *Porky Pig*, you have the writers and whoever's doing the stories totally in conjunction with each other."

What are the biggest lessons you've learned in your ten years in animation? What has made you a better animation writer?

"I think it's personal in that I take it very seriously. Just because it's animation I'm not going to have an attitude that it's the ghetto of writing. You're either a good writer or you're not. There are plenty of feature films that are made where the writing's terrible. But, on the other hand, you can write a great cartoon episode."

Did your animation work help you as a writer?

David Titcher

"Yes, it did. As a matter of fact, since then, if there's one thematic thing in a script sense that all my scripts have taken on, it's that anything is possible. I must have gotten that from animation because anything can happen in an animation script. It sort of loosens you up to possibilities. In my scripts now, if I am confronted with something that seems impossible such as, 'How are they going to escape from this place? It's the most well-guarded place in the world,' from animation, I know it's no real problem. On the other hand, the downside of animation experience is that in live-action writing, you have to avoid becoming too cartooney in your writing. You'll be criticized for excessive broadness in the comedy, and that is something that, if you are writing features or sitcoms, executives don't like, even though audiences do seem to like that kind of humor."

FIVE

Developing and Producing a Low-Budget Feature:
A Look into
The Glass Shield

This is an important chapter. At the heart of this chapter is the classic struggle of fighting your way through the system as an unknown outsider and winning.

The Glass Shield *was produced in 1993 for around $3,500,000, a miniscule budget compared to the current blockbuster budgets of fifty to one hundred million dollars or more. This film was of special interest to me because the initial story idea came from John "JJ" Johnson, Jr., a former policeman. JJ had no formal writing training nor any Hollywood contacts when he started. Yet, five years after he set out to pitch his* story, it was being filmed with distinguished acting and directing talent attached.

I wanted answers to the following questions: How did a Hollywood outsider get something produced? What notes did the writer have to deal with from the technical advisor, executive producer, production company, and actors? How were the various people brought on board? How did they get their funding? What enticed both producers and actors to come on board? What were the snags, and how were they resolved? Why this story?

Fortunately, the whole production staff embraced the interview process and were very candid with their thoughts. I interviewed Chet Walker (executive producer); Thomas Byrnes and Carolyn Schroeder (producers who also raised the funds); Charles Burnett (writer/director); Michael Boatman (lead actor); and John "JJ" Johnson, Jr. (technical advisor and the one upon whom the story is loosely based).

CAST MEMBERS (partial list)

ACTOR	CHARACTER
Michael Boatman	JJ
Lori Petty	Deborah
Richard Anderson	Massey
Michael Gregory	Roy Bush
Michael Ironside	Baker
Don Harvey	Deputy Bono
Ice Cube	Teddy Woods
Elliot Gould	Greenspan
Bernie Casey	Locket
Ernie Lee Banks	Mr. Woods
Erich Anderson	Ira Kern
Natalija Norgulich	Judge Lewis
M. Emmet Walsh	Hall

MAIN CHARACTERS

JJ is an idealistic, young African American assigned right out of the Police Academy to an all-white Southern California sheriff's department.

DEBORAH is an outspoken, young, white rookie police officer in the sheriff's department. She becomes JJ's only ally in the department.

MASSEY is the police chief. He also leads the internal police "muscle" clique affectionately called The Rough Riders.

ROY BUSH is one of the founding Rough Riders, assigned by police Chief Massey to train JJ.

STORY LINE

JJ, a young, idealistic, African-American police officer is assigned right out of the Academy to a formerly all-white Southern California sheriff's department. This is in response to intense community pressure following the suspicious death of a popular black athlete while in the custody of the sheriff's department. Once inside, JJ becomes the object of prejudice and demeaning practical jokes. He befriends Deborah, a fellow rookie also under the gun, and together they struggle to have a career in the sheriff's department. However, their lives are put in jeopardy by the Rough Riders (a muscle group within the sheriff's department), who want to return the department to its former all-white, male status quo.

JJ, in an attempt to fit in, lies under oath about an illegal car search that led to the discovery of a gun. His testimony is crucial in the case because the car's driver is being tied to a high-profile murder through the gun supposedly found in the car. Later, JJ discovers that someone in the police department substituted the murder weapon for the gun he found in the search. He realizes that he has unwittingly been used in an attempt to convict an innocent man and protect a high-profile guilty man. He is then faced with a moral dilemma.

Does he tell the truth, set the record straight, and set free an innocent man, or does he remain silent, allow this man to be convicted, and thereby take a big step toward his lifelong dream of becoming accepted in the police department as one of the boys? The truth will end his career and the careers of those involved in the conspiracy. The lie insures they will be indebted to him.

For the reader's information, these interviews were conducted in 1993, while the film was still in production.

HOW *THE GLASS SHIELD* CAME TOGETHER

John "JJ" Johnson (technical advisor)

"As I left the police department, I thought back on my experiences and the problems I had at the station regarding racism and a controversial death, and I had a strong conviction to get my story out. My main motivation was that I felt so cheated. I worked hard to get to the police department, and once I got there I felt I was treated in an unprofessional manner. When I decided to leave, I just had a conviction that this would make a good story."

At about the same time, Chet Walker (executive producer) wanted to tell the story of the controversial death of a popular black athlete while in custody of the police at the station where JJ had worked.

Chet Walker (executive producer)

"I was trying to do a story on Ron Settles, but there was so much litigation surrounding the story, I couldn't make it happen."

JJ first attempted to tell his story through a book deal.

JJ

"In the latter part of '89, I wrote to five publishing companies: Time Warner and other top-notch companies. I went to the library, got their addresses, and sent them each a brief synopsis of my story idea that dealt with the Ron Settles hanging incident, the way I was treated, and how I felt that the police department hired me as a scapegoat as if to say, 'We have one here. We have a black police officer now.'

"I got two responses out of five. One said, 'No, thank you,' the other one said, 'Get a literary agent.'

"I didn't know how to go about getting the story published. For eleven years my whole thing was police. What's a literary agent? I called around but got no help whatsoever. So, I kind of scratched that idea and forgot about the project. I mean, what are the odds of me coming out of South Central LA, going to a police department—and then coming up with a book deal? Pretty low.

"Then in '89 an ex-girlfriend told me about something in the *TV Guide* called the *Hollywood Producers Directory*. She said, 'Hey, you could put your story in there. It goes out to about three thousand producers, and maybe somebody will pick it up.' [As of this writing, this directory is no longer published.]

"It cost me one hundred dollars. A guy, Michael Johnson, was running the company at the time, and we became acquainted over the telephone. He loved the story.

"The way the *Hollywood Producers Directory* worked was, they'd send you a package and you'd do a brief synopsis of what you had, either a script, an idea, or, I forget the other category. Mine was the idea category: this is what I have, a brief synopsis of the incident (the same thing I sent off to the book publishers). He loved it. He said, 'Yeah, I think we can kinda raise some eyebrows. Let's put it out.' And it got in the book.

"As a result, I got calls from five movie companies: Paramount, REM, London, and a couple of independents. They all said basically,

'We have your deal here. Do you have a script?' And everyone I talked to did the same thing. When I said 'No, I don't,' they'd hang up. Literally hang up. Just hang up, and I'm thinking like, 'Whoa, what's the deal here?'

"Well, after the fifth call like that, I called Michael back and said, 'Look, this is what's happening to me.' He explained, 'When a company calls, they're ready to go with it right there, basically, and they want something written or in the bag. They don't have time to sit down with you and go over it with a writer.

"So, I scrubbed the idea again. But Michael said, 'I have this writer, Ned Welsh. He's a good writer, he's written a few things, and he'll probably do a script for you for like $2,500.'

"I didn't have $2,500 dollars, and, in the back of my mind, I scrubbed the idea, thinking, 'I'll never do this.' But, because I like to finish what I start, I also figured, I may just go ahead with it later. So, I took his number.

"I had Ned's number for two months. Then on a whim, I called him to see if I could come up with some kind of deal. Maybe do it on a payment plan or half price. He wasn't home, so I left a message on his machine.

"He called me back and said he had the directory, and in that instant there was a bond, an instant bond. I explained everything to him, and he wrote up the treatment to do a TV movie. He also wrote up the agreements for the rights for me to give him the power of attorney to basically go ahead and shop the story around. Ned wrote a treatment and then shopped it among his contacts. We ran into a bunch of dead ends—CBS didn't want to do this, NBC didn't want that. It was all a dead end.

"Eventually, a friend of Ned's introduced him to Chet Walker."

Chet Walker

"I met Ned before he wrote a script. He had a treatment plus some articles about JJ. When I saw that, I thought, 'Maybe we can touch on the Ron Settles story by telling JJ's story.' Then Ned and I together developed the original script, called *One of Us*. I supervised the development of it, Ned wrote it.

"I shopped it around, but I couldn't get anybody to take it. Then I gave it to Charles Burnett because Charles and I had developed a story at Warner Bros. called *My Word of Honor*. I let him take a look at the story that Ned had written. He liked the concept, but he thought it was a little too much in the television genre, so Charles rewrote it. More than that, he reworked it."

Charles rewrote Ned's script and broadened the story.

Charles Burnett (writer/director)

"When Chet brought the *One of Us* script to me, we had just finished writing a story for Warner Bros. called *My Word of Honor* that didn't get picked up. He had the idea that we could do this film really quickly. So, I said, 'OK, let me read it.' After I did, I said, 'Well, we could probably do a little better job on it.' The script was basically about JJ's experience at the station and trying to be a part of it.

"I think Ned's script takes place barely before a lot of the revelations about the police department came out. So, I wanted to put in what was current, to some extent. Not just what happened to JJ, but what has happened throughout the country and LA particularly. I say throughout the country because there is a scene in there that sort of resembles the case in Boston where a guy killed his wife and said he was attacked. So we have that in the story, and we have things that happened in the police department in Long Beach and turned it into a murder-for-hire scheme. A bunch of those things happened and are still in the court system right now. So, it was basically adding all those things together and trying to tell a story about a man who wants to be a cop so badly that he ends up compromising himself in a way that could happen to any of us. I wanted to incorporate all the things that were happening in the country racially and how it's institutionalized and the sort of things like that—the problems the police have, to some degree."

The next challenge for Chet was to find a production company to back the project. Although local production companies were not interested, Charles had recently worked with producers Tom Byrnes and Carolyn Schroeder, who were experienced at getting financing. He introduced them to Chet, who immediately brought them into the project. Their first step was to buy the rights to JJ's life story as it applied to this police situation.

Tom Byrnes (producer)

"Carol and I raised the money to buy the Johnny Eddie Johnson script and also got the money to pay Charles to do a rewrite."

As the script was being written, Tom and Carolyn started to search for a production company to back the project. They found potential CiBy 2000 (pronounced "See Bee"), the French company that backed The Piano.

Carolyn Schroeder (producer)

"We ran into CiBy 2000 at Cannes 1992. The gentleman that was their consultant was also on the Cannes film selection committee, and he picked Charles's film *To Sleep with Anger*, so he knew of Charles Burnett. He was excited that we had a project with Charles and introduced us to CiBy 2000 when we went to Paris."

Tom Byrnes

"It took us a year or so to get the financing, and the film is entirely financed by CiBy 2000. They got involved because they wanted to be in business with Charles—they liked his other movie, *To Sleep with Anger.* It's very remarkable because Charles tells very American stories. This is an American theme story, too, about police relations set in Los Angeles made by a highly respected, talented American filmmaker. Yet all the financing has come from a French company. Nobody else had the courage to back this project.

JJ

"I met Chet in '90, the last part of '90. In the latter part of '91, we came up with an agreement. Then they shopped it to Carolyn and Tom. All of them liked it, and they were going to go with it and see what they could do. So, we got our agreement signed, and for me it was just cross-your-fingers-and-wait time. We waited and waited and waited. We had start dates, and then no's, and we're going to go with this date, and then no. The company that put up the money for it backed out and I felt like, 'OK. Well, it's dead fish in the water.'

"Six months later, the company decided, 'Well, I think we want to do this.' So, it finally gets there and we're on again. The next thing I know we have a start date set for July '93—we're gonna start and I'm jazzed. Then I got a confirmation stating it's going to go August 3, but it really didn't hit me until I was invited down to preproduction at the Hollywood office."

DEVELOPING THE STORY LINE AND MAIN CHARACTERS

As mentioned earlier, Charles wrote The Glass Shield *to address, in a fictional story, many of the race and police issues of our time.*

Charles Burnett

"I tried to make JJ as human as possible.

"The theme is that aspirations and reality are two different things. That belonging (in this case, being one of the boys) shouldn't distort your vision, shouldn't compromise your morals. So, if you do the right thing and are honest, then you won't get into trouble.

"The dilemma for JJ (the lead character) is that he lies under oath believing he's doing good—lying to convict this guy. He thought his action was an innocent gesture in the sense that he truly believed that the guy on trial for murder was guilty. However, in reality, the guy was innocent. He was framed, and JJ unwittingly helped to convict the guy, to defame the guy."

Another vital writing consideration for Charles is texture. The Glass Shield *is a strong ensemble story. In fact, there are some 70 speaking parts, 75 locations, and 180 scenes. All this on a budget of $3.5 million. Even more unbelievable is that they attracted quite a number of prominent actors, like Elliot Gould and Michael Ironside on favored nations contracts.*

Charles Burnett

"Life isn't as simple as most modern Hollywood films make it out to be, and it involves more characters than just the three principal characters that most films of this budget could afford. In old Hollywood movies, I think mainly because they had a stable of contract actors on the lot, they could use tons of actors, and I think the films seem richer. I am a little influenced by that. I think the more people the main character confronts, it is in essence the same as conflict. It adds layers or texture to the story, and characters have more dimension."

Charles understands the collaborative effort inherent in film and accepts input from many sources. As the writer/director, he worked with actors, producers and technical advisors to make subtle changes.

Charles Burnett

"To me, the script is like a framework. To arrive at something more than just what's on the page, I think in terms of making the performers create rather than being mechanical and just doing what you want them to do. Allow them to develop the characters and play with it, if time allows. I think they feel better when they can create and feel as though they're helping you, and they are helping you."

WHAT'S BEHIND THE SCRIPT AND CHARACTERS?

Tom Byrnes

"Charles is very cautious about the kind of images that he is responsible for putting before the public. I think it is a very nice responsibility the filmmaker has. Some people don't consider it at all. If it's commercial or marketable, they'll make *New Jack City*, then they'll make *Menace II Society*. And it's not that there aren't areas like those depicted in *New Jack City* or *Menace II Society*, but you don't have to keep telling stories about that segment of African-American culture.

"*To Sleep with Anger* is a very interesting, well-told family drama about a black family, and it won lots of awards and got lots of attention. There's no violence in it, no profanity. It presents a black family the same way a white family was depicted in *Ordinary People*, a drama about the tribulations of a family.

"Charles will make the piece more humane or show that there are various sides even to someone as bad as the Baker character. Baker is a character who is a rogue cop, who is like a hired killer, a gangster. Yet he has a real affection for his partner, Hall, and you see the camaraderie and friendship of the Rough Riders. Yet they can go out and be very brutal to other people. They are not stereotypical bad guy characters."

Carolyn Schroeder

"I think personal integrity is pertinent to everyone as well as what happens when you compromise yourself. What are the ramifications of that compromise? There's great hope in the tragedy of the end because the good guy goes down with the bad guys, and yet he has a spiritual renewal. Charles has always had European sensibilities, and he's always been a little bit of a poet. I think this is one of those films that will lead everyone to the coffeehouse to sit around for hours discussing what it meant because it's going to mean something different to everybody."

Michael Boatman (lead actor)

"When I first started, I had this image of a man living in a pressure cooker or furnace. We're talking about a job where you don't know if you are going to survive from one day to the next, literally."

THE CASTING PROCESS

With the script finished, financing in place, and Charles lined up to direct, the next step was to cast the show. Having recognizable names attached is like money in the bank. But to get them on a low-budget movie requires something more than money, in this case, the opportunity to work with Charles. Here's how casting went on this movie.

Carolyn Schroeder

"Well, we did have financing, which always helps. For a long time, we had Cuba Gooding, Jr., from *Boyz N the Hood* attached. Then he got a new agent, another movie for more money, and he went that way. So, we were looking for a new "JJ" when a friend of ours told us about Michael Boatman.

"We went over to his manager's house and watched a videotape of his excerpts from *China Beach*—which just knocked my socks off. We said, 'This is it.' She also represented Lori Petty, and we started considering her for the character of Deborah, who was pretty feisty. Lori Petty in real life was close to being who Deborah was. Fortunately, she's an excellent actress and did a wonderful job bringing Deborah to the screen. And I could certainly understand why, when Lori read the script, it appealed to her.

"Michael Ironside, believe it or not, came in and read for the part. And I can't even remember whom we had offered it to. We made some other offers to some big names but were having trouble scheduling people. Michael wanted it so badly that he completely rearranged his schedule so he could be in the film.

"Before we went to Cannes this year, we gave the script to Elliot Gould for the part of either Baker or Massey. He called back and said, 'No, forget it. I can't do it.' And when we started talking about it, the guy from CiBy said, 'You know, he'd make a good Greenspan' (a character who murders his wife and blames it on another man). Then Elliot called back and said, 'Nobody told us it was Charles Burnett [directing]. I want to meet with you when you get back.'

"After we returned, he came over to our house and met with Charles for about forty-five minutes. All they talked about was basketball, I mean, nothing about the script, and then he left and he did it.

"The below-the-line production attorney, Harris Tulchin, represented Ice Cube. Harris and Tom used to be law partners together, and we got the script to Cube through Harris. Of course, Cube wanted to do it because it's like the characters he sings about—young black men getting rousted by the police for no reason whatsoever and assumed guilty."

ADDITIONAL THOUGHTS

Below are highlights from the interviews. Among other things, I felt it important to understand how scripts get into the hands of producers, directors, actors, and agents. And, since careers are made on finding good scripts, I also wanted to get their thoughts on the common flaws they find in the scripts they reject.

In general, how many scripts do you go through in a month, and how many do you think you go through to find one that you really like?

Tom Byrnes

"I've slowed down. There was a period in time when I used to read several scripts a week. I now have enough projects that I want to do. Although I still read scripts, it's nowhere near as often as I used to. It's because, I know, for example, as I finish this project, I have others that are lined up in the wings that I need to take care of. So, I now have a couple years' worth of work that I have optioned or own. I have paid for five, six, or seven scripts, and I have to pay attention to those. And I also have my own ideas I want to develop. Things that I'd like to see done.

Sometimes you pay others to develop an idea you have?

"Right. I pay them to help flesh it out, or I give them a step outline and say 'This is kind of the way I see it.' Then I ask them to write it."

Michael Boatman

"Well, at this stage, when I audition, I often meet the directors and producers right away. I've reached the point where, now that

I've done two series, several TV movies, and things like that, when they do call me in for something, I generally always meet with the director, at least. I don't get offers at this point, I still have to audition. Although I was offered this film based on a meeting between my manager and the director, who saw my tape on *China Beach* excerpts. As a result, I read a lot of scripts. I read about ten to fifteen scripts a month for me to audition for—feature-length scripts or TV movies or pilots for TV shows. Out of that fifteen, I'll probably find three that I really, really like. And out of that, there will generally be one.

"I think I find one script a month, although it doesn't break down precisely month to month, but it averages out to about one script a month that I really have a chance to get and that really clicks with me."

How do scripts find their way to you?

Chet Walker

"Word of mouth. Friends that I know who are writers. Friends who know writers. But, I've been doing this for twelve years. So, I've met a lot of people. I read probably five or six a week."

Tom Byrnes

"I don't know quite how scripts get to me. What will happen is that, for example, soon people will know we made this movie. Then I'll probably get lots of scripts from independent filmmakers saying, 'Oh, you and Charles. Great, I have something . . . ' and there'll probably be these sensitive dramas and stuff, and I will look at them.

"Personally, I am trying to do films that entertain and make some comment on the human condition, but I also need to make some money doing it."

What are the common flaws, if any, in the scripts you reject?

Tom Byrnes

"I don't know if there is a common fault. I think, well, one of the things that I notice and when I ultimately see something that I don't like I say, 'Geez, it doesn't work.' Part of it is my own frame of reference. Initially, what I hunt for—not that I restrict it—but I'm not in the market for finding a big science-fiction picture like *Jurassic Park* or *Star Wars*. I don't even want to see a low-budget one, or a period piece.

"I have this wonderful story I'm considering about an Indian. It's a human drama about the future and how people are going to cope with genetic engineering and stuff. The big reason I'd reject this piece is because of the producer/businessman side of me.

"I'm a lawyer seventeen years by training. I was a lawyer before, and I'm still a lawyer. I was a lawyer before I became a producer, and my introduction to law was through producing and entertainment school of law. The point is, there are far fewer buyers for big-budget films. It has to be a big studio. It can't be an independent company because it's either expensive or it's going to be very cheesy. You can't do a period piece without having all the wardrobe or costumes and props and things. You can't do science-fiction films without lots of money for special effects and, again, set dressing and design, wardrobe, or automobiles.

"So, I hunt for pictures that initially can lend themselves to a smaller budget. There are more buyers for that kind of a film, which means you may lose or have to exclude certain types of scenes. For example, you can't have eighty people having a gunfight, nor can you do gigantic stunts with cars careening on the freeway and stuff, even though they're very impressive scenes.

"Hopefully more people will see *The Glass Shield*. Then I may have a few more inroads into studios where I'd say, 'I've got a wonderful script. You ought to make it.' But, by and large, most of the buyers at those companies end up doing business with people they know. So, they go back to the same people they've made movies with. Or they go to the big agencies. They phone CAA and say, 'We're hunting for a science-fiction picture. Why don't you send five scripts over to me? Your five best writers.' He will do the same thing with William Morris, ICM, and a couple of agencies.

"Pretty soon, that one production executive who is hunting for that movie will get twenty scripts. (If he got five each from the three big agencies and five from buddies or friends or people he knows that he tells he's looking for a science-fiction picture, then he's got twenty scripts.) And he'll choose something from there. The odds are of me bringing mine in saying, 'Hey, I've got this great script . . . ' and getting them to read it—I just think the odds are so against me that I don't even waste my time. I just don't think it's the best use of my time.

"So, I'd rather develop things that I think can be done by a lot more people, that can be done by a lot of independents. Sometimes I even develop projects that can be done simply for video and cable TV budgets. I've got some projects I've budgeted a million four or a million five. And they're smaller dollars. They're small-town stories where a drifter comes through town and somebody from town wants to leave. That kind of a movie. Then the writing has to be very good because you can't keep the people turning the pages simply with tremendous action and dynamic fights and other things going off. You've got to create interest in the story and characters.

"What I ultimately hope for is an interesting story. And I think a lot of scripts superficially glaze over those kind of things. I sometimes find I get more people who are very good with sentence syntax and grammar or write in a nice way but ultimately don't have much to say.

"I like to find stories where the people are very interesting or there's a potential to make some very interesting characters inside an interesting story."

Chet Walker

"A lot of the scripts I get, because I'm not a huge major producer, come from writers who don't have a lot of experience. So, the major flaw is the construction of the script and the story line. The script is an outline for the director, so writers not only have to know stories, they have to know camera angles and all that stuff in order to really make a script work. A lot of people I read don't have the experience to see all those things. Even though the story may be good, the construction of it may be flawed."

When you are looking for a script to produce, what are you looking for? What elements are important to you?

Carolyn Schroeder

"Well, there's not a genre of films that I'm looking for. I mean, everybody wants to do something of substance. I take that back, some people don't want to do anything of substance. I do, however.

"I have to be really honest. First time I read it, I have to be wanting to turn the page, so it has to hold my interest. Then, when I get past that point and I start to analyze it, if I like the story and I like what has transpired in the script, I look at the structure of it. I look to see if there is a through-line and that the story is clearly told. At the end of the first twenty pages, this happens and at forty pages, et cetera. It's like composing a sonata, A-B-A sonata, the structure is the same, but the variable is the talent. I look to make sure it hits all the right spots and yet has something unique and interesting or the characters have something unique to them. Something has to stay with me after I put the script down.

It sounds as if you look for scripts that are both story and character driven?

"Either, or. It doesn't have to be both. But everybody wants a well-defined character. You don't want an interesting character introduced on page five who just fades out on page twenty. You get to the editing room, and you realize, 'Oops.' Or the audience says, 'Who was that guy?' It needs to make sense.

"Hollywood is very star driven, and so you've also got to get the right stars attached. But the agents say you can't submit it to the star without backing, but you can't back without the star. So, you've got to figure out a way to get to people without having to go through the proper channels. Or, you get to the point, which Tom and I are trying to do, which is where your reputation is such that you can follow it all through, properly.

"But, starting out, you've got to get people attached. Or sometimes they will say, 'We'll consider doing the script if you get these three names attached.' There are lots of different ways to skin that cat, and then on the strength of that, you can go out.

"And you can see this process in movies. There are some reasons that are warranted—why they would like to attach a star with a script. Look at *Unlawful Entry*. I think that's a perfect example of a film that could be a B film. It could have had three completely unknowns in it. It's still a genre film, a suspense thriller that could have lent itself to a one-million-dollar budget. But it had Ray Liotta, Madelyn Stowe, and Kurt Russell and so it was a big-time movie. Whoever is attached to it makes a big difference in terms of marketability.

"But, sincerity goes a long way in a script. It is apparent to me when people are trying to skim the surface, and I sense too much of a formula like, 'Oh, remember when another film had this in it or that in it?' Things like that that don't ring true. There are scripts I have read that have elements that are similar to other scripts, but there's a certain amount of sincerity in the writer's attempt to express it. It's like the difference when playing a pause in a music piece, when you have a rest. You can either have no thought in your head while you play the rest (or don't play the rest, as the case might be), or you can continue with the inspiration of the piece and that moment of rest will have some weight to it. The more back story the writer has in his or her own mind, whether it's expressed on the page or not, the more fully it will be realized what he or she is writing about and who the characters are."

As an actor, how do you approach a script to find depth in a character?

Michael Boatman

"First of all, certain things come to me viscerally. I think that's when I become attracted to a script in the first place. The minute I read something, it goes into me, and I find images forming. I think, at that stage, it's sort of beyond my control, and all I do is lasso it and pull it in and then work it from there. But when things don't come viscerally or when things don't come immediately out of the script, I look at the character's motivations as outlined by the script. I think about where the character is going and what he seems to want in each and every scene.

"So, it really is a breakdown process. I call it pencil work because I use a pencil, and it's a process that's constantly changing. For this show, I had ideas about where JJ was going, where he was coming from, what was happening to him in between those two points. But they were constantly changing as things went on. I had a basic idea or basic arc in mind, and there is an image that I generally found compelling about JJ. I saw him as a man living in a pressure cooker.

And what happens with other shows and other projects is, I'll get a recurring image from the script. A visual image will hit me such as the one of JJ living in a pressure cooker. Sort of a theme, I guess, but it happens in my mind when I first read the script. And then obviously when you work with the director, that becomes a little fine-tuned or changed. But I think you go in with a certain attitude—I go in with a certain attitude."

From your perspective, what advice would you give to screenwriters?

Charles Burnett

"I went to UCLA when film was an art form. There were some good writing instructors. I think Bill Adams was there, Mark McCarty was a writing teacher and so was William Menger and some others that come to mind. At that time, in the sixties, UCLA was sort of anti-establishment, and anything that was very slick in Hollywood was, well, you were in the wrong boat. The master's program taught you film as an art form because it was a social movement at the time and film was a means of social change. It really affected how you wrote and what you expected to gain from writing. And, also, at that time, Hollywood was basically closed. Now it's changed a lot. I think everyone now is writing a script thinking about a three-picture deal and things like that. I think people look at it more as a business, as opposed to an art.

"When you look at it as a business instead of an art form, there are a lot of considerations, it's not as creative. You don't have the range of flexibility. I mean, you have to be understood because of the economic considerations. For example, in *The Glass Shield*, one of the problems I faced was having so many characters in it, I think there were around seventy speaking parts. It was an issue. The number of scenes also becomes an issue. The nature of the film, or the subject or the theme of the film is an issue. And they're not all commercial, most of them. Because of all those different factors, *The Glass Shield* is not a commercial script in that sense. Because it doesn't really fit the pattern, it took someone with vision to say, 'OK, I'll take a chance on it.' It's not about car chases, even though there are some car chases in it. That's not the theme. It's not about drugs. It's a story that tries to make a social statement, and that's not something Hollywood wants to hear about."

Chet Walker

"Well, you have to be persistent. You can't give up. And you have to believe what you have is going to work. You have to keep writing. You have to keep going to movies, and, when you watch a movie, you have to watch each aspect of it. You have to look at everything. No matter how bad a film is, there is at least something technical about it that you can learn from. So you just have to keep watching all aspects of it and keep doing it."

JJ

"Just believe in what you have. Believe in what you are putting out, go all out, and don't give up. I've given up at a certain point, then turned around and used my disappointment as strength to continue. Believing in my own mind, I can continue, I can do this.

"I don't know about the business, but I will get on the phone and punch numbers until I reach the right person who will listen and say yes or no. They can't do anything physical to you, all they can do is say no."

SIX

Show Runner:
An Interview with Stephen J. Cannell

Strictly speaking, a "show runner" is an executive producer of a TV series. However, the title carries more weight than that. A show runner wields a significant amount of Hollywood clout. These are the men and women who can make deals happen, whom the networks trust to create and run shows. Studios and networks with a series idea in mind will turn to a show runner to develop the idea, or they'll look to the show runner to come up with new ideas. Then when it goes into production, the network and the studio have complete faith that the show will come in on time, on budget, and with a better than average chance of doing well in the ratings. This is a person with a ton of experience, powerful contacts, and a long string of successes—a champion in the TV business.

I was extremely fortunate to interview Stephen J. Cannell, an icon in this industry for decades. Prior to the interview, I got a printout of his credits; it was seven pages long. Overwhelming, to say the least.

When I did this interview, my goal was not to dig into every aspect of creating a show and dealing with the studios and the networks, but to get a sense of the process and why things happen the way they do. I think this chapter properly rounds out the previous chapters that deal with writing for television.

How did you get into writing and producing?

"Well, I always wanted to be a writer, but I have dyslexia and so early on it never really occurred to me as being something I could accomplish. I mean, I always liked to do it and always wrote short stories, I just never really thought I could be a writer. Then I went to college and an instructor named Ralph Salsbury convinced me that spelling isn't what writing's all about. He told me I had talent and that I should keep up with my writing—that I had something worth giving.

"I took him at his word, and when I got back from college, I went to work for my dad who had a furniture store. I drove a furniture truck during the day and wrote every evening. My wife would hold dinner until ten o'clock, and I'd come home around five o'clock and write until ten. I would get in five hours every day Monday through Friday like that, then I'd write a half day on Saturday and a half day on Sunday. I did that for about five years without a whole lot of success. Nobody bought anything. I was struggling: trying to get an agent and doing all that stuff every writer tries to do."

How old were you at that time?

"I graduated from college when I was twenty-one, and when I first started to sell, I think I was twenty-six. The first thing I sold was an episode of *It Takes a Thief*, which was never shot. Then I did a couple of stories for *Mission Impossible*—they bought two stories from me. Then I started to write scripts that actually got shot. I did two episodes of *Ironside*, and an *Adam 12*.

"When I did the *Adam 12*, I had to write it over the weekend—it was sort of a last-minute script. They had run out of material and needed an episode for the last show of the season. I got the assignment on Thursday and had to turn it in Monday morning. Thursday I plotted it and typed it up as an outline. The network approved it, and I started writing on Saturday and turned it in on Monday. The producers and the actors liked the script so much they made me the head writer on the show.

"I was then put under contract at Universal Studios and was there for eight years. During that time, I created about eight shows and became an executive producer. That was (actually it still is) a time when writers are the most important element in the television series.

"Once you have your concept, and once you have your actors cast and your time period, the only real variable is the writing. Sure, the director is a variable, but nowhere as strong a variable as the writing. So, what ends up happening is if the writers are consistently good or are perceived to be, they begin to get real power in the equation in television. That's what happened to me. I went from head writer to executive producer in about three or four years.

"I had a huge career at Universal, and by the time I finished my eight years there, I had created or co-created *The Rockford Files, Baretta, Ba Ba Black Sheep, City of Angels, Chase, Richie Brockman Private Eye* (which I did with Steve Bochco), *Stone,* and *The Duke.* I had a lot of projects at Universal, and they went to series from pilots I wrote.

"After eight years at Universal, I set up my own studio and then had to compete with majors. In fact, by the seventh or eighth year that Cannell Studios was in business, we were the third largest supplier of television in Hollywood."

Do you rent space from existing facilities or do you have your own studio?

"I built a studio up in Canada. But more important, it was a completely free-standing television studio. I had no protection from a major [studio]. I had no partners. It was just me and my wife. And at the height of our volume, we had six or seven shows on the air simultaneously with something like fifteen hundred employees all on our payroll. We did all the bookkeeping, all the payrolling, and all the legal and business affairs. I had a six-story building on La Brea [a street in LA] just packed with people. Then I built the studio up in Canada, in Vancouver—I still own it, it's on fifteen acres. It has seven sound stages, and it's a beautiful, state-of-the-art production facility."

How do you approach story development and scriptwriting?

"I write stories that have a three-act structure. Act One should define the problem. At the top of Act Two you should complicate the problem. That's usually when something in the back story hits the heroes on the back of the head that makes the problem much more complicated and dangerous than it originally was. Then during Act Two, your protagonist should be moving to solve this new, more complicated problem. And, very importantly, your antagonist should be moving to try and prevent the solution of the problem.

"Lots of people don't move their antagonist. They let the bad guy just stand there and wait to be caught. You've got to put that antagonist in motion, and he or she has got to move in Act Two. At the end of Act Two is the second-act curtain, which is the destruction of the hero's plan. Also at the end of Act Two, I like to have the hero in the most devastating and emotionally conflicted place in the drama. Act Three should be the solution."

How about four-act television scripts?

"We just add an extra act to sell soap. But when you're structuring, there's only three acts. There are other ways of doing it. I believe that the way I just described is the correct way. If you take any great drama, and dissect it . . . any movie that's stood the test of time, you'll find that three-act structure in it."

That's what they pound into your head at UCLA.

"Well, it's true. I guest lecture occasionally, and one of the things I always like to ask is, 'How many of you are writing spec features?' And I'll get a bunch of hands. Then I'll ask, 'How many of you have got broken scripts, that you can't finish?' And I'll get twice as many hands. 'And how many of those scripts go around page thirty-five or forty?' And they go, 'How did you know?' and I say, 'Because that's the beginning of Act Two, when you have to complicate your problem.' If you think about it, it's absolutely true because everybody knows how to define the problem—you have to have the idea to sit down and start at all.

"Here's an example of what I mean by a complication . . . and I'm just making this up right now, so it's not going to be very good. The problem is . . . this guy's going to lose his house. How am I going to define that? . . . Okay, he's lost his job, et cetera. What's the complication? . . . The complication is . . . there's a million dollars buried under that house, and there is an entire plot to get this guy fired so he would lose the house. So, the situation is not what you think it is . . . it isn't that you lost your job; you now realize that there is a conspiracy to get you. As the writer, the minute you get that complication you can keep writing."

Concerning writing, what are the most significant changes you've seen in television? It appears to be so different today.

"Well, there are a couple of changes. I don't know what are the most significant—I think that would depend on the individual. But, one thing . . . when I first started, we always got at least a thirteen-episode order and generally got twenty-two. I mean, a show would really have to be a breech birth before they would rip it off the air. At that time, we didn't have demographic information, just Nielsen household numbers. And the numbers came in slow; it took about a week, and network people weren't slavishly tuned in to the numbers. The Nielsens were simply used to sell advertising. Networks believed in the process. They would say, 'Well, we might not be making quite as much on this right now, but we'll stick with it because we know it will become something.' There wasn't this notion that you have to have a success immediately. There was not this whole slavish dependence on testing.

"Now, network executives can flat level a project. It can be their favorite project and then they'll get a bad audience test on it and this show they loved two days ago will immediately become a pariah, 'No way. We're never going to program that. Forget it. It's gone.'

"There's some part of me that wishes there was a little bit more passion involved in this from the network's side. There's just damn little. There used to be a lot more back in the early days. The people at the networks were more broadcasters, and they were more passionate about the projects. I mean, Brandon Tartikoff kept *Cheers* on the air for two years before it became a hit. It was the same with *Hill Street Blues*. *Hill Street Blues* was on forever before it became a hit. It premiered in the bottom of the heap, but NBC liked it. And I got the same advantage with *Hunter*.

"I was out thirteen episodes and blowing taps over that show, but I had a two-hour episode we made that really turned out great. I could see Fred Dryer and Stephanie Kramer maturing as actors, and the relationship between them was strong. But I knew NBC was going to cancel it, so I went to Brandon and said, 'Take a look at this two-hour with me.'

"I took it over to NBC and we just looked at it on the screen. Mind you, this was a show that was getting clobbered on Wednesday nights; it just wasn't doing anything. Afterward Brandon said, 'You know, it's really strange. We work and work and work to try and get a show where there is some kind of chemistry between the stars and something good is happening on the screen. Then when I find it, I'll be damned if I'm going to throw it away. So, I'll tell you what I'm going to do, Stephen. I'm going to pull *Hunter* off the air right now while we still have five episodes left to air. And I will bring it back in a good time period prior to scheduling meetings and give it a real solid test.' And that's what he did.

"He brought it back on Saturday nights in *Remington Steele*'s time period. They hiatused *Remington Steele* and gave me the Saturday ten o'clock time slot. It performed not quite as well as *Remington*, but almost as well. Pretty remarkable given the fact that *Remington* had two years to build in that time period.

"The following fall, he then put us on Saturday nights with *Remington Steele* as our lead-out. We were on at nine, and the rest is history. It was on for seven years. Now, that's an executive with guts. He was willing to say, 'You know, there's something here,' and not, 'Oh, well, the audience has rejected it. They don't like it.'

"You have to do programming a little bit with your guts and your passion and your emotions. It's not all testing. Why should we believe what fifteen people pulled at random out of a supermarket tell you is going to work.

"The thing I perceive to be the most salient change is today, we have split-second cancellations where a show goes on and it's literally canceled after one airing. Sometimes even before the national Nielsens come in. A lot of shows have been canceled off the 'overnights' (a smaller sample than the nationals).

"I say, if you don't care enough about a show, believe in it enough to fight for it, you shouldn't make it. There's too much work that goes into making a show to have it be treated that way. I had a show on last year called *Profit* that got huge reviews. If I had written them myself, I couldn't have written better reviews. Yet, it lasted four episodes and then was gone because of the numbers. Certainly it was the kind of show that was going to take the audience some time to get into—it was about a sociopath who was in a business environment. He was in this company, and he was Machiavellian the way he went after people. It was interesting and different because the star of the show was the sociopath. The whole thing was upside down. And the reviews on the show, . . . 'Groundbreaking television . . . The best show Fox has ever put on.' That's kind of strong stuff from really tough critics. Yet it was on just four weeks and gone."

135

Was this a pure business decision?

"I guess. I don't want to vilify anybody because I know the networks are under a lot of pressure to deliver. They've got a board of directors in New York who don't have a whole lot of sympathy for this. But then again, today we find that conglomerates are controlling our networks. What does Larry Tisch really know about programming? He's an asset trader. But he needs results, and you can't blame him for wanting results, he's got a lot of money invested in CBS. But sometimes, to get those results, you have to take your time. You have to make a bet on something like a *Cheers* and be willing to stick with it for a couple of seasons to let it grow.

"Yet, I've heard people at the network say, 'I can tell from the test results after two airings whether a show's going to work.' I say, 'Bullshit,' unless it's a poorly made show or it's a breech birth of some kind nobody can tell. If you could tell by testing, everything on the air would work and, of course, it doesn't. For me, that's the most significant change in television.

Another thing that has definitely changed is that our Nielsen numbers all used to be based on households. I don't know whether I really believe that Nielsen can actually tell you who's watching television anyway. But, let's say that you accept Nielsen as being a valid sample, which the networks don't really even accept, and they are all over Nielsen to improve their reporting. Anyway, it used to be household numbers. Now we have demographics, and a show can actually be marginal in households but do very, very well demographically in the eighteen- to thirty-four-year-old female/male demographics. So that becomes a show you can sell on Madison Avenue for more money.

"The first time I saw a demographic hit was with a show that, on household ratings, appeared to not be doing very well, but the network kept renewing it. I couldn't figure out why until they said, 'We're making so much money on it. We've got to renew it,' and that was *St. Elsewhere.* It had a very strong eighteen- to thirty-four-year-old demographic, a very young show, and they sold [the commercial time] for a lot of money, thus making it too valuable to cancel.

"I think there is a lot of fuzzy thinking in all of this, too, because on Madison Avenue they basically feel that if you are over fifty, you are not worth having as a consumer. The only viewer they want is the eighteen- to thirty-four- or forty-year-old. The reason for that is that they believe younger people are impulse buyers. They truly believe you can show them something on television and they'll go, 'Oooh, I've got to have that,' and they'll run out and buy it. So, therefore, they believe eighteen- to thirty-four-year-olds are more susceptible to television advertising than older people, who tend to be a little more set in their ways and less apt to go running out and buy something because they see a cool-looking commercial or because Michael Jordan is wearing it.

"Again, I think they are full of it on that because what that particular philosophy fails to take into account is that the fifty-year-olds of today were raised on television. They are used to getting all of their information from television. I'm fifty-five, and I'm a runner. If I see a cool pair of running shoes on television, I'm down to the store to buy a pair. And, I'm not married to Crest toothpaste or any other damn product. I mean, I'll try all kinds of stuff if it looks good on television. I'll think, 'Hey, that's something I can use,' and I'll go out and buy it. The fifty-year-old today is a much younger person than when our parents were fifty. And, again, it's a television generation.

"By favoring the eighteen- to thirty-four-year-old viewer, Madison Avenue has cut out the viewer who has all the cash . . . who can go out and actually spend money. I remember when I was eighteen to thirty-four, I didn't have a pot to piss in—my wife and I were saving up to go to movies. What kind of customer am I? But now, you look at people in the fifty-plus age range, and that is where all the disposable income is in America. And, yet, they are not being solicited by television because Madison Avenue is of the opinion that they won't impulse buy.

"I think that's one of the great fallacies operating today. But you know what? Perception is everything. If they perceive that to be the truth, then, in fact, it becomes the truth. And I think that's a mistake because what you end up having is just a whole lot of duplicate programming. Everything is trying to be hip, young, funny half hours. Everybody is trying to do his or her version of *Friends*. It makes television one kind of thing . . . you don't get a lot of variety, and invariably the clones aren't as good as the original, so quality suffers.

"As a result of all this, the networks are experiencing this tremendous peel-off of viewership. They are loosing between five and seven percent of their whole pie every year. And they are scratching their heads and asking themselves, 'How can this be happening?' Well, the answer is because you are programming to a smaller and smaller demographic group while the larger demographic group, the war babies, is left to go begging. Pretty stupid philosophy, and the minute CBS starts to put on shows that appeal to older people, their households go up but their demos go down. Their eighteen to thirty-four demos go down and they panic.

"I just read the CBS schedule and again they are going for youth, and they're going to get killed because their natural viewership is older and has been for years. The people who watch CBS are traditionally older people. But, they're caught in an economic bind because they can't sell their [commercial] time for as much money when they've got Dick Van Dyke as a star. So, it's a strange time in television. I think, eventually, it's going to get sorted out or the networks will go broke. You can't continue to lose the percentage of viewership they're currently losing and stay in business."

That can kill the ability to put up quality shows by diminishing the money that can be spent.

"That may be a blessing in a strange way because they may finally get back to the idea of not making pilots. Pilots are a strange part of our business. Paramount has been making one-hour pilots for up to six or seven million dollars. A one-hour pilot for six million dollars was made at Paramount this year.

Which pilot was that?

"I don't remember. All I know is that CBS didn't cover all the money. Paramount deficit financed probably three million dollars on that. The pilot looks great, but you know damn well that's not the show [the networks] are going to get when they buy it. Paramount's not going to put up three million dollars every week. You're buying a dressed-up version of what you're going to get. My feeling is that the networks get fooled into buying a wish. Then when the show comes in, it's not what they thought it was going to be.

"I think the whole pilot process needs to be examined. If I were running a network, I'd say, 'If you're going to make an hour pilot for three million dollars, then you ought to make the series for three million [per episode]. Obviously, that isn't quite accurate because you have an amort [amortization] account and a group account which, when you are doing a series, gets divided up over the number of episodes made. In other words, if it costs you a dollar to build your set and you have twenty-two episodes, you can divide twenty-two into that dollar and average the cost of construction. Each show pays four or five cents' worth of it. The overall costs on each [episode] go down the more shows you make. When you do a pilot, you have to pay for all those group costs at once. The networks should demand that if the studio's going to spend that much on the pilot, they ought to spend the equivalent amount [per episode]."

Which leads into my next question. How do you create a series? What is the process? Do the networks come to you with ideas? Do you approach them?

"It happens all different ways. I've created forty shows that got on the air, and every one of them has had a different genesis. Some of the ideas were from network executives, some of them were from me, some came as a result of putting two ideas together, and some happened when a star got into the mix, such as, 'Oh, this guy would be great or this gal would be great for this.' I can't tell you how different each genesis is, but at some point, as the writer/producer, if I am going to be the creator of the show, I have to decide how I'm going to make the show. I have to ask myself: 'What about the show makes it special for me? . . . Why do I care about it? . . . Why do I want to watch it?' Most critically, I have to answer the question, 'Why do I want to do it?' If I can't answer that question, then I shouldn't make the series.

"If the reason for making a show is because they are going to pay me a lot of money, then I'm a whore. What I need to do is, I need to love my show. On those few occasions when I thought I was not making a good show, it bothered me. It really made me unhappy because I don't want to spend my time doing something working seventy hours a week and then going in and looking at the answer print thinking, 'This is no good.' "

During the life of a series, what is the network influence?

"It depends on a lot of things. If the show is on the bubble (meaning it's marginal—it might get renewed, it might not), you tend to get a lot of help—people trying to figure out how to fix the thing, how to make it better. If they hate the show and if they believe they're going to cancel it, you can't get them on the phone. You're a walking dead man. It's like nobody talks to you.

"Once you become a big hit, then the network usually leaves you alone. They don't come in that often when you have a big hit. Generally, by the second year you've solved the network problems.

"I don't want to imply that the only good ideas come from the writer/producers. Sometimes the network has good ideas. In fact, lots of times the networks have real good ideas. And you have to keep your ears open to that, too. When the network brings you a thought that doesn't seem to make sense, you've got to try and talk them out of it or find an acceptable compromise. But lots of times the networks are very helpful on shows. I don't mean to characterize them as being

140

an adversary. After all, it is their system, and in a sense you are playing on their field (even though it was chartered by our government). When it gets right down to push comes to shove, the fact that it's their field and they are giving you permission to play there can be a pretty heavy card. We all know that. They don't have to threaten, all they have to say is, 'Really, that's the way you feel? How strange.' If they lose interest in you, all of a sudden you're on against *Friends* or *X-Files*. And you go, 'Geez, what did I do?'

When a show runs several seasons, how do you keep it fresh from year to year?

"As an executive producer, you will find that your writing staff will get bored with the show way before the audience will. Audiences only see your show for one hour every week and they're not bored. They're not doing what you're doing, working on it eighty hours a week. The writing staff is writing it every day, Monday through Friday—Saturdays and Sundays included. I mean, when you're on staff, you are writing weekends every weekend. All you are doing is writing that show. You come in and go to dailies . . . and you cut film . . . and go to story meetings . . . and you talk about the characters . . . and you talk about plots and, 'Ah, shit, didn't we do that last year?' . . . and so on.

"What ends up happening is that very often by year three the writing staff is bored with this thing. They've thought about it too much. They've been working on it too long. That's when you start to get the crazy show. It happened on *Hunter* where we'd look at ideas like 'Hunter ends up in jail for the weekend and he's in the loony bin at Atascadero and everybody thinks he's crazy. Ha, ha, ha . . . that would be a funny one.' It's a bunch of writers playing with themselves because they're just tired of the show. They just don't want to do another cop drama.

"What you have to do is you have to be alert to it. We had a bunch of those on *Renegade* in the fifth season where they were the sort of shows that weren't the real drama normally done on *Renegade*. They were like, 'What would happen if this happened? The road not taken. What would happen if this one thing changed and we had to abandon the adventure for an hour? Where everybody's got a different role.' That's the writing staff getting bored, and as the executive producer I'll look for those signs. And when those scripts begin to come across my desk, that's the time to call a meeting and say, 'Are you guys tired of this thing? Maybe we need to bring some new people in. That doesn't mean we're going to fire anybody. Let's just bring in some fresh blood to stir up the mix.'

"I've often done that—kept all those same writers but brought in a couple of new people, and they are in the story meetings and going, 'What about this?' because it's all fresh to them. You just have to make sure the staff doesn't get bored."

When you staff your shows, what process do you go through to find writers?

"I'm usually looking at story editors and staff writers that I already have who are on other shows. I look to see whether they could be brought up to become writer/producers. I try very hard to promote from inside because it's good for morale. You want to be part of helping build another person's career, not hold them back, but to try and bring them forward. So, that's one place to go, and then you read scripts. We will generally give out freelance assignments as audition assignments.

"When we put an assignment out to a freelance writer, it's always an audition, whether they know it or not. If that writer hits the ball, the next thing you know, the producer on that show is going, 'You know, this person really did a good job. Maybe we ought to bring him or her in? He or she could really help us get out from underneath our script problem.' We're always looking in that way. But, generally, we use the freelance assignments to find people."

Say you've brought on a new staff writer. How do you help him or her grow as a writer? Is it simply a matter of getting out scripts?

"In order to get on my staff, you have to write what I think is good dialogue. That's the only requirement. If you write unexpected dialogue that's sharp and isn't full of clichés and if I'm reading lines and going, 'Oooh, shit, I didn't see that coming. That's a great line,' and it's right for the scene . . . that's all I care about. I'll teach you how to structure. I'll sit with writers and explain the three-act structure, and I'll work out a story with a writer. We'll plot it scene by scene so that when they leave, they've got a beat sheet with fourteen scenes in it and a perfect three-act structure. Then I know they'll be able to deliver because they're going to be able to write dialogue that will fill up that script.

"If they can't do the dialogue, generally what happens is no matter how good the structure, you've got a mushy script because the people don't sound right. So, I'm looking for someone who can write dialogue because I can always show him or her how to do the structure. Then after we've done that for a while, they usually become disciples of the structure I just gave you, and they can do it themselves.

"Another advantage of a good three-act structure is that if you screw up the movie . . . you put bad actors in it, your director had his camera in the wrong place, the pace is wrong—it's too slow, it's dragging on the floor, etc. . . . you can always cut to the plot. The plot will always work because it's got complication, it's got a second-act curtain, it's got those moves that keep your interest up. So you just start shredding the thing down. You get rid of this, you start cranking up the dialogue . . . you can always make it work. It won't be great, but you can sit in a room and the audience will watch and it won't put them to sleep."

Do you have any last thoughts, especially that may apply to show running?

"I think one of the things that is important to be a good show runner is to not be autocratic, not be a dictator. I believe that a good show runner encourages people to have ideas and doesn't stomp on them. There are some show runners I know that if it's not their idea it's no good, 'I am the only genius in the room,' that kind of stuff. I've always felt that's the egotism of insecure people.

"You have to be secure enough in your own head to surround yourself with people that you think may even be better than you. Then when they succeed, you've got to applaud them. If you do that as a show runner, you end up getting the best out of everybody. Don't become that person who takes the writer through a three-ring rewrite and then shakes his head and says, 'Don't you see what's wrong? God, nobody can do this but me. I am the only guy who's got the touch for this show.' And you hear show runners all the time saying, 'I'm working my balls off. Nobody else can write this show.' And I'm going, 'Come on. Get out of here.' You aren't letting any-body else write it . . . that's the problem.

"A good show runner needs to encourage other people. You've got to realize that if you take three or four really good writers, and if you give them the same story to write, they would all write it differently. And if they are really good writers, all the scripts will be equally defendable. If you're saying, 'Okay, this is not the way I do it. The way you do it is this way,' and you're rewriting a young Steve Bochco, you're a fool.

"You've got to be able to look at a young Steve Bochco and think, 'Hey, this guy's great. I'm not going to rewrite him. I wouldn't do it exactly this way, but given the way that he wrote it, it's great.' And it takes some security to be able to say that. A lot of people just can't do it. I see it all the time, this 'I'm the only genius in the room' bullshit.

"I'm not saying that you let this thing run itself. Good show run-ners have to be strong and when people are making mistakes you've got to make corrections. My point is that you've got to encourage other people's creativity, and accept solutions from other people that are different from what you would naturally come to . . . if they work.

"I remember that I had one writer working for me, and I didn't ever rewrite him. And we did a lot of stuff together, but we didn't write in the same way at all. I used to read his scripts with a pencil in my hand, wanting to change lines. As I'm reading I'd think, 'No, it's gotta be this.' But I would stay my hand because I knew he was a good writer; yet sometimes I would feel that he really failed. And he was a guy I was paying a lot of money and I was confounded. Then I would go to the dailies and see it on film, and it would work great. My way would have worked, too, but this worked. So I was right not to change it.

"This writer and I had a different rhythm. So it was always hard for me because I would have written it differently, but I always worked hard not to rewrite him or to get in his way. Only to help him when I could say, 'Look, the reason this doesn't work is because you're creating confusion for the audience.' But it would have to be some specific thing where he could go, 'Oh, I see. You're right,' and he'd fix it.

"I purposely try not to put scripts from my show writers in my typewriter. Instead, I give the corrections but don't physically re-write. If *they* do the rewrite, then they are coming closer to the center of the show—they become more valuable because within six or seven scripts they are writing the show exactly the way you want it written. Not exactly in the same words you would choose, but they are writing it with the same attitude you want.

"I think it's insecure people who have to have all the answers. I think that's also true with cutting [a film]. Often, people will argue with me in the cutting room. They'll go, 'I think you're wrong Steve.' . . . I encourage argument. I don't want to be the only smart person in the room. If I am, I've done a bad job of putting good people around me. So, a lot of people argue with me, and I'll listen to them. And sometimes I'll violently disagree, and I'll say, 'Okay, let's edit it your way. Go ahead and cut it your way and we'll look at it.' Then when I do look at it, I try very hard not to prejudge it just because it isn't the way I wanted it.

"Sometimes I'm surprised and I'll say, 'You know what? This is good,' and if he or she feels this strongly about it, I'll leave it. Some-times I'll say, 'It's better, damn it, you're right.' And sometimes I'll say, 'You know what? I'm not convinced.' But I always give it that chance, and then I really try hard not to prejudge it. I'm surprised at how often I'll find that somebody else's idea was just as good as mine when I was convinced I was right.

"And that makes for a lot of fun in the shop. That makes for people having a good time together because you're not hitting them over the head. So, you have to have good people . . . you have to do the most difficult thing of all, which is to select people that you think are as good, if not better, than you. And that's hard to do because the insecure egotist in you says, 'You're kidding? You're bringing somebody aboard who can actually write this thing better than you? My god, what if other people notice?' I say, if you do that, then in the long run you improved your whole operation.

"You know it's funny because when we were doing *Rockford*, I had two really wonderful writers working with me: Juanita Bartlett and David Chase. And I used to read their stuff and think, 'God, I'll never be as good as David. I'll never be able to write as lean as Juanita. If I tried for a hundred years, I'll never be able to say as much with as few words as she does.' And they told me they felt the same way about me. That made for an exciting and highly effective workplace. And as a show runner, that's probably the most important thing I can do."

SEVEN

Interviews with Writers

This chapter contains interviews with three very successful writers: David Koepp, a young, highly successful feature writer who made it big almost right out of school; Michael Werb, whose first big break feature, The Mask, *came after many years as a relatively unknown writer; and Joe Gunn, a retired policeman who built a second career in television.*

David Koepp

Screenplay credits:
Apartment Zero
Bad Influence
Death Becomes Her
Jurassic Park
Carlito's Way
The Paper

The Shadow
Mission Impossible

What did you study at UCLA?

"Undergraduate film and TV. So, I guess, primarily, I did a little of everything as an undergrad."

What courses stand out as having made a significant difference to you?

"I felt, in general, the film history courses were terrific. I learned a lot from just seeing a number of films; thinking about them, writing about them, and discussing them. I liked Steve Mamber's film authors class a lot. Those made a difference for me and then, of course, the screenwriting courses, although I wasn't able to take the ones I really wanted, the smaller classes that mostly were for graduate students. I had Richard Walter (fellow chair of the UCLA MFA program in screenwriting; see chapter 9) once, and I found that enlightening. However, for me, the best thing that came out was my relationships with other young writers, which I still have today. A community of people who trade ideas, trade material, and discuss it in a reciprocal way, that is enormously helpful."

When you say you found it helpful to have these other writers, you mean that you get together and bounce ideas and scripts off each other?

"Yeah. There's no official group or anything, just friends you make. Sure, you would bounce ideas off of people or ask for notes on a draft. And you could never be too cruel to somebody because you knew three weeks later you were going to give them yours and they would have a chance to get even. And it was all people who were at similar stages in their career. I thought it was a very healthy environment in that way."

By drafts, you mean treatments?

"Drafts of scripts: first draft, second draft, third, fourth."

How did you make it? I realize this is an open-ended question, but is there any one thing that singled out your projects?

"Well, I don't know. I think there's a certain combination of hard work and luck in any business venture. I know I work very hard. I just wrote as often and as well as I could. Why did my scripts get produced? I don't know. It's a hard question to answer. You just do the best work you possibly can and hope that others see it as you do."

Were you in the screenwriting graduate program?

"No, undergrad."

What did you do at UCLA that contributed toward your success?

"I got an internship. I got a couple, actually. One was with an agency reading scripts, and that was illustrative. But I don't think it's anything you want to get involved with for more than a couple of months. After reading five or ten scripts a week (or two or three or how ever many you agree to do) for a couple months, you get a pretty good idea of what's out there. It's the sort of job that doesn't really lead anywhere. I can see where it can make you just kind of bitter and overwhelmed.

"But I did learn from that. I had another internship with a guy named Morrie Eisenman. He had just advertised at the film school for an intern. He represented foreign producers and distributors buying and selling their films in the U.S. That was very intriguing because I saw a lot of interesting films and a lot of uninteresting films. I got to go to the film markets like Cannes and MIFED and AFM (American Film Market). I think I learned a lot about the business end that I didn't necessarily have to know, but it was helpful."

Do you mean as far as knowing how to tailor your scripts?

"Not as would affect your writing, because I don't think you want to do that. Just about how movies are made. It helps to understand that. In *Apartment Zero*, my first film, I was also one of the producers. That film wouldn't have happened, I don't think, without the film-makers getting involved as producers, and I was glad that I knew something about the world of independent film."

Having read all those scripts, are there certain common flaws that you find in most specs that keep them from becoming marketable?

"Well, I don't know about marketable because I think you sort of stumble into that. I think *good* is always marketable. I think the hardest thing to find in a screenplay in Hollywood is the writer's personality. I think that's what people are most looking for. In my own work, the things that I'm proudest of are the things that I put the most of myself into, and the things I'm not as proud of are the ones where I felt as if I tried to please others or write to a certain audience. I think a lot of young writers, in particular, are so eager to please and so impatient to get their career going that they give up the only vital quality that they have—their own perspective on the world. I guess young writers sometimes don't realize that all of Hollywood's producing entities are desperate for a spark of originality or humanity, and that only comes from putting yourself into your script rather than writing what you think others want to see."

You've written wonderful stories. What attracted you to them? How do you recognize a good story?

"Well, in the case of an original, it's usually something I've been feeling lately in an emotional or psychological sense that I'm then able to match up with a story idea. If it's been on my mind a lot as a personal issue, then I know I have the desire and interest to write about it as a movie. I'd want to spend that much time with it. In the case of an adaptation, it's pretty much binary for me—either I get it or I don't. If I read a book, my mind either swims with possibilities of how to make it a movie or it doesn't. If it doesn't make your mind spin, you'd better not do it."

What is your definition of story structure?

"I guess I would say setup, complication, and resolution. I'm pretty much a three-act guy—I believe in the traditional three-act structure. I pretty much follow that."

In general, what are your writing habits, especially when you're in the middle of a script?

"If I'm in the middle of a script, particularly the first draft, I try to work as early in the day as I can; that's when I'm the freshest. I'd say if I can put in five good hours, that's a great day. I mean five uninterrupted, actual writing hours."

When you write, do you go away so that you're not at your office at Universal where people can call or drop in on you?

"Well, I have an office at Universal, and it has its advantages, but home also has its advantages. If I'm out of town on something, at a hotel, obviously that's the easiest of all because you've got nothing to do. The office I like because it's a work environment, and I feel that if I came all this way, I might as well sit down and get something done. It's pretty easy to barricade yourself; just close your door and don't answer the phone. Then again, there are temptations because Universal's full of people and actually has an amusement park, so there's a lot to do if you wish to distract yourself.

"Home, however, has its advantages, too. It can be quieter, but then again, if you have a family, you're tempted to go spend time with them. So both places have good and bad sides. Ultimately, it doesn't matter where you are; the decision to write is always yours, and if you really want to do it, it doesn't matter where you are."

Tell me about your first sale and the struggles of getting that completed, and what doors opened once you made that sale?

"Well, *Apartment Zero* wasn't a sale because we didn't get money, we just went and made it."

You raised the money for *Apartment Zero* and just produced it?

"Yeah. The first outright sale was *Bad Influence*. That was the script that got me an agent. I originally was going to sell it to Universal, but they wanted a bunch of changes that I just didn't feel good about. So, we went elsewhere and made it as a lower-budget independent film for Transworld for about seven million dollars, which I thought was quite an accomplishment in LA. That one was just a matter of being patient enough to not jump at the first deal we got, then making sure that we were clear with the people about the movie, about what kind of movie we wanted to make and making sure they were in agreement. So, it just required some patience, particularly on the part of the producers. Morrie Eisenman and Steve Tisch produced it, and I was grateful that they gave me the chance and didn't muscle me into a deal I didn't want. They were patient and let me set it up where I felt comfortable."

What doors did that open?

"Casey Silver here at Universal was impressed that I went elsewhere with *Bad Influence* rather than just take the deal and make the changes and try to live with it. So, he offered me an overall writing deal here, which I took. So, I guess it opened a pretty big door."

How did you raise the money to do *Apartment Zero*?

"Several ways: some equity investing, Martin Donovan, the director/co-producer/co-writer raised some from a real estate guy in England, and I put in some of my own."

What was the budget on that one?

"A million four hundred thousand dollars.

"And the rest through more traditional financing. Morrie sold the foreign rights, excluding North America, and we banked the contract. It's called a negative pickup. It's where you sell the rights to a film that doesn't exist yet. You take the contract to the bank and borrow against it, which is what we did."

Are you now moving more into producing?

"No. I would never do that again."

You don't want to do that?

"It's a really hard job, completely different from writing."

You said that Universal wanted *Bad Influence,* but that they demanded a lot of changes you weren't comfortable with. What kind of changes did they want?

"Basically they wanted it to be a comedy. Which is a big change. I don't know if you saw the movie, but it was a reasonably dark thriller about the good and evil impulses in people. They thought that would make a pretty funny comedy."

Is that what inspired *Death Becomes Her*?

"No. *Bad Influence* could have been a comedy, but I didn't see any reason to take what I thought was a pretty serviceable thriller and reinvent it as something it was never meant to be. If you want a comedy, why not start out with a comedy premise? So, that was a pretty wide gap between their vision and ours. I believe we were wise to avoid that."

What's the major difference between your approach to comedy and drama?

"Well, I've never written a comedy. So, I don't know."

You don't consider *Death Becomes Her* a comedy?

"Well, black comedy, which is pretty different. Maybe I'm drawing too fine a point. Actually, as we were working on it, Martin and I never did consider *Death Becomes Her* a comedy. We certainly tried to be funny, but I think we saw it as a lurid drama. We were delighted that people found some things in it to be humorous, but I don't think we conceived it as a comedy. Sort of a horror-drama with funny stuff in it. It's hard to categorize.

"I just feel that I'm not a comedy writer. I have nothing but respect for people who write them. I tried to write a flat-out comedy once; it just didn't work out."

Did you study screenwriting before you came to UCLA? And, did you come here with the intent of becoming a screenwriter?

"Yes, I did. I was at the University of Wisconsin studying playwriting, and I wrote a couple of plays there and really wanted to write movies. Then my playwriting professor there urged me to go west because, as he said, 'We don't make movies here,' and I did very much want to be a screenwriter when I came to UCLA."

Now that you're in a position to get things done, are there any unproduced screenplays you have written that you will get produced?

"No. Certainly, there are several scripts of mine that haven't been produced, but I tend to feel that that was probably right—my early scripts weren't terribly mature. I think they were valuable. They all taught me something different and moved me forward in my learning, but I don't think that they would make wonderful movies. I'm looking to the future, not to the past."

How many plays did you write and how many scripts did you write before you sold one?

"Plays, I don't know because they were one-acts, it was college . . . it's hard to say. I don't even know if they count. Of the screenplays, I think *Apartment Zero* was the fifth."

What was the biggest change between the first and the fifth?

"Well, let's say the sixth. Because *Apartment Zero* was Martin's story idea. Let's say *Bad Influence* because I think that was my first really solid solo.

"The big change was a deeper understanding of film structure and a greater commitment to creating characters as opposed to story for story's sake."

So you found ways of writing more scenes that showed the characters as opposed to just pure linear plots.

"Well, I think it's realizing that they work in unison, not opposition. It's not one scene for story and the next for character, one for story, the next for character. They both exist in the scene or it's not right. The story is the result of the character. It happens because of who they are. I think the commitment to that concept made a big difference in my writing."

Is there anything on a broad scale that you would like to suggest to aspiring writers in the UCLA programs?

"Yes, I say it all the time, and it's not exactly controversial: by far the hardest part of screenwriting is writing a good screenplay. If you really concentrate on that and commit yourself to that, the business end will almost sort itself out. I know when I was looking to break in, I spent so much of my mental energy worrying about agents and producers: how to meet them and how to keep them. As it turned out, that was the easiest part compared to the daily struggle of putting words on paper. If you can redirect yourself toward learning how to write well, the other problems will just sort of melt away once you lick that part. But it isn't easy to write well. I certainly don't do it all that often, but when I do, that's when the business life becomes easier."

Michael Werb

The Mask
Face/Off

Tell me about your writing background.

"I took one screenwriting class as an undergraduate at Stanford—I was a journalism major. After graduating, I didn't know what I wanted to do with my life. I worked for an architect for about six weeks, then left the country with three hundred dollars in my pocket, a one-way ticket to Paris, and was gone almost two years.

"I picked up jobs in England, Southeast Asia, Australia, and a couple of other places—basically working my way around the world. I came back to LA, still having no idea about what the hell I was going to do for crust [money]. So, I joined a New Wave band called Girl on Top, which I'm sure Lew Hunter and Richard Walter remember. I wrote songs, sang backup, and attempted to play bass.

"Writing music was really great, but we had a lot of problems in the band. There were a lot of drugs and general infighting, and the band kept breaking up so many times and getting back together. I couldn't take it anymore. Fortuitously, my old Stanford roommate called and asked if I had any ideas for a cable access show.

"I came up with a bunch of ideas, and the cable company accepted one of them—something called *Young Psychiatrist*, which, as it turned out, ended up being fairly similar to what was to become *Doogie Howser*, only with a psychiatrist—a very young psychiatrist. I discovered I really enjoyed pounding out scripts fast, and I thought, 'Maybe I'll go to film school.' "

What year was that?

"That was 1982. I bought a Syd Field book and wrote my first script, *Picture Me Deadly*. It's about a psychotic boy who keeps trying to murder his mother. I sent the script and a forty-five single record the group had released along with my UCLA application. I was accepted to UCLA in the fall of 1983."

In the master's program?

"Yes. The MFA program."

And that's where you met Lew Hunter?

"Yes. That's where I met Lew, and Lew was the first screenwriting teacher I had. Richard Walter was second and Cynthia Mandelberg, now her name is Cynthia Whitcomb, was the third. I learned a lot from each one."

When did you graduate?

"In '87."

Is *The Mask* the first screenplay you sold?

"No. I've been working very steadily since 1986."

What are some of the other things that you have worked on?

"Well, I will include things that did not get produced."

Sold but not produced?

"Correct. My first assignment was something called *Vice Capades*, a dumb institutional comedy for New World pictures, which was a non-union job. Immediately after that I got my first union job at Cannon Pictures, I sold a pitch to Susan Hoffman.

"I always feel it's important to acknowledge the person who first gave you your leg up in the business and that was Susan Hoffman who was then a vice president of development at Cannon. That was how I got into the union. I wrote a movie that was called *Death Sentence*, which was an action movie written for Chuck Norris. It was eventually shot as *The Human Shield* with Michael Dudikoff.

"Then Susan went over to Carolco and hired me to do a rewrite on a horror film; a sequel to the 1970s Ida Lupino grade-Z classic, *Food of the Gods*. This was called *Gnaw—Food of the Gods II*. I did a production rewrite on that. Then the writers' strike hit, and, from what I can see in the movie, most of my work was rewritten during the strike, not by me. The movie turned out very bad, and I ended up spelling my name backwards on the credit. So, I'm E. Kim Brewstar, which is 'Rats Werb, Mike'; it's about giant rats that attack a college campus.

"It was a fun experience, and I'm in the movie. I appear as a college student who is eaten by a giant rat. I can be seen convulsing and spitting up blood capsules."

Ah, the life of an actor.

"Really. Not for me."

Where did you go from there?

"From there, I was approached by Lou and Sam Arkoff, of AIP [American International Pictures] fame, to write a movie called *Machine Gun Kelly*. I did some research on the real guy and found that he had a completely fascinating life and this was really a great story. George Kelly became public enemy number one, and he never took a shot at anyone. He and his wife planned a number of minor bank robberies in the early thirties, and the only reason they became famous is because J. Edgar Hoover built them into media stars so he could capture somebody big.

"It's a sweeping, Depression-era romance. Frank Price bought it and took it over to Columbia with him. It was, I would say, roughly ten weeks away from production with Billy Baldwin as the lead, when he dropped out. I understand the reason he dropped out of the project was because he could not find an actress he liked. Although the studio had approved several actresses, I was told he passed on all of them and ended up making *Three of Hearts* instead. It was the biggest disappointment of my career because it was so close to production, but it didn't happen.

"But that script did get me a job, shockingly enough, adapting the *Curious George* children's books for Imagine. At first, they didn't want to see me. I had not written anything in that genre. But, to my agent's credit, she convinced them to just take the meeting, and they liked my take. So, I did *Curious George* for Universal-Imagine and *hope* they'll shoot it next year. I underscore the word 'hope,' because you can never really expect anything in this town. I've learned to be very skeptical after having the plug pulled at the last minute on *Machine Gun Kelly*."

So, you wrote the screenplay for *Curious George*, which is now sitting over at Universal?

"Correct. The guys who wrote *Who's Harry Crumb?* are rewriting it now, which is ironic considering I've written one of the biggest comedy hits of this summer but somebody's always rewriting your work. After I finished *Curious George*, I spoke with two of my best friends, Michael Colleary and Christine A. Roum. Both of them were down in the dumps about the business, so we all decided to get together and form a writers' group. We first met in Century City in March 1992 and decided to act as if we were still in screenwriting class at UCLA. We met once a week, each time giving ourselves a new assignment. It was a great experience.

"Out of those meetings, Christine wrote and sold *Dead Reckoning* to Warner Bros., and I sold *Hamlet* to Fox. The Joe Roth regime at Fox loved my script, but soon after they bought it—Joe left the studio. Almost immediately, I was thrown off my own project. They wouldn't even meet with me. It hurt more than you can imagine.

"It's a nice little comedy about a drug-sniffing pig who works for the DEA. My grandfather was a pig farmer, so I've always been very fascinated with pigs and wanted to write a comedy about a pig. Through our writers' group, I got that out of my system, and, surprisingly enough, I was able to sell it.

"Right around the time I was finishing *Hamlet*, one of my agents at Triad, Michael Chessler, insisted I take a meeting with director Chuck Russell (*The Blob*). He had read *Curious George* and thought I would be perfect to write *The Mask*—because *Curious George* is basically about a monkey careening around New York. He thought that

I would be the right person to write a movie about a manic cartoon careening around Edge City.

"I owe Chuck a lot. He talked me into doing the project even though I had just sold *Hamlet* and was not really interested in taking on something else. He insisted I write it for Jim Carrey—someone I had never heard of at the time. After several meetings working out the story, I wrote the script. It took me six weeks and now the movie's out and it's made over a hundred million dollars. It's very exciting and very strange. It was, perhaps, the easiest thing I've ever done."

How did the script get changed along the way, between the time you wrote it and what ended up on the screen?

"Chuck took over from the day I handed in my draft. This was very frustrating, initially, but he had a vision for the film as a whole, and he did keep me involved. He rewrote some dialogue, cut scenes for budget, et cetera, but the script did not change significantly. I was welcome on the set at all times, attended all the test market screenings, and was a part of the editing and mixing process.

"The script that I had written was more of a love triangle than what you see on the screen. For example, I had written a scene that was cut which I considered important to the story line. In the scene, Stanley has to confront both of the women in his life at the same time: reporter Peggy Brandt and singer/moll Tina Carlyle.

"After Tina leaves, Peggy tells Stanley, 'as a friend,' that Tina cannot be trusted. Her big speech about trust sets up the twist when Peggy betrays him. Then the villain, Dorian, ends up killing Peggy by tossing her into the printing press.

"It's a cartooney death scene; as the newspapers emerge, there's a photograph of Peggy's smashed face and the headline 'Reporter Killed in Freak Accident.' Before he tosses Peggy in, Dorian says 'Honey, you deserve to have your name plastered all over the front page,' and, of course, she is. The scene was shot but ended up on the cutting room floor. Test audiences apparently did not want her to die, so that was pulled out at the last minute.

"Also, I had written a much more expensive climax which took place on the water in the marina. It was basically the same action beats that you see in the movie with the dog, but it took place in a much more expensive location.

"Milo, the dog, by the way, was not in the comic book. I created this character from a Jack Russell terrier I know who lives in Berkeley."

I loved the dog. Very funny.

"The dog was funny. The actor playing Milo is named Max. I understand he's getting offers all over town."

This certainly has to have opened bigger doors for you?

"Yeah, I hope so. Now that the movie's a hit, the people calling me are at a higher level. I'm going to assume that the price of my next assignment is going to rise."

I understand you sold two more scripts. Is this correct?

"Yes. Michael Colleary and I just sold a script to Paramount this year."

What's that one about and what's the title?

"It's called *Face/Off*. And it's a *Fugitive* kind of a thriller with a sci-fi bent to it. The ultimate cops and robbers story. It's very, very strange."

Is it a comedy?

"No, no. It is not a comedy. I mean there certainly are some humorous moments, but they're only for relief."

Let me back up a little bit. Tell me more about the writing group you formed with Michael Colleary and Christine Roum.

"One of the most important things about being at UCLA was the structure it provided. Every ten weeks you had to turn out a product, guided along the way by great teachers.

"Writing is tough enough—having to motivate oneself. The hardest thing about writing is sitting down and doing it every day. So, we decided each of us was going to be the teacher to the other two. We gave each other assignments, and week after week we all brought something to the table. It was very, very productive and kept the UCLA film school spirit alive."

Do you guys still get together?

"We're going to start meeting again, probably this fall. Although we are all working on assignments, it's important to keep writing spec screenplays, and not necessarily for sale. Writing for oneself is sometimes the only way to keep creativity youthful."

The group reads your work in progress?

"Absolutely. We read the outline, the first act, and give notes and assignments for the following weeks. We're very specific and sometimes very brutal. We don't dance around story problems or character problems or dialogue problems. The important thing about our writers' group is that we check our egos at the door. If somebody is very critical of something, it's okay. We have that basic respect. The friendship is never threatened."

Up until this point, have you had any day jobs, so to speak?

"No. I've not had a day job since I was a secretary for a lawyer in '86. At that time, I was taking the bus to UCLA from the Valley. I became friendly with Michael Colleary because he lived in the Valley, too, and was able to drive me home sometimes. We were both in the master's writing program. Christine was in the production program."

Tell me some of the greatest lessons or skills you learned in the MFA program at UCLA. Certainly the writers' group was significant.

"That certainly was one of the best things. Learning how to keep going after graduation. The program also taught me to work fast, and it also taught me the importance of rewriting."

How do you approach rewriting?

"I try to keep an open, fresh mind. It's very important to be able to recognize when something doesn't work. Then, if something really sucks and I've got my blinders on, there's no doubt that my writer's group will let me know."

Any last thoughts?

"Yes. It has to do with rewriting, or, rather, being rewritten. I've worked for six major studios: Paramount, Columbia, New Line, Disney, Warner, and Universal. With only one exception, the studio has brought in other writers to replace me. If you care at all about your work, it can be frustrating and humiliating, but it's part of the insanity of the business. I've learned to just keep my head above water and swim faster."

Joe Gunn

Screenplay credits
(a partial list):

Features

The Wild Pair
Capital Hell

Television

Delvecchio
CHiPs
Ohara
Dragnet/ Adam 12
Get Christie Love
The New Mike Hammer
Superboy
Hunter

Movie of the Week

San Antonio Cops
Trackdown, The Night Stalker
Mallory

Tell me about your writing background.

"I wish I had this grand story about taking all these writing classes in college, but I didn't. When I was in the police department, I ended up with a lot of writing assignments: rewriting the department manual, in charge of rewriting all the special orders that came out on the police department, and so on. In college, my major was English, so I guess that all leads to a background in writing.

"Back when I was with the LAPD, I became very close friends with Bob Cinador, who was the creator of *Adam 12* and *Emergency* on television. Bob used to always say, 'Why don't you try writing one of these scripts?' I used to always reply, 'Bob, I'm a commander with the police department. I just enjoy coming out here and sitting in on your casting sessions and going sailing with you. I don't want to be a writer.'

"Then one day, twenty years ago, I was going to buy a new house with my family, and we discovered we could make the monthly payments, but we didn't have enough money for the down payment. I said, 'Bob, I'm ready to write a script.' He said, 'Great, but how do I know you can write one?' He was doing a show called *Chase* for Universal with Mitchell Ryan. A terrible show, but he gave me a bunch of scripts, and he said, 'Take it home and spec a script. I'm not going to pay you anything.'

"So, I sat at the dining room table and wrote an entire script start to finish, dialog, action, everything, and I brought it in, and Bob bought it and shot it. I remember when I got my first check. It was for sixty-six hundred dollars, which was about half of an annual salary. I couldn't believe it.

"So, I wrote three more in a month and a half, and he bought all of those, and I was on my way to becoming a screenwriter."

Were you a staff writer on *CHiPs*?

"I produced the last year of *CHiPs*. Prior to that I created *Delvecchio*, and, subsequently, I've been on seven or eight shows on staff."

Delvecchio sounds familiar.

"It starred Judd Hirsch, for Universal. I created that when I was still with the LAPD."

How has your writing changed over the years from when you started out? How has your understanding of screenwriting changed?

"Oh, tremendously. When I first started writing, it was a monetary investment. I was writing only because I needed money. That probably lasted for about a year. Then all of a sudden, I started to enjoy this, and I started to get artistic. When they started to rewrite me, I was going, 'Hey, wait a minute. I have an investment in these words.'

"But I came up in a very advantageous time. I started writing in the late seventies and into the eighties, when writing in television was much different than it is today. It was a freelance market. You usually dealt with the producer and no one else. You didn't have what you have today, which is this huge committee that you have to go in on a television show, and there is very little freelance opportunity. Very little chance that your original script will remain in its ultimate form by the time it hits the air. Back then, what you wrote was yours.

"So, what I used to do was get sample scripts of top writers in the industry. I used to take them home and read them because I was greatly interested in the mechanics of writing. Studying the tricks they used to get their message across in their scripts. How did they get from A to B? How did they get from the first act to the third act?

"I think from reading writers that you respect, getting hold of their original scripts, is probably the best way to learn how to write. I think you have your own ideas and your own story, but getting down the mechanical, script format of conveying it is the tough part, to me. That was the tough part all along. I read several books, *The Ten Greatest American Screenplays*, and the two additions, and seeing how those great writers put their words down into script form was an eye opener—because they're all different, and I learned techniques."

Who were the top writers you studied?

"E. Jack Newman, who created *Police Story* and *Room 222*. He's won at least five or six Emmys for Movies of the Week. Joel Oliansky, who won an Emmy for the miniseries *The Law* and did *Masada*. These are just a couple of the writers who were in their prime—still are in their prime (a writer never gets out of his prime). They were selling and were recognized as the top writers in their field."

Do your stories always focus on police issues?

"Yeah, you know, unfortunately, or fortunately, financially, you get pigeonholed in the industry and, as much as I would like to, and have, on a couple of occasions, branched out into something else, you go where the buyers are. In my case, the buyers have always been on police-oriented stories. I sold a comedy once, and then after I had sold it, the head of NBC comedies left and the new guy came in and said that they were canceling the order: 'Because you're a cop writer and you should stay with what you do.' So, it's hard to break out. So, primarily, I do work in police-oriented shows."

Have you written many scripts that are not police issues, other than the one comedy, even if it's for personal enjoyment?

"Oh, yeah. I've written action-adventures. I've tried comedy, but I can't sell 'em."

Have you ever co-written?

"I've attempted. I've co-written when I'm on staff because it's a natural evolution. On a freelance basis, I tried one time to co-write something and found that it didn't work for me. I'm a fast writer. I like to sit down and whip out ten to sixteen pages a day. I want to quickly get through what I'm doing and then go back and do my rewrite. In this one particular case, I was writing with somebody who wanted to argue on words. Then argue on the sentence. Then argue on the paragraph. We were doing a half page a day, and it drove me crazy. After a week, we just abrogated the agreement.

"I have a style of writing, and I just have to sit down and write."

You say you like to write ten to sixteen pages a day. What work has gone on before you sit down and write those ten to sixteen pages?

"It depends on what I'm doing. If I'm doing a television show, I like to work off the briefest of step outlines. I mean really the briefest. I'll map out each act into scenes, but I'll only do a one-line scene. I don't like to do dialogue, and I don't like to do extensive mapping out of the scenes—it bores me. I'd rather do just a little road map of where I'm going to go and then get into the writing and let the scene take me.

"I'm currently doing a novel, and I have to confess that I didn't do a road map because I've had this novel in my head for about twenty years, and I've been going free-form on it. It's taking me places so that I don't know where I'm going each day. It's been a wonderful experience doing it this way."

You made this road map in your mind over these twenty years. Is that now becoming a hindrance?

"No, it's been an asset. I know the story. I know where the story started. I know the beginning and I know the end, and each day I start knowing what the next scene is going to be in my novel. It's the characters that are taking me places as I type that are just wonderful, and I just go with them."

In your career, what have your writing habits been like?

"I'm a very disciplined writer. I think it started because in my first six years of writing, I was still with the police department and I had to write during nights and weekends and on vacations. I think I was still earning in the top 10 percent of Hollywood writers. So, there wasn't any such thing for me as having a bad day and walking away from the typewriter or the computer. I had to sit down. And if I was having a bad day, I had to fight through those bad days and get something down on paper—good or bad. At least it was something to come back and correct.

"So, I think the force of doing that for six years disciplined me to the point now, that when I'm working on something, I put in six or seven hours a day, every day. I just can't walk away from it. I think it's worthwhile to devote that time because during bad times when you have writer's block, the time has to be spent doing something. You're going to have writer's block somewhere along the way, and if you don't waste that time, it's going to come back to you. So, you might as well fight through it and sit there and get it over with. Then walk away. To me it's going to return.

"So, I do my five, six, seven hours a day when I'm working on a project. Now, I may start at different times. I like to work out at the gym every morning. I go in at 6:30 every morning and play basketball and work out and then come back and read the paper. So, normally I start around 9:30 or 10:00 in the morning. Then I work through the afternoon."

So, primarily you write early in the day.

"Yeah, I'm not a night person, and I'm new to the computer. This is only my third year with one. I used to write longhand, printing on a legal tablet for seventeen years."

How did you get it printed?

"I made a secretary very wealthy, especially when it came to rewrites."

How did you land the series *CHiPs*?

"I had just gotten off of a two-year contract at Columbia, and, along with a friend of mine, we went over to do the last year. We were just selected."

How many years did it run?

"It ran six years. We did the last year. It was an interesting show. It was a different kind of writing because, and not many people know this, if you stop and think about it, at no time on any *CHiPs* show did they ever remove their gun from their holster. Ever. Since it was a show geared toward kids, what you had to do was come up with shows every week where the officers didn't look stupid by putting them in a situation where they should have had their guns drawn.

"So, it was a different kind of writing than doing *Hill Street Blues* or *Miami Vice*, which are more gritty and dirty. Ours was a type of writing geared for teenagers and lower age groups. It was educational."

Did they have a bible?

"It wasn't a written bible, it was an understood bible where the purpose of the show was 50 percent educational, which was traffic safety and to teach integrity and morality to children. That was the purpose of the show. So, a lot of people say, 'Oh, you work for *CHiPs*. What kind of show is that? It doesn't compare to *Hill Street Blues*.' Well, it does in that we accomplished what we were trying to accomplish, which was to educate people on traffic safety. To teach kids that good is good and bad is bad, yet not look stupid by putting them in situations where they should have had their gun out.

"I think writers tend to be snobby. Writers tend to think if you're not working for an *L.A. Law* or a *Hill Street Blues*, then you're not doing quality work. Well, there are different shows for different age groups and different time slots on television."

On my printout, I see *Manimal*. I remember the name, but I don't remember the show.

"Well, that's a joke. I only did one script for *Manimal*. Of course, *Manimal* is the show that Brandon Tartikoff always takes heat on as the worst show he every programmed for NBC. I didn't work on it. I wrote a script for it. *Manimal* is the guy who turned into a bird and a tiger and all the animals. It was a Glenn Larson show that lasted for about thirteen episodes and was canceled. What's funny is that it's now a cult series in France. Still, American critics say it's the worst show ever in American television history. Whether it is or not, I don't know. But I took an assignment on it."

What was your involvement in *Dragnet*?

"I did *The New Dragnet* and *The New Adam 12* for two years in syndication three years ago. That was interesting because we did 104 episodes in two years. We were shooting two shows a week, and there were three writers on the show. We hired a lot of freelance writers because of the time constraints. A lot of the freelancers we didn't ask to do rewrites because we didn't have time. So, we were doing complete rewrites, plus I wrote thirteen of the episodes. These were half-hour shows, and we would shoot two shows back to back every week. So we were really pumping it out, and these shows can still be seen on Channel 11 every weekend. They show *Adam 12* and *Dragnet*."

Why were they in such a rush?

"In order to meet the budget, you had to keep the deadline."

What were your primary duties as executive story consultant?

"I used to take the meetings with the freelance writers. I'd listen to their pitches, make recommendations to the producers as to stories that we ought to buy, then work with the freelance writer on the outline and on the format of his story. Then I'd send him or her on their way. Then when the first draft came in, I'd work with the freelance writer on the rewrite. Send him on his way again. Then when the second draft came in, we didn't have time for a third, so I'd rewrite the final product."

So, if it came back the second time and it wasn't completely what you wanted, you took it.

"And rewrote it. But we didn't take credit for it. We never went to arbitration on it. We left the original writer with the credit.

"Then we'd have the meetings with the director, and there would be changes because of location. At the location meeting, we would make further changes to the script. Then we'd fine-tune the script into final shooting preparation."

Were you also involved with the selection of the directors?

"No, the producer took care of that. I was strictly involved in the writing preparation. It was a great experience because we were doing it so fast."

Did you ever deal with nonrepresented writers?

"I had one team who was not represented. They came to me through a very close friend whose opinion I respected who said, 'I've read a spec script by this writing team, and it's very good. You ought to take a look at it.' I read their spec script, and it was very good. So I called them in."

Was it a spec script for the show?

"Not for the show. It was entirely different. But it was a very good spec script. I called them in and gave them the opportunity to pitch a story. I didn't give them a story, we gave them an opportunity to pitch a story. They came in with a good story, and I gave them an assignment. They turned out to be very good, and they were not represented by an agent, and that story was their first assignment in the industry. Which allowed them to join the Guild.

"They were not represented, and they were recommended by someone whom I had also given a first writing assignment to, on a different show."

Do you read scripts of beginning writers?

"When I'm working on a show on staff, I read a lot of scripts that are sent to me by the agencies. It's very difficult to read scripts that are submitted by people that are not represented. Not because of time restraints for the show, but for the legal ramifications involved. Their story may hit on something you already have in development, and then you're in for a lot of problems trying to convince them that you really didn't steal their idea—that we had this in development already."

Of all these scripts you've read, what are their common flaws?

"Again, it depends on what show I was working on. I'm character driven. I look at how characters are created and react to each other. If the plot is a little weak, I figure that's my job on staff to work with someone to totally develop a plot. I'm not as worried about that. But, if someone's characters in their spec script are poorly developed and the dialogue is bad, I don't feel I can put out that much time in the limited amount of time I have on staff to stand over someone at the typewriter and write dialogue. I quickly recognize that someone is basically weak as a writer in dialogue, and, if they get an assignment, that means I am going to work that much harder on staff rewriting complete dialogue when the finished product comes out.

"Plot we can always fix because the person is not going to leave the room unless we've mapped out the plot. But, we don't do dialogue in the room. That's something the person does when he or she gets home.

"So, if I'm reading a spec script, I am really fascinated by really interesting characters and great dialogue and interaction between the characters. More so than I am by plot."

You're talking about pitch sessions. When you are diagramming the story, is that part of the pitch session?

"Well, that's part of after we buy it. See, a pitch session is, let's just say I'm doing *Dragnet*, they come in and say, 'We think we have a great story for *Dragnet* and it is . . . ' and then they tell us the story. They don't have to go into great detail because we don't expect them to. A great story is, the two partners go out and get themselves involved in a hospital scam where old people are getting cheated out of their Medicare checks.

"Now they have given us enough to know just by that one line whether we think that is a viable plot for a *Dragnet*. That's enough. We say, 'You know, that's a good *Dragnet*. Okay, we'll let you know.' Then we run it by the people, and they say, 'Yeah, that's a good *Dragnet*.' Now we say, 'You've got a deal.' They've just made story money now. They've made enough for us to pay them story money. Now we sit down at the blackboard when we call them back in, and we say, 'Okay, let's get to work.' This usually takes about four hours.

"We go to the blackboard and plot it out: Act One, Scene 1. Our two guys are in a car, they get a call. *Dragnet* always starts with a voice-over, 'We were working Fraud Division out of . . . ' You know. Scene 2. Now we're going to see this. Scene 3 is this. We map it out all the way down so that there are no surprises, and the writers copy it down.

"By the time they leave, all the scenes are mapped out for them. Now, as a writer, they have a certain amount of freedom. Maybe when they are doing the script, they discover that it worked better doing it this way. If they can justify it, sure. Justify it and come in. We're flexible.

"But there's no dialogue coming out at this session. It's just structure."

If the writers do decide to make a big change, are they required to call you?

"No. They can if they want. If they don't, and they come in and it works, fine. If it doesn't work, then they have to go back to the original. We'll send them back and say, 'It didn't work. In your rewrite, go back and do it as we originally plotted it out.' "

How do pitches originate?

"One way is for an agent to call up and say, 'I think I've got a couple of guys who would be great for the show.' The second way is when someone you know, whom you've worked with in the past, says, 'I'd like to come in and pitch you.' The third is when I know a writer who has delivered for me in the past. I'm selfish, I want to get good material, I want my job to be easier, so when I'm on a new show, I'll call writers whose work I trust to be good and say, 'Hey, how would you like to come in and pitch for the show?' "

Tell me about being a writer/producer. What extra burdens do you have? How does it affect your writing?

"Well, I like to produce. The extra burdens, I don't look at them as burdens as much as extra responsibilities. You're involved with the overall production and look of the show. You're involved in budget. You're involved in casting. You're involved with the crew. You're involved in post-production. I like it, especially when it's my script because you're involved with picking the director. You can make sure that what you've written is being interpreted the way you've written it.

"I've had very few finished Movie of the Weeks or telefilms or especially feature films ever come out the way I had written them. By the time it goes through the production process, by the time every writer's nemesis, the director, gets through with it, and by the time it goes through post-production, it's a different product altogether.

"As a producer, you are now in direct control, where you can make sure the director is giving it the interpretation that you want in that picture. You can go in during post-production and make sure the post-production team is putting the emphasis where you want. So you get that extra power, and, as a writer, I enjoy that.

"Television is a producer's power medium, whereas film is a director's power medium. But in television, the producer has the power."

Is there anything else that you feel that students should know that I haven't asked?

"No. I'm sure it's just old hat. I love to write, and I'm sure if you, too, love to write, then you have to write. Selling is the hard part of all of this. As much as you love to write, you have to go out and sell."

How has that changed? When you got in, it seems as if it was very open.

"Yeah, it's changed drastically. When I started writing in the late seventies and early eighties, as an individual writer, you used to have access to the networks. You could go in and sell a pilot or sell a Movie of the Week. Then after you made the sale, you'd go out and shop that sale to a studio. So, I'd sell a Movie of the Week and then I'd go over to Columbia or Warners and say, 'I have a sale. I sold a Movie of the Week, are you interested?' That put you in the bargaining chip [position] because you now have a network sale and you'd let the studios bid on it, whoever wanted to make the deal with you. What was even better was a pilot.

"Today, as an individual, I can't go in to any of the television networks unless I go in with a partner, which is a major independent production company. Either a studio or one of the giants like Spelling or someone else or Cannell. You see, they won't even meet with you on that basis. So, they've squeezed you out as an individual. Unless, of course, you own the biggest property of the day, which is very rare to get.

"So, that has changed dramatically. Also, in television today, they've done away with almost all quality long form. They've gotten more into sitcoms and reality shows, in which I, being a long-form drama writer, have a limited area of access.

"Movie of the Week is a shifting genre. I mean right now, as we speak, today, it's the woman-of-the-week-in-jeopardy genre. So, unless you have a woman-of-the-week-in-jeopardy, you're not going to make a sale. The network executives today are primarily in their twenties, and it's very, very tough if you're not in your twenties to go in and sell them. But that shifts. I mean the industry shifts back and forth. But, if you write, and, if you're good, and, if you have a piece of property they want, you can make the sale. It's just as simple as that. It's hard. It always has been, and it always will be."

EIGHT

Interviews with Literary Agents

This chapter contains interviews with two literary agents: Jim Preminger and Sandy Weinberg. Jim's business lies primarily in television, whereas Sandy's lies primarily in features. Each openly discusses how he finds new writers, develops a writer's career, or helps to resurrect a stagnant career.

Jim Preminger (Jim Preminger Agency)

What's your background and how did you come to be an agent?

"I grew up in Los Angeles, the son of a successful literary agent, Ingo Preminger, and the nephew of Otto Preminger. I studied political science at UCLA and at the University of Chicago, where I did some teaching.

"I've been an agent for twenty-two years. The last seventeen years

I've had my own agency in the same location. Prior to that, I was with an agency known as The Artists' Agency. I got the job kind of serendipitously and actually started their literary department in 1975. Between the time I got out of graduate school (University of Chicago in 1971) and 1975, I was just trying to get into the entertainment business as a producer. I worked on two movies in production and optioned some material. I hired a couple of writers, in one case, to do an adaptation, and, in the other case, to rewrite an original screenplay. It was in the course of trying to package and produce one of those properties that I submitted a screenplay to The Artists' Agency, although it was called Bresler, Wolff, Cota & Livingston at that time. They represented Jack Nicholson and I wanted to see if I could interest him in this property. They accepted the screenplay, covered it, and then informed me that Nicholson wasn't available to do it; however, they wanted to start a literary department in their agency, which up until then was just a talent agency, and they offered me the job."

This was a script that you had commissioned?
   "Correct.
   "So, in brief, that's how I got started. I accepted that job, and in my first couple of years, I looked to graduates of writing programs and industry contacts I had to find new writing talent. I signed a few people and managed to get them going, and my business began to take hold."

Why did you choose to focus on TV?
   "One of the first people I signed was Gary Goldberg, who, at that time, was finishing up school at the University of California in San Diego. He was viewed as someone who was going to be successful based on the writing he had done in school, and he had an agent already, but the agent was leaving the agency business. I knew the agent, and he suggested that I read Gary's work and meet with him. So, I met with Gary and fell in love with his material, which was TV

spec scripts primarily. Even though my background and my interest was more in features, finding such a strong television talent drew me into the TV arena. After about six months I was able to get him working in half-hour television."

So, his specialty was sitcom?

"Yes. He became very successful very quickly. He wrote for *The Bob Newhart Show*, he became a story editor and a producer on *The Tony Randall Show*, and then a producer on *Lou Grant* very quickly. In his second or third year in the business, he even created his first series, which was on CBS called *The Last Resort*. His career just took off, and he created *Family Ties*, *Brooklyn Bridge*, and now *Spin City*. I no longer represent him, but I did represent him up until three years ago—a twenty-year relationship.

"I'm very happy to say I've had several long-term relationships, including Peter Casey and David Lee (two of the three creators of *Frasier* and *Wings*), whom I began representing in '77 or '78 and who I still represent."

What was it about Gary's writing that caught your attention and led you to believe that he was a strong TV talent?

"This goes to the heart of what you do as an agent, which is a combination of exercising creative judgment and business judgment. The important thing to do as an agent is to decide how to spend your time—where to invest your efforts. You read somebody's material and see whether or not the person has talent based on what you see on the page, and you decide whether you relate to it or not. If there's something there, then you meet with the person. You see what kind of person they are, they see what kind of person you are and whether there's a match or not.

"Getting a new writer started is a very time-consuming occupation, even with someone as talented and motivated as Gary Goldberg. Because he was starting from scratch, it took several months to get him his first half-hour writing assignment. People would acknowledge that he was talented—I think everyone who read him could see he was very talented—still, it took time to find a producer who would give him a job."

How do you get over that?

"You have to knock on enough doors and sometimes repeatedly. You also have to have an instinct for where this writer could be successful, if they did accept him. I had this feeling that Gary would be a great match for *MTM* [*The Mary Tyler Moore Show*], which, at the time, was in its heyday of half-hour comedy production. It turned out that my instincts were right—he had a great five years."

What specifically do you look for in a new writer?

"It's partly subjective. To begin with, I look to get excited by their material. I look for a voice, a fresh voice, that, if it's a comedy, it's got to be funny and humanistic and appealing. If it's a drama, I might look for something edgy and penetrating. But it's that voice. I look for someone whose writing is distinctive, that sets itself apart from other people's writing.

"If it's a new writer, I also want to get a sense that he or she is 100 percent involved in getting a career launched, or, if it's a writer who's already experienced, that he or she is totally committed to moving up to the next level. The relationship between an agent and a client has to be a collaborative one. It's a team effort, and if I'm going to spend my time on behalf of a client, I want that client, at the very least, to put his or her share of time, effort, and ingenuity into promoting himself or herself. By promoting, I don't mean going out there and making contacts—although sometimes that can be helpful—but by providing me with the material, with the ammunition, and with the tools, that I will need to sell the person."

You mentioned levels of writing. Would you please define the levels?

"In a television series, it's fairly clear what the progression is. Writers start, sometimes, as freelance writers. They try to get on staff any way they can—that's the key on a series. They would likely start out as a staff writer, move up to story editor, to executive story editor, to co-producer, to producer, to supervising producer, then to executive producer. That's the standard progression in series television. Once you're an executive producer, and once you've gone through that process, which might take several years, the best people will be recognized by the networks, and the networks will approach them to create and run their own shows."

Do you have people who are not interested in progressing up this ladder? Who are satisfied to stay at one level, say they enjoy being a staff writer or story editor?

"Yes, I do. Not everyone has a natural instinct to want to take command. Not everyone wants that much responsibility or is that ambitious. I've had both kinds of clients. I've had several who really like being a consultant on a show, which gives them some free time to do other things—either writing or nonwriting activity."

I've been a technical consultant on a number of shows. What do you mean by consultant? Are you talking about a writer?

"I'm talking about a writer. There are different kinds of consultants. On a half-hour comedy show there are two kinds of consultants. There's a creative consultant, a fancy name for a story editor—which is a full-time staff writing position, in the lower to middle level of a show's writing staff. Then there's a consultant who's a punch-up person, who comes in one or two days a week, isn't a full-time member of the writing staff, but maybe comes in on rewrite day. The punch-up person comes to the table reading, stays late, stays until 2:00, 3:00, or 4:00 in the morning once a week and can be very valuable. That person tries to pitch a lot of new jokes. That person is also looking at a script with fresh eyes and usually is very experienced, very much sought after, and very well paid, who the show looks to, to help fix some scenes that might be problematic. He or she helps to give it that extra quality, a last-minute polish, so the script will be as good as possible on shooting day.

"This year, I even had a consultant on a one-hour drama show. A client that was offered a job as a writer-producer on a one-hour drama, but because of a family illness and other obligations, she didn't want a job that was quite that demanding. However, they wanted her badly enough that they offered her a consultant job where she was allowed to write at home. She would come in for occasional meetings, maybe one day a week, and was, in general, given more flexibility than full-time staff writers are given."

Now I'd like to explore getting representation. First, how do scripts from new writers get to you?

"I have a rule, as a lot of agencies do, that we will accept material only from writers who are referred to us by people we know. I do that because we have to have some type of a screening process. I get, on average, five to ten letters of inquiry a day. Even with the help of a reader or an assistant, there's no way I can cover that volume of material. So, I have that rule, and it's pretty standard throughout the industry."

How many scripts do you read, on average, in a week?

"Given the amount of reading and work that I do for my ongoing clients, I would say I read no more than two new writers a week, and I might sign, maybe, one writer a month, at the most. That would be a lot, actually."

How many scripts do you read from your client base? And, are these spec scripts or scripts from writers on staff, scripts that will be produced?

"For some shows, I'm very intimately involved, for example, with *Frasier* and *Wings*, I'll read a lot of the production scripts. I also handle a lot of movie for television writers and feature writers, so I'm reading all kinds of scripts at different stages for different purposes.

Sometimes, a writer will give me a spec screenplay and I'll read it and give notes and then the writer will revise it. In fact, we'll go through that process two, three, four times before we agree that the script is ready to be sent out. There's a lot of that kind of reading.

"I also get treatments of various lengths from clients who want to set up pitch meetings to sell an idea and go into development on an idea."

For your freelance clients, how involved do you get in the stories or treatments?

"If you're talking about freelance writers for episodic television, I generally do not help prepare for those pitch sessions because the requirements are very specific to each show. For pilots, movies for television, and features, I frequently help clients prepare for pitch meetings, and that varies from client to client. Some clients like me to be involved creatively. Other clients see me as their business advisor, they want me to get them the contacts. Then, once they meet people, if they are successful in selling the idea, they look to me to negotiate the deal."

How do you shop a script or concept?

"Let's start with a script. If it's a finished spec script, I'll draw up a list of producers who have a strong relationship with a studio. I will also try to identify at least one producer with each studio or each buyer. There are now a lot of buyers who are not full-fledged studios but who do have full development and production financing, so I'll draw up a submission list. The submission should reflect both the relationship that the producer has with a studio or another development-production entity and what I understand to be the taste of the producer. This is critical, because, I think, some producers are better suited for comedy, others for action, and others for drama. So, in that respect, I try and do a bit of casting.

"The reason I focus on producers is that I try and get a champion for the script involved as soon as possible. That means someone who, on a day-to-day basis, is involved with setting up and packaging feature screenplays. Someone who can advance the project and who has contacts with directors, actors, and studios."

What makes for an enduring writer?

"Fundamentally, the writer has to have talent. However, I think, it's vital that a writer realizes that television and screenwriting is a business, and to remain viable in this business, you are partly creating a product and partly creating yourself or reinventing yourself all the time. One of the things that makes a writer successful is a willingness to always be writing on speculation, even if the writer is employable and employed.

"I can't tell you how many times, particularly in series television, clients of mine have successfully changed the course of their career by writing on spec, and I'm not just talking about in the beginning of their careers. I'm talking about writers employed as producers or employed in some other capacity. If, for example, a client wants to write on a different kind of show, either a better quality show or a show in a different format (a sixty-minute show instead of a thirty-minute show), the only way to do that is to write in the format for the kind of show that he or she aspires to write for and do it well. Since you're *not* always going to be employed to do that, you have to do it on spec sometimes."

Can writers transition between television and features?

"That's a really interesting topic for me as an agent because there are two contradictory pulls involved. On the one hand, for most people it's very hard to make progress as a feature writer, or a series television writer, or a movie for television writer unless you specialize in that field and stick with it and don't jump around. The people I've seen rise to the top in series television are the ones who stuck with it year in and year out. The ones who have been on staff year in and year out and paid their dues, moved up the ladder, and who have not taken a year off to write their spec feature script. If they wrote a spec feature script, they did it during hiatus but then jumped right back into the staffing season for television the following year.

"Similarly, in features, an equally competitive arena, I think, the need to constantly renew yourself, to stay competitive, requires that you constantly write new treatments and screenplays and pitch new ideas and stay in that arena on a continuing basis. Having said that, I would now say that these days it's very easy for people who are established in one arena to cross over into another arena and get hired. I don't find it that hard as an agent to sell a successful television writer to features and vice versa."

Is it easier to go from one to the other?

"I don't think so, anymore. I think it used to be every television writer's dream to write features, and that used to be a hard transition to make. Now, it appears that feature producers and studios are very interested in successful television writers. They like the qualities that seasoned television writers bring to a feature project, such as discipline, speed, and the ability to rewrite—the things you learn over the years as a television writer.

"In features, I find that the allure is just as strong the other way. Feature writers who have spent years seeing projects take three, four, or five years or longer to go from conception to production are very much attracted to the pace of television. They are very drawn to the opportunity of seeing their work on the screen quickly, and seeing more of it, more regularly. Also, feature writers are very aware of the big paydays television writers have. I strongly feel that there are just as many allures drawing people from features into television as the other way.

"But, as I say, just to finish answering your original question, I do have a number of clients who can and like to switch back and forth. I have one client who, in the last three years, has written two cable movies for television, two or three one-hour drama pilots and has had two feature writing assignments. He's happy doing all these things; he loves the variety. Sometimes he feels the need to satisfy his desire for more serious writing by doing feature-length material. Other times, he just loves the one-hour format—he likes the speed of it and the things that the television format offers.

"Now the dilemma for this writer, who is highly regarded throughout the industry as a very talented, very employable writer, is that he has, nevertheless, failed to reach the zenith of either of these areas. That may be due to his penchant to sample different arenas and not devote himself exclusively to any one arena. I don't know."

Is he happier doing that? Or does he want to reach the zenith in one of the arenas?

"Well, I'm sure that there are times when he wished he were at the top of one of those professions, but, in general, he's professionally pretty happy and is enjoying being able to function and work in these different arenas."

What are your thoughts on the fact that the business is not very writer-friendly? Writers are constantly fighting for recognition and credit. The industry seems to want to quickly dismiss the writer, to take a writer's work and immediately pass it on to another to be rewritten.

"That, too, is a really interesting question and in my mind is related to a bunch of different things. One of the things, I think, it is related to is that no matter the attitude of the industry, it can't do without the writer. Every project starts with the script—the writer *is* indispensable. What the writer does is indispensable to the process. It's not like someone can come along and say, 'OK, on this one, I think, we'll do without a script. We won't have a writer. We'll just go out and start filming.' I don't think you've seen that very often. The industry probably has some kind of love-hate relationship with writers for that reason.

"Your question is very much on the minds of the whole writing community, and writers are taken advantage of in many, many ways. I can recite some of them right now. The Writers Guild is trying to clamp down against this practice, but even when a writer is employed to do a feature or a pilot or a television movie, there is an industry practice where the writer is expected to do free internal rewrites. To do extra drafts for free. It comes out of the writer's desire to always want to have his or her best work seen. A producer will say, 'Sure, I can turn it in, but do you really want this draft to be seen this way, or do you want to do X, Y, and Z to make it that much better?'

"Perhaps another way in which today's writer is in a weaker position is in the way writers are treated. In the twenty-two years that I've been an agent, I've seen significant changes. It used to be that, if I had a viable writer available for an open writing assignment and the producer wanted my client for that assignment, I would never show material to that producer until I had a firm offer for that job. Today, for many assignments, that still holds true but, particularly for a lot of the more interesting assignments, I may get a producer who will call and say, 'You know, I'm very interested in your client and I've got this great, new project. I'm going out to a very short list of writers, maybe two, three, or four writers whom a network is interested in working with and that I'm interested in working with. I'd like to see what kind of take your client will have on the material. I'd like to send your client the book (or the pages, whatever it is) and have him or her take a look at it and prepare an audition presentation for me. I'll be getting similar presentations from two or three other writers.' "

This is a nonpaid writing assignment?

"It's an audition to get a paid writing gig. Now, you can refuse to do that, but if you do, you take your writer out of the game, and you want your clients to be considered for good jobs. So, in general, today it seems that even experienced writers who are very employable will have to submit to a certain amount of auditioning. This has been frowned upon by the Guild for various reasons and, in the past, frowned upon by literary agents who want to protect their writers from doing work for producers without getting paid.

"On the other hand, there are many ways in which the writer is not taken advantage of. There are times when the writer is the key person on the project. There are also lots of very powerful feature screenwriters who are the centerpiece of feature projects. Certainly, this is true on nearly all television series. In television, it's usually a writer/executive producer who's in control. Occasionally, it's a star. We are all aware of shows that stars control and where the writers are replaceable."

On finding representation. What steps do you recommend that new writers take, especially people outside of LA or New York City?

"The first thing a writer has to do is prepare writing samples; that's number one. The second thing is get his or her material to someone in the industry, like a producer or a studio executive or a story editor someone who will read the work, not necessarily with the idea of buying it, but with the idea of helping that person find an agent. As I said before, most literary agencies will only read material when submitted by people that they know. They won't take it directly from the writer. Therefore, the first business goal for any new writer who wants an agent, is to find that person in the industry who will respond to their work and who then will call an agent or a few agents recommending the writer."

Is there other advice you would give to those writers who are new to the system?

"Write the very best script they can, and *do not* send out work that you know isn't ready. Target your spec material to the arena that you want to go into. If it happens to be series television, then write sample scripts for shows that are relatively fresh, successful, and high quality. If you want to be a screenwriter, then write the best *original* screenplay you can. I don't know how to define it better than that."

Sandy Weinberg (Paradigm Agency)

What is your background, and how did you become a literary agent?

"I began as an attorney and became a disgruntled attorney—I think there are a lot of those floating around. I was certainly one of them but decided that I wanted to have a working relationship with clients other than just negotiating their deals and fighting over their money, which is what I was doing as a lawyer."

Were you a literary attorney at the time?

"No. I negotiated and drafted a lot of motion picture and music contracts. At that time, I worked for a very prestigious entertainment litigation firm where I litigated a lot of breach of contract actions, artists' rights issues and First Amendment issues regarding artists' privacy and intellectual property. I practiced for two years then became an assistant to an agent—a secretary. I went from having a secretary to being one.

"I was a secretary for about a year. Then I got an agent position at a company called H. N. Swanson, which is one of the two oldest literary agencies in Los Angeles; it no longer exists in the same form today. Swanny had been around for sixty years as an agent and represented the biggest authors of our time. He sold *Roots*, the miniseries, and he was a really big agent. I was there for a little less than a year; then I came here. This company had been called Harris & Goldberg and the name changed about four years ago to Innovative Artists. So, I've been here for about 5½ years."

Since the time of this interview, Sandy has moved to Paradigm Agency.

What is your personal focus here?

"It's on writers and directors (literary) and primarily, it's studio features and two-hour TV movies. I've also sold a bunch of pilots, in episodic TV, and occasionally I will sell true life stories and books, but, most of it's representation of writers and directors."

What do you look for in new writers?

"What I look for is in the material. The background of the writer can vary, but I look for a couple of things. One is often referred to in the industry as the 'original voice,' which is someone who can write characters vividly and in a way where I can see them in my head as I read them. Someone who can project those characters in the very first sequence of pages of the screenplay; that's very important.

"The first sequence of the screenplay or movie is where you set up the characters, and there is an art to doing that. There are a lot of mechanical tricks to doing that, but there is also an art.

"The second thing I look for out of people (who don't have the mechanics down) is writing that evokes a visceral reaction. I read a lot of screenplays, as do a lot of other agents and executives and producers, and if this is a screenplay that makes me laugh or makes me cry or makes me sweat or evokes some sort of reaction—if it can do that in me—then I know it can do it in other people.

"I'll tell you now, I hate everybody. So, if one can hit me in a way that literally evokes a visceral reaction, then I know there is something really great there, even though I may not be able to articulate exactly what is great, or what is bad. I mean, when I read a horror script that I find to be truly scary, that's a great moment for me during my Sunday afternoon. That's an important moment."

How many scripts do you think you read in an average week?

"It depends on the time of the year and it depends on what clients are doing because some clients want me to read drafts and some don't, so it does depend. I would say on average no less than seven and no more than twelve because you can't read more than twelve in a weekend or your mind just goes blank."

So it's all done on the weekends?

"I try not to read Monday to Friday. Occasionally I will, if someone needs an opinion of a writer who's looking for an agent—you gotta go fast sometimes—or if it's a client's script, I will do it in the middle of the week. However, my fresher reads are after I've had my nap on a Saturday or Sunday afternoon. I'll wake up and read. That's when I do my best reading. I'm just too tired at the end of the workday. I'm usually here until eight or nine at night, so it's not a good time to go home and evaluate material."

What's the busiest time of the year for you?

"It's cyclical."

Is it consistently at a certain time of the year?

"No. There are years where sometimes August is a slow month. This has not been a very slow August; this is a very busy August for me. I've been very lucky and a bunch of my deals have come in. We sold a bunch of stuff to studios and to networks this August.

"January is often slow because people are still getting back from the Sundance Film Festival. It depends. There's no saying, really. The market's been pretty hot for the past couple of years, so there hasn't been a lot of downtime. Certainly, around holidays things slow down, and it's not a good time to shop material because a lot of the buyers aren't in their offices, they're on vacation.

There seems to be a long time between sale and release of a feature. What is the progression from script to sale?

"I've got two movies on the air: the Gotti movie on HBO, I sold that movie almost four years ago, and a Disney Channel movie that's done very well for them, I sold five years ago. And that's television, where it's supposed to be fast.

"Do you mean the progression of what I do with the material?"

Yes. How do you shop a script you like?

"You don't sit on good material. You get it out there. However, really good material doesn't always sell the first time out. Sometimes it scares people."

Why?

"Because, if it's really, really good they don't always trust their instincts that they can market it to a mass audience. They think it might be too special for a mass audience."

Really? You mean the production companies?

"Yeah. It's interesting. Some of our most evocative scripts that have been turned into movies have taken long periods of time to set up and get into production. That's not always true, but sometimes it is true.

"We look at the process in two ways. Depending on the client and the client's desire, we can take a piece of material and try to sell it, which is a different process from taking the material and trying to sell it in a manner that will help the writer's career."

What do you mean?

"It's the difference between throwing scripts up and seeing if they stick and sending the scripts into the system where the writer can benefit. A lot of agents follow route one that I just described, which is where they really don't care so much about what happens to the writer, they just want to see if they can sell the material. Philosophically, that is not how we do it here. Philosophically, particularly with a newer writer, we make sure that we use the material in a way to make an introduction for that writer to the system.

"There are various systems. There's the studio feature system, the television network system, the cable network system, and there's the independent feature system. The writer's material needs to be introduced in such a way where producers read the material and, whether they pass or not, we make sure that the writer is equipped and ready to go with a pitch for another story that's in the same tone as the material. Chances are, most people will pass, even on things that eventually sell, because their inclination is 'nothing is ever good enough.' And if something is really good, they're afraid of it because they think it's too difficult to get it made.

192

"So, you're in a situation where a lot of people will pass and then you have to ask yourself, as someone who represents writers, 'How can the writer benefit here?' And the writer *can* benefit because, if they like the material, but they don't love it enough to take it to the studio and see if the studio will buy it, we can then get the producer to take a meeting with the writer. We do this by telling the producer, 'Joe wrote the script and, yeah, it's good, but you should meet him and get to know him.' And the producer will say, 'Well, you know, I would, but I don't have enough time right now. I'm in production on my movie. Let's do it another time.' And I will say, 'Well, you know, they have a pitch, Joe has a pitch.' And immediately the producer will make time to hear the pitch because they are afraid of missing something.

"So, armed with the pitch at the time that the script goes out, the writer has given me a tool to get them into the room."

Oh, so the script is like a writing sample . . .

"Exactly. What was a spec just became a writing sample because it was turned down for purchase. So, in an instant I've converted it into a writing sample and I've used the pitch to get him into the room. And the pitch is a fully worked out story that a writer can tell in ten to fifteen minutes where the producer will come away from the pitch remembering that writer for coming in and telling a great story, even if he doesn't want to try and sell the pitch [to the studio]. A writer who he has never read before, except for that one time, who he'd never met before, except for that one time, has proven twice that he has the ability to tell a story—which is a very powerful thing for a writer. It's the only power a writer has when coming into a room for the first time.

"Producers have a lot of things. They have a lot of money usually, they have superior social skills, they have great ties to people with big checkbooks, usually, because they usually don't make a weekly check themselves, so someone they know is paying them something big. The power a new writer has is in his or her ability to write stories and tell stories. It proves to the producer that this is someone they can pick up for assignments because they've read one script that was good and they've heard a pitch that was fully worked out.

Later, when an assignment comes up with that producer, the [writer's] agent can call the producer and say, 'Well, you know who might be good? It might be Joe Shmoe, who wrote that script. Remember that script.' And he'll go, 'I don't remember.' 'Well, you met Joe. He pitched you the story blah, blah, blah.' And he'll go, 'Yeah, I remember that guy. You know what? What the hell, show him the script. Let's hear his take.'

"So, now Joe Shmoe wrote a script, that didn't sell; he's pitched a pitch, that didn't sell; but now he's being sent material that is an open writing assignment. So, he may have an opportunity for work even though none of the other two opportunities have sold.

"As agents, that's what we try to do to get writers into the system. If you send out a spec that's really good to a lot of producers, a large percentage of those producers will take a pitch meeting and the writer has an opportunity to meet a lot of people and get into these systems. And every studio is a different system with different producers they like to work with and different needs as a studio in terms of product."

Just to back up a little. Do you work out a pitch with your writers?

"Yes. I don't work it out, but I hear it and we talk about it. There are some stories that are unpitchable, and there are other stories that lend themselves well to pitches."

By unpitchable you mean that it's a good story but it doesn't lend itself to a short ten-minute explanation?

"It's hard to convey that particular pitch in a room.

"Pitches that are well received tend to be pitches that have no more than two major characters, that are male driven (because it's a fact most studio movies are male driven), that have a beginning, middle and end that is clear, and that has a clear character arc for each of the two characters.

"It's very difficult to boil down a story to ten or fifteen minutes, but there are certain guidelines in pitching that some writers will rely on that can be useful in boiling stuff down. We also don't want writers pitching with notes. They can have an index card in front of them, but a pitch is a performance. A pitch is keeping the attention of a producer who normally has a very low attention span because they have a lot of things going on. It's not because they are stupid, because they're not, they're very smart. They just have a lot of stuff going on, and it's hard to get them to focus in the middle of the day on something other than their crisis at hand. They are very smart people. They are producers for a reason; they have a gift for making things happen."

You mentioned studio features, television, cable, and independent feature markets. Do your clients write a script and then you decide which of these markets it best fits into?

"No. We try to develop a game plan with each writer by looking at what that writer seeks to achieve in his or her career and then mapping out a path for the writer to pursue. There's a lot of crossover between film and television now. But there are still some basic guidelines, and one is that studio features have male stars. Writers who write studio features for female stars are writing for the smallest market of all because it is very rare that the commitment of an actress will green-light a movie for a studio.

"There are almost no women today who can do that, absent Michelle Pfeiffer, Sandra Bullock, or Demi Moore. At this moment in time, I don't think there is another woman who, if committed to a movie, will green-light it at a studio—which means a budget of twenty million and up. At an independent, yes. But at a studio, a film which normally has a budget of at least twenty million dollars, no. It's because the box office doesn't prove they can do it. Right now this is the case. By the time the book comes out, there probably will be more.

"So, you try and focus on male-driven properties because there are a lot more male actors who can green-light films by attaching to them. Television two-hour movies are just the opposite. They are totally female driven; their audience is female, and the demographics are clean, all except for Fox which has a large male audience. HBO and TNT have primarily male audiences, as does Showtime, but Showtime is actually more of a mix. USA has a primary female audience, which a lot of people are surprised about, but yet they do. Their programming is for women, at night. They tend to go for sexier stuff than the networks."

How about shows like *Silk Stalkings*?

"Think about *Silk Stalkings* for a second. The lead detective is the woman, not the guy. The guy is often used as what we normally see in detective series as the woman's role. He's usually the object of a sexual foray and the woman almost never is, well, Robb Estes was much more than the girl was. We saw him scantily clothed much more often than you ever saw her. That's for the women in the audience—and the new guy is even more so because his character's not nearly as quick. He just isn't."

They just got a new male lead.

"Yes, and he's more of a cover model than even Robb Estes. Robb Estes actually turned out to be a good actor and women love him and now he's doing two-hour made-for-TV movies because there is an audience for him and he's readily cast in these network movies."

When you say that an actor can green-light a film you mean that . . .

"If Tom Cruise wants to do your movie, a studio will green-light that movie if it's the phone book."

So, do you first go after an actor that you can attach to your script?

"No. Some agencies will package movies, but we tend not to do that here. If it's a script that has a director attached to it, we will then go to actors first. But for just a writer, no. Because then the writer's agenda is not being met, which is to get into the system. It's the actor's agenda that's being met or the agency's agenda that's being met, not the writer's. So, we're very adamant about not doing that."

Does that hurt you as an agency?

"No. It helps the writers."

It does? Well, I guess it does makes sense. You wouldn't have a game plan for your company that wouldn't be good for your clients.

"Well, that's actually true because we are sort of an alternative agency that way. We're not a packaging agency."

You mean like a CAA or an ICM.

"That's correct."

Out of their millions of writers and actors and directors and so on, they can pull all these elements together.

"Well, that's what they're supposed to do. That's what they say they do. We don't say we do that. Sometimes we still do it, but we don't say we do it and we don't do it on a daily basis. We don't develop material internally for our actors like the big agencies do. We're not scurrying around town looking for the right script for Bette Midler like CAA is."

When we spoke before, you said that the business is not writer-friendly.

"No it's not. The writer's the first guy that gets fired. That's another reason you don't want the star to be attached first because the star may pull in his best friend to rewrite it—or the director does that. The writer is the first one to get fired. He's the first one to get blamed when something goes wrong. They fire the writer."

Are you able to work around that in your game plan? Or does that still happen a lot?

"Of course it happens. What are we supposed to do? Once they buy a script they own it, and they can do anything they want with it."

You can't write in . . .

"You negotiate contractual guarantees. The Guild gives protections to the writer for a certain number of steps, and we contractually can get more than the Guild protection. But ultimately the studio that puts down money for the material controls the material, and they can develop it however they want. The studios often take dramatic material and make it more comedic or comedic material and make it scary or action material and make it a love story. They can do whatever they want. So, the writer's the one who is fired first.

"Every time an actor is hired or a director is hired, your writer is vulnerable to the reconceptualization of the project by the actor or the director. Writers who are highly experienced or respected don't face that problem as much. It's hard to fire a writer who is highly respected because people want to work with that writer. That's part of the draw. For newer writers, it's a hellish experience and it's something you always experience with a new writer. You always know they are going to get fired."

The Hollywood system is a furnace, and no matter what direction you go in, you're going to be tempered in its fires.

"It's a very powerful system. There's only a few studios. This isn't a business that proliferates."

What can you tell me about the politics of studio writing? I'm referring to when we spoke before and you talked about "A," "B," and "C" lists . . . about how the real world works.

"It's not the real world, it's the studio world, which is not a real world. In the studio world, no one gets sick and dies. In the real world, they do a lot. There's almost nothing real about a studio world. Anyone who has been on a studio lot knows that."

I meant that many of the doors are closed anyway.

"No, no, no. Once you're in, they're open.

"Studios generally make genre films, and that's because they know how to sell them to people. Rarely do you see studios sell mixed-genre films. Big movies (expensive films) are very clearly genre films. They are comedies, action films, horror films, and thrillers."

So as a writer breaking in, you're going to want to clearly define your story as one of these genres and not a hybrid.

"That's correct. Particularly a larger budget one. Because they want to be able to market them. Marketing is half of what studios do; making movies is pretty much the other half. They will sometimes spend millions and millions of dollars marketing a movie. So, it's really important that it be clearly genre specific and that's particularly true for new writers who are trying to define themselves in the market.

"What the studios do is that they have lists of writers. If it's a comedy that needs a rewrite, they will look to their comedy list. If they have an action movie that needs a rewrite, they will look to their action list, and if it's a horror film, they will look to their horror list. The top of the action list is the guy you would expect, Shane Black. And they go down the list from Shane Black until they get the writer that makes sense.

"Sometimes if there is a star attached, the star will insist on certain writers or a director will insist on certain writers. But the studio hires writers off their wish list. And the object of representing newer writers is figuring ways to get them on those lists. And you don't enter a list as number one above Shane Black. You enter at number forty-nine, and you have to keep coming back to the market with original material until that system hires you. So, say you work your way up that list and maybe you're number twenty-six, and the first ten are busy, the second ten don't like it, the next four are on vacation, and number twenty-five has the flu. So now your client is twenty-six, and your client gets an offer. And that's often how it works the first time out when a writer's getting an assignment. And they get the assignment because studio executives hear their pitches and read their material even though no one ever buys it.

"If you sell a spec, you get on the list a lot faster. If you sell a pitch, you get on the list a lot faster. You get a movie made, you go much higher on the list. If you get sole credit on a film, your name goes right up there on those lists, for a while. That is, until you do something the studio doesn't like; then you go off the list and you have to work your way back into it again. We do a lot of that, too.

"For our clients who have fallen off the lists, we work hard to get them back on. I just did that with a writing team who hadn't worked at a studio in three years and now they are working at a studio. At two studios, actually (sold two projects). But we really had to hustle; it's been three years and they've only been clients here for six months.

"Rejuvenation is a very gratifying thing for an agent. A very gratifying experience to help a client rejuvenate their career.

"You asked me, 'What attracts me to writers?' A writer who had a big career and who has blown it is very attractive to me as a client because there are ways to rejuvenate careers. That's different from a new writer who's new into the system, which is what you originally asked me to talk about.

"When a writer who was a big writer years ago has fallen off the turnip truck and needs help getting back on, that's someone who is very, very helpable. That is if they are willing to stick to a game plan of pitching and speccing and being politically savvy. Usually they fall off the turnip truck by being apolitical—by pissing people off. That's usually how you fall off a list. You can also fall off the list by doing a lot of development for a studio where nothing gets made. They may get tired of you."

What defines a high budget movie? Is it because locations or effects are expensive or it requires a big star?

"Because someone at the studio decides to make it for a high budget. There's not always a rule about that. *Independence Day* has no big stars, but they decided to spend a lot of money on the movie. They could have made the same movie for forty million dollars, for half of what they made it for.

"Why studios do anything is purely a matter of the internal politics of the studio. It has nothing to do with outside forces at all."

Is there anything worth getting into about studio politics?

"Probably not. Because, unless you want to be a studio executive, there's really no reason to get into it too much. But there is a very strict pecking order. There's also a lot of relatives working at the studios. Seriously. And that's not necessarily a bad thing. They just happen to be there. It's hard for an outsider."

What makes for an enduring writer?

"One who writes great characters. Studio movies are all about characters. They really are. Plot is secondary. They can always change the plot, but they can't change the characters. Ultimately it's someone who can continue to come to the market and show one's ability to write great characters."

Jumping back to the "system," what type of movies do cable and independents make? You made the point that studios go for the clear-cut genre films and TV movies are female-driven. What about cable and independents?

"It's all changing. I don't know if there are any fast rules anymore.

But cable does have higher sexual content than other networks. That's one of the reasons why there is cable—because the network standards have always been so strict that they would have had a monopoly had they controlled more channels based on those standards. For diversity purposes, the government has allowed lower morality standards to exist for cable programming, pay cable being the least strict. Free cable is more strict. On some networks, you still cannot have open-mouth kissing. Watch TV movies and you'll see a lot of pecks on cheeks; particularly one network is notorious for taking sex out of the movies."

Do you see the independent film companies as arenas for more experimental formats?

"No, not always. Studios are starting to get more experimental. Independents tend to have very much lower budgets, they tend to be more director-oriented as opposed to any other driving force— they really are, they really are director-driven and they do cross-genre more. You see more black comedies, more serious horror films, and the human condition dramas in independent films. Studios don't know how to market them. They really don't. I'm certain they wish they could but they don't. Very rarely do you see a character drama make a lot of money at a studio."

I get the impression that studios are going through a change right now.

"I think it's opening. I think it's really opened up in the last couple of years."

That's a change.

"Yeah, it's growing. The system has been growing since the strike of 1987, when everything shut down and then some studios went out of business. A few of them dropped out of sight."

Just never recovered?

"Oh, no, a couple of them that fell out of sight in the late eighties have just reemerged. Orion just got back on its feet again. And Turner and New Line, these are companies that were not in this same business ten years ago that they are in now. So, it's opened up a lot, and Polygram has now made a firm commitment to Hollywood and has various companies under its arm, unlike they've ever had before. They're making an enormous number of movies now.

"At studios, they are trying to reduce their risk. There's more money here now, and studios are trying to reduce their risk up front by sharing risk financially. Studios used to insisted on owning the whole movie. That simply is not as true today."

You mean that they will bring in foreign investment?

"They will sell of pieces of it. For example, Paramount will make a movie and cofinance it with Universal and one will take foreign rights and one will take domestic rights. They will each put money into the production budget and each one will want certain rights, and they divide them up before the movie's ever made. That's new. Studios didn't used to do that. That's also because they are public companies, so they have to reduce their risk."

Of the writers you represent, are they all trained through film schools?

"Oh, no. Oh, God, no. No, no, no. Send me a truck driver who can write a great action film. Films schools tend not to—things are a bit more homogenized sometimes. I think film school students feel sometimes pressured to second-guess the market in the material they are creating because they are living around people who are in the market and they are barraged by information. And I think they get defensive and try to guess what the market wants or needs and try and create that while at film school and use that as their sample. Sometimes that works. For a writer it's hard because you have to show your own voice and that's not always the best way to do it."

Are there any topics that I've missed that you feel are important to talk about?

"We talked about access. About how people find agents. For me the most powerful way to get material to me is through a referral, and Los Angeles is a very big place and no matter where you live, you know someone who knows someone who lives here who knows someone who knows someone. And I am fairly obligated to read material that is sent to me from someone I know. As opposed to material that is sent from someone who I don't know. So, referrals are very important and they come from lawyers or development executives or from my Aunt Betty—someone I know."

How about the person who is in middle America who doesn't know a soul in Hollywood?

"They need to do their homework. They need to first decide if they are looking for representation to sell their material or looking for representation to support their writing career. Those are sometimes two different things. Many agents in various cities co-agent with Los Angeles agents. I co-agent with agents in Minneapolis and Chicago and New York and Washington, DC and San Francisco and Canada. So I get material from agents I co-agent with, whom I share clients with, from all over the place. So, I think that the yellow pages are a good start."

Do you think it's critical for a writer who truly wants to write features to live in Los Angeles?

"Yes. Do they have to live here forever? No. We have clients who live all over the world. Writers who come here for X number of weeks per year that are concentrated in terms of meetings and in terms of pitching. So, they have to spend time here, you can't avoid it. This is where the buyers are. But, yes, you need to build relationships."

Are there other cities that could work? How about New York?

"Sure."

Or Florida . . .

"Not in Florida."

Nothing's happening that's big enough in Florida, but New York's possible?

"Sure. It's difficult from New York because the studio executives are here. We have writers who live all over the place, but you have to spend time here if you want a career as a screenwriter. If you just want to sell material, you can live anywhere. You can live in Alaska."

So, if you want to be a feature or a television writer, you pretty much have to live here to be practical.

"Or Toronto."

Americans living in Toronto can get work?

"No, but Canadians can."

"I also think it's important to mention that I really do believe that no one really has answers to a lot of the questions. I mean, I'm telling you answers that I think might be true. There is no single truth to all this. People find employment as writers from various backgrounds, and 'no one really knows anything.' I think William Goldman was absolutely right, 'No one really knows anything,' but we have to have some framework for what we do during the day with our clients, and that's where we've developed ideals and foci to empower writers a little bit so they don't feel like they are totally at the mercy of the system. That they are using their power of the pen or computer and that they are pitching to attract opportunities."

There's security in a game plan.

"For writers who embrace the plan that they have chosen, when they stick to it and embrace it, we've seen a very, very high level of success. Extremely high level. Sometimes it takes six months for the first job, sometimes it takes a year, but for writers who stick with the plan and develop material that is true to their voice, we see success. That's why we practice it.

How many writers do you handle at any one time?

"As a group, there's four agents here. We handle about sixty. The agents here don't have their own list; we represent them as a group. So, we're all working together here to give the writers unified representation and that's different from other places. It's a pretty low ratio actually. Some agencies have four, five hundred, seven hundred writers. We don't."

Here you have a better chance to work out an individual game plan and get personal attention rather than be a small part of a large system

"It's true. Most successful writers in those larger systems are very self-starting. If you interview them, you'll find out that they are doing a lot of the things that we're advising our writers to do. It's just that the agents aren't taking the time at some of those agencies to talk to the writers about it. The writers are just doing it on their own. We are working with our writers in that process. So, it's a bit different that way."

NINE

Why Film School?
A Look at the UCLA MFA Program

Half the professionals in Hollywood say, "Screw film school, learn by the seat of your pants. Get out there and get a job as a PA [production assistant] and work your way up. Learn by doing and observing." The other half of Hollywood says, "Film school is the only way to go. You need a critical understanding of the history and art of film." Certainly jumping into the water and learning to swim firsthand is one option; however, I wanted explore the value of attending film school. What are the benefits or advantages of film school? What, in general, will a screenwriting MFA student learn while in the program?

In recent years, UCLA has been singled out as having the best screenwriting program of the big three (NYU, USC, and UCLA film schools), so they must *be doing something very right. So, who better to address the above questions than Professor Lew Hunter and Professor Richard Walter, fellow chairs of the UCLA MFA screenwriting department? Both were successful screenwriters prior to coming to UCLA. In fact, Lew came to UCLA after a long, successful career in Hollywood.*

Professor Lew Hunter (chair)

Lew has been an exceptionally good friend and mentor for years. Without his help and contacts, I would not have had access to many of the people I've interviewed. I was looking forward to this interview and was anxious about it at the same time. It turned out to be a mixed blessing. I know Lew and his wife, Pamela, so well that I'm aware that he's worked closely with many of the biggest names in the business, and I strongly encouraged him to bring out those relationships. Without a doubt, he felt comfortable enough to say things he normally, out of modesty, would not express so directly, and I welcomed the tangents we went off onto.

The interview took place at his house where he invited me to his writing shack in the backyard. It's a tiny space, barely enough room to walk in and turn around. There's a small work desk, a small daybed for resting, a chest of drawers for miscellaneous papers and scripts, and a window that opens out, giving him a view of the yard. Overhead, a loaded bookshelf protrudes like an extended eyebrow covering three walls.

I plopped down on the bed, and, as I searched for the ideal spot to set up my recorder, he simply grabbed it, reclined in his writing chair, and placed the recorder on his chest—how's that for relaxed! In this setting, we delved into his life experiences, thoughts, and advice.

As a reader of Lew's interview, you should know that in this past year, he has been an instrumental part in setting up the new European Conservatory for the screenwriting program at the Sorbonne.

What is your writing background?

"We can start out as a farm boy in Nebraska with a mother who graduated from the New England Conservatory of Music, who had me dressed up in Easter Bunny clothing singing 'Here Comes Peter Cotton Tail' or as George M. Cohan on the Fourth of July belting out 'It's a Grand Old Flag,' simultaneously learning a variety of instruments: piano, violin, xylophone, and trombone—I believe the musical saw also was taught for some strange reason.

"My father was a 'not-so-simple farmer.' No, wrong, he was actually a simple, wonderful farmer. My father was known throughout the county as the nicest man in Webster County *and* the strongest. How does a son, even at age sixty-one in 1996, live up to that? I can't. He has . . . now and forever . . . been my truest hero. No hidden psychobabble agenda . . . Number One . . . Ray Lewis Hunter!

"Now, my mother, or, 'Take my Mother . . . please,' I was discussing with a musician last night about listening to Milton Cross from the Metropolitan Opera on the radio on Saturday afternoons with *Tosca, Barber of Seville*, et cetera—and loathing it, by the way, because I'd much prefer to be playing ball. But, actually, I guess I would have been working the livestock or in the fields.

"My mother loathed the concept of me being a farmer/rancher. Ergo, after a variety of miscreant James Dean–like episodes, I found myself in Wentworth Military Academy for my senior year in high school. Then Nebraska Wesleyan University, majoring in business administration, which is what people still major in when they don't know what they want to do when they grow up. In Year One, I found out what I wanted when auditioning for the theater.

"It's the familiar story of me going over with somebody else to audition, and I was the one who got the part. A tobacco-spitting preacher in a play called *Sun Up*—which I have never heard of before or since. Recently, when I dedicated the Nebraska Wesleyan theater in my tuxedo, in front of a tuxedoed and coifed audience, I spit on the floor (hardly an elegant thing to do) and said, 'On this very stage, in this very spot, I became attracted beyond my wildest dreams to performance art when I got a laugh spitting tobacco. By the end of the play's run, I had mixed licorice with my saliva so I could better arc my spit across the stage. And, of course, the laugh would accelerate every evening with the further I spit.'

"I then became an acting major. God smiled again and got me into television producing for KFOR-TV and KOLN-TV in Lincoln. Doing everything, literally, from floor manager, to sweeping floors, to directing, to performing. Ergo, I was sort of drawn away from acting into television production because I couldn't memorize lines very well. Even today, if I'm asked to remember something, I write it down, or it simply doesn't get remembered or done.

"At the time the two best places for television study were Syracuse University and Northwestern University. By that time, I was nineteen years old because I had skipped grades, and I got a master's in radio and television. My master's thesis was on *Goebbels* . . . different, eh? And I've always said, 'I would prefer to be Richelieu than King Louis.' I suppose that's far better than saying, 'I'd rather be Goebbels than Hitler.' With my now teaching at the Sorbonne with Richelieu glowering down from behind me in the world's oldest lecture hall, I always think of that.

"I then wanted to get into network television in New York or LA. Again, God touched me on the shoulder by pointing me westward, young man . . . page staff, mail room, and music clearance in a one-year period. That was the progression. At that time in network television, the typical entry-level jobs started with the page staff and mail room. Many of our famous directors, like Sydney Pollack, Franklyn Shaffner, and John Frankenheimer, had begun on page staffs. I then applied for a nationwide RCA-NBC David Sarnoff scholarship, saying I knew a fair amount about live television (we didn't even have taped television at that time).

"I wanted to now know about film. They were kind enough to give me the scholarship, which allowed me to go to UCLA and get a master's degree in cinema, as it was called at that time, a rather arch phrase we have since dropped. We now simply call it film, soon to be changed as new technology will render the word 'film' obsolete.

"I came back to NBC after getting my second master's degree. I went into the broadcasting promotion department . . . made trailers . . . got awards . . . all the time wanting desperately to get into programming.

"ABC hired me away from NBC, and I became manager of the on-air broadcast promotion department. Harve Bennett, one of our intrepid UCLA alums responsible for a great many of the *Star Trek* motion picture series and Irwin Shaw's *Rich Man, Poor Man* and *Six Million Dollar Man*, hired me to be a program executive at ABC where I was put in charge of series such as *Batman, The Addams Family, Peyton Place, Bewitched, Voyage to the Bottom of the Sea, Combat,* et cetera, most of which are being made into movies today.

"After two years of being a program executive and telling writers how to write (and closet writing, too), it seemed to me I should learn about scripts beyond sixty pages, the length of an hour-long episode at that time. I seized an opportunity at Disney to become their story editor. I was thrilled at the opportunity, as I had worked with Walt back in my broadcast days.

"In 1968, Walt had since gone to his substantial reward, and, of course, his rewards are now reaped by Michael Eisner in this day and age . . . and, well, they should be. They are well deserved. In my opinion, Walt would have been very, very pleased. Yet when we went to picture, Walt would say, 'Well, I think we're ready to shoot.' He never told anybody, 'It was a great picture, it was a great script, or a great performance.' He was an interesting paternal figure . . . sort of a beloved dictator. I idolized him and still do. A hero, right after my father.

"I was at Disney when Ray Bradbury and I tried to get *The Martian Chronicles* shot at Disney because of our wonderful technology breakthroughs, well exhibited with live television with *Twenty Thousand Leagues Under the Sea* and *Swiss Family Robinson*. We could really do *The Martian Chronicles*. I said, 'Ray, I've been here for two years, and

I'm more and more self-conscious about telling writers how to write.'
Three years at ABC, two at Disney supervising the writing at various
shows and movies, and again writing on my own. (I have some perfectly dreadful episodes of *The Dick Powell Theater*, *The Zane Gray
Theater*, and a couple of original motion picture scripts I hope have
decayed in my files by now. Training-wheel scripts that fell off the
interim bicycle years back.) I've read two thousand scripts over a two-
year period, and I just can't believe that I can't possibly be in that
top-ten-percent-of-shit.

"I was sort of brought up in this business to be a bit irreverent
about your ability, particularly your writing. It's all a facade, though,
because we all are, hopefully, very proud of what we do. But to get
objectivity on our own material, often we denigrate a false form of
humility.

"Ray encouraged me to read Dorothea Brande's book *Becoming a
Writer* (which, to this day, I recommend) and a Zen Buddhist book
by Alan Watts, *The Wisdom of Insecurity*. And this Saturday, in one of
life's ironies, the circle, or *La ronde* as they say in poetry—where the
end is the beginning or Alpha and Omega in the Bible—I'm mod-
erating a day-long screenwriters' conference in Woodland Hills for
the Alameda Writers Club where I get to happily introduce their
keynote speaker, Ray Bradbury. Of course, I've seen him a number
of times since the Disney days. To say I love him is a solid understatement. In my book, *Lew Hunter's Screenwriting 434*, I refer to him
a great deal, particularly in my closing chapter about why we write.'

"From Bradbury at Disney, I came home, talked to my then-
wife, and said, 'I'm going to take a year off.' Bless her heart, she
said, 'Fine.' Just like that! I was giving up a lot of money at Disney,
probably $40 or $50K per year, which today is worth about $150,000.
Between that and unemployment insurance . . . I'd say the government does subsidize the arts.

"I remember going to what we show-biz folk called the U1 line
and waiting. Quite a sociological experience . . . people of different
ethnicities and vocations. We'd stand there and wait, collar turned

up, hoping nobody saw us, to pick up our weekly dole. I understand they now mail the check to you to subvert that regular humiliation. But it wasn't . . . well . . . it was what it was. God forbid anyone should know. We/I/We're/was OUT OF A JOB! I lasted an entire year, writing six scripts during that time frame. Six full-length feature, motion picture scripts. Gold! Stan Sherman, the head writer on *Batman*, said, 'You know, Lew, I think it's probably as simple as— the more ponies you put in the race, the better your chances are of coming in the money.' I repeat, 'Gold!'

"I teach that today. You must get out the scripts. F. Scott Fitzgerald said, 'Hollywood is full of writers who never write.' Ergo, producers who never produce, directors who never direct. But writers are the luckiest in the entire entertainment business because they're never without a job. They may not be getting paid, or they may be getting their pay from U1 or whatever the 'dole' department is now called, but they still have an opportunity to develop their ability and to create properties which will hopefully someday be of some value to them in, not only the learning curve, but in actual dollars and cents on the marketplace or, at the very least, a calling card that can stimulate people to say, 'I don't want to do this script, but I really like the writing. Would you be interested in doing something else for us?' And ergo, marriages are born, children are named after each other, and all those good procreating things.

"I then sold a movie, which was the first script I had written, about what happened to the Japanese Americans before, during, and after Pearl Harbor. It eventually was called *If Tomorrow Comes*. I took *Romeo and Juliet* and overlaid it on that era with the Montagues, the people of Japanese heritage and, of course, the Caucasians the Capulets, with a Nisei Romeo and a Caucasian Juliet, played by Patty Duke. We had the nurse parallel as an English literature teacher, played by Anne Baxter. James Whitmore was Patty Duke's father. Mako played the Paris role as well as the cousin to the Romeo played by Frank Lui. Pat Hingle, a wonderful actor, played the sheriff. John McClain was the priest/padre.

"I sold *If Tomorrow Comes* at the end of this trial year. I was so desperate . . . desperate meaning I was about to go get a real job—I had been offered associate producer work, but I didn't feel that would enhance my writing. I thought it would surely make me a 'Hollywood hack.' Whether I am, or I ever was, is almost immaterial. In my mind, I was trying to get Diogenes to put away the lamp.

"So, I sold *If Tomorrow Comes* to Aaron Spelling and ABC. The movie was made and, thus, a career started. I wrote episodes for a variety of series, worked on movies that never got made, wrote films for Billy Graham's company, World Wide Pictures, which tips off my role as a lay minister in the Methodist church. I then had an opportunity, in 1972, to go to NBC with far more authority than I had at ABC. I would be in charge of movies, series, and eventually became the director of development for movies and dramatic comedy series. Deanne Barkley, a secretary, and moi were doing the equivalent of what it takes fourteen to twenty people to do today.

"Our philosophy was that we were overseeing, not making, the series or movies. If we liked them, we would pick them up. Just that simple. It was a very exciting time because the bean counters, specifically the GEs and the Westinghouses, had not come to the fore. It was truly show business with the emphasis on *show*. There was no control by advertising agencies, the case prior to my entry, because by then, television advertising was so expensive, few sponsors could afford an entire program, so television networks began to have the power.

"In the meanwhile, I continued to be fascinated with writing, but one of the reasons I took the NBC job was to give me the cachet to become a producer. I was never very happy with the filming of any of my scripts. I wanted to be involved with helping the baby walk. I didn't want to be Santa Claus, who brings the toys but can't play with them.

"After four years, I had the opportunity to leave NBC. I then had the background, the connections to be able to get a meeting, to be able to be heard with the proper amount of respect. I was saying to the president of a small studio just yesterday, working on the *James Dean, an American Legend* movie I am writing right now, 'All the people I grew up with are the heads of studios right now.' I'm plugged in now at such a high level, it's almost as ineffective as starting out because you don't want to call Michael Eisner, Peter Chernin, Ronnie Meyer, or Michael Ovitz and say, 'Oh, would you help me get a movie going?' . . . or whatever.

"Peter Gruber, whom I worked for at that particular time, up until recently, was head of Sony. John Calley is now chair of Sony. Barry Diller was another ABC vineyard grape gatherer. Sherry Lansing of Paramount used to sell me shows when she worked for Leonard Stern. I think I've covered the big six in Hollywood. Oh, Warner Bros.' Bob Daley was a vice president at CBS, and Barry Meyer, still at Warner Bros., was a wonderful ally. Sid Sheinberg, ex-president of Universal, and, of course, Lew Wasserman, our God at that particular time—he was, to the entertainment business, when I started, *the* power in the fifties, sixties, and seventies. Then in the eighties and into the nineties, Michael Ovitz and his warriors, as Joseph Eszterhas called them, became *the* power.

"The first movie I produced and wrote was the movie that continues to be the seminal point of my creative career. That was *Fallen Angel*, which won a number of international awards and got New York Film Festival, Writers Guild, and Emmy recognition. From there I produced *Desperate Lives, Playing with Fire*, and a good number of other television movies. Concurrently, I produced three television series, *Yellow Rose, Mississippi*, and *Other World*. Also, concurrently, as I was producing and writing for different people, networks, and studios, I used to do a great deal of doctoring of various motion pictures (that gentlemanly discretion keeps me from naming).

"I made much more money as a script doctor than I did as an NBC executive. Another epiphany that propelled me into writing . . . there's more money. Willie Sutton was asked, 'Why do you rob banks?' He replied, 'Because that's where the money is.' Why do many of us write? That's where the money is.

"Writers are also the creative power of the industry, theater and television most specifically. Motion pictures are going to be that way soon. Of all the students who have come through our writing program, a great collection of them have also become directors. We at UCLA can go back to Coppola, Higgin, Ballard, Schrader, et cetera. More recently, Greg Widen, David Koepp, Neil Jimenez, Alex Cox, Allison Anders, and probably a dozen that don't come to mind immediately. See? Screenwriting . . . that's where the money is.

"My mother used to say, 'Why did you leave NBC? They were grooming you. They wanted you to be president. You could have worn a nice suit like Mr. Schlosser,' the president when I was there. 'Mom, I make three times his money!' She still didn't get it. I guess she only got the power. But I was much more drawn to playing with than to buying the toys, if you will.

"But en route, incredibly, I became a professor at UCLA. Bill Froug asked me if I would take over his position while he went on a year sabbatical producing a show for Universal. I said, 'Gee, Bill. I've never taught before on a continuous basis.' Studios or networks used to send me to schools when somebody asked them for a speaker. They would say, 'Send Hunter to those schmucks and schmuckesses because he's got two master's degrees.' But to Bill I said, 'I've never taught on a continuing basis, but, OK, I'll try.'

"After one quarter, I went into the then Film Department chair, John Young, and said, 'John, this has been one of the most wonderful experiences in my life. If I don't get asked back again, "I'd be crushed" would be an understatement.' They asked me back, and I've continued to teach a full-time load, in academic terms. You see, UCLA is a research university, so it's not like a nine-to-five job at a normal university. I teach two classes a week, five courses a year . . . three hours each week for each class . . . one course in the fall quarter, two in the winter, two in the spring. There is a great deal of time for research, which, in my world, does not include boiling things in biology test tubes, but writing and working on scripts, such as this

James Dean script I'm looking at right now, which is glowering back at me in return.

"I am well able to concurrently write and produce, for you should know that studios, when they want you, will do anything, probably including fellatio in the middle of the studio commissary, to get you to do something. If they don't want you, a gun wouldn't even get you an opportunity. I would say, 'I have to be at UCLA every Tuesday and Thursday afternoon from three to seven. I'll come back, though.' And, of course, I did come back. In the case when I was working on a series, I not only came back, but I'd work until one, two, or three o'clock in the morning to try to get the pages to the set.

"As time has gone on, education has more and more consumed my attention and career. I have written a book that is cleverly called *Lew Hunter's Screenwriting 434*. I learned from Frank Capra . . . get your name in the title. Actually, I didn't do that. The publisher said, 'If they're going to ride the horse, make people know who the horse is.' Ergo, my name in the title, and, of course, Screenwriting 434 is the number of my graduate screenwriting class.

"I had been asked to write books early on but said, 'No! No! No! There's Syd and Richard. They'll do!' Someone said, 'Why don't you put your class on paper?' That made sense because we start with an idea and sweep all the way through the screenwriting process from idea, to roughing out the story line, to sophisticating the story, developing the characters along the way, doing the step outline, the first draft, and then, the rewriting. Putting that on paper seemed to be useful. I have felt, even to this day, that all of the books talk *about* screenwriting . . . they talk *around it*—but they don't actually tell you *how to write a screenplay*. A how-to book seemed timely and appropriate.

"In Southern California, without shrinkese dialogue and words like 'validate' and 'empower,' we call it a process book. In terms utilized around the world, it's a how-to book. And I'm quite pleased and particularly proud of it because I wanted to write it for a young boy at the end of a pier in a bayou, or a young woman atop a fire-watch tower in Montana. If they had no access to the education available to urban people, they could get this book and be able to utilize the same form, the same process 90 percent of our screenwriters use when writing screenplays.

"I have had hundreds of people call me and write and thank me. A young man was in Silver Springs, New Mexico, even remote in terms of New Mexico (sixty-seven miles north of Demming). He had written four screenplays and used my book as his only reference.

"I'm also proud of the fact I have been living as a screenwriter for twenty-seven years; and the fact that screenwriting has been my basic vocation gives me pride and pleasure. It all ties back to my self-consciousness about telling writers how to write yet needing to write for a living myself to gain that authoritative posture. For moi.

"George Bernard Shaw says, 'Those who can do, do, and those who can't, teach.' So, I am, hopefully, one who can do and teach. Don't anybody please break that balloon!

"Now we come up to today where the book is going beautifully. I do an enormous amount of traveling. People call me (I don't solicit). They simply call and say, 'Would you come to Croatia and help us with a screenwriting workshop, or Israel, or Denmark, China, et al? I have also become sort of a godfather/designer for the new European Conservatory for Screenwriting based at the Sorbonne in Paris. And I guess I can say, without stretching, I am also a professor at the Croation Film Academy, as well as UCLA, as well as my own career as a writer running alongside it all.

"But, with advancing senility and trying to beat total senility, I have these fabulous opportunities, so my wife, Pamela, and I travel, teach, and learn. That seems to majorly be my life at this time ... and the longest possible, winded answer to a simple question thirty minutes back."

I know that you've read thousands of screenplays. What are the common flaws you see?

"Between being a professional writer, a producer, and an educator, I read an average of 1,000 scripts a year. I've been doing all of this since 1968, so that's, whoa, *28,000* scripts of various lengths and levels of quality. *The most common flaw writers have is believing they are writers before they are writers.* It's generally fatal because they put themselves out in the mainstream of the marketplace way too early. They get drowned by rejection and criticism, which couples with their lack of personal assurance. They do not have the med school, the law school type of foundation to allow them to withstand the slings and arrows of a very, very critical, sometimes hostile, professional world."

Tell me more about a proper foundation.

"People call up and say, 'I'm a writer.' I try to say, somewhere along the line, politely, because I try very hard for the world to love me, number one, and, number two, I try not to be rude, 'How many scripts have you written?' With an open-eyed voice, of course, they'll say, 'Oh, one.' Usually an *X-Files* or a *Seinfeld*. To that I'd like to say, 'How can you call yourself a writer! That's akin to calling yourself a doctor if you learn how to put on a Band-Aid . . . or to call yourself a brain surgeon after you've learned how to fix a broken leg.'

"Doctors, lawyers, ballet divas, opera singers, and musicians of every instrument, must have teachers . . . oh, and painters . . . (where would Monet be without Boudin?). *Everybody* has a mentor, and *every* artist goes through a learning course, and part of the learning curve, in my opinion, particularly in writing, is not five-finger exercises. By that I mean, some screenwriting professors want students to spend a year doing a whole bunch of exercises on character. A whole bunch of exercises on dialogue, et cetera . . . bullshit, jump in there and learn from the experience. Learn by doing and not by practicing in the way that practicing relates to exercises in music. Leap in the pool, and swim or flounder, but get to the decking rather than do exercises. Learn your craft before you go out with your material.

"People, generally, when they go out in the market too soon, drown. Few, actually zero to my considerable knowledge, survive. For, as my pal, famed screenwriter (*Star Trek*'s *Wrath of Kahn* writer) Jack Sowards says, 'In Hollywood, people don't fail, they give up.'

"But people are less likely to give up if they educate themselves or attend film school or the multiplicity of workshops available in urban areas by my dearest pal and colleague Richard Walter, as well as Linda Seger, Michael Hague, Bob McKee, sporadically, as I said, Lew Hunter (since I don't go out and do that for my living), Syd Field (the grandfather of us all), and others that don't come to mind immediately. All the people I've mentioned are very special people, with a particular nod to Richard Walter, a once-in-a-lifetime friend. In the seventeen years we've been working together, not one cross word, not even a syllable resembling acrimony, has crept in our conversation. That is bloody remarkable, particularly in education where ex–UCLA Dean Robert Gray said, 'Lew, remember, in education never is so much made out of so little.' Men and women try to stake out territories and create tremendous adversarial situations. Richard and moi have never had that.

"There are other screenwriting educators around I don't respect either very much or at all, so I won't even mention them, for as a comedy writer pal once said, 'Some people *do not* have a right to their own opinion.' And that would be my sentiments on charlatan screenwriting teachers. They are not professional writers. They are like snake oil people of old. Men and women rolling across the prairie, throwing up the sides of their wagons and slapping on the canvas to Buy This Elixir. Or 'Take my screenwriting class,' or 'Read my book, and I will reveal to you the secrets of screenwriting that have never heretofore been revealed.'

"The publisher put on the cover of my book: 'Lew Hunter, industry premiere teacher' which is wonderful hype . . . 'reveals the secrets of a successful screenplay.' I earnestly don't like that because *there are no secrets*. They're all clearly illuminated by Aristotle two thousand years ago, and most recently in 1946 by Lajos Egri in *The Art of Dramatic Writing*. Those, in my opinion, are the two bibles of performance drama/comedy. The rest of us—myself, Syd, Linda, Richard, and Michael—have really put screenwriting clothes on them, but we're all talking about narrative storytelling. We're all talking about character. We're all talking about first, second, and third acts, shorthand, of course, for beginning, middle, and end.

"So now people can and should avail themselves of this information, plus reading the books, plus seeing movies with a new eye, and with the information they have utilized, they will see and learn structure . . . Aha! . . . the magic word.

"Bill Goldman is so right when he says, 'Screenplays are three things: structure, structure, structure!' When he and I were in a panel once, I said, 'Bill, could they also be three other things: conflict, conflict, conflict?' He agreed. In the immortal words of my pal and just-mentioned fellow chair of the UCLA screenwriting department, Richard Walter, 'Nobody wants to see a movie about the village of happy people.'

"You may best learn screenwriting techniques by experimentation. By your own learning curve. By jumping into the deep water and by swimming via all the aids of classes, workshops, books and, very often, support groups. Sometimes writing cadres are useful; sometimes they are the blind leading the blind, particularly in the outback areas where most people do not have screenwriting experience; yet some want to give people the impression they're quite gifted when, in fact, they're *not*.

"Today, there are many want-to-be screenwriters out there, and a number of classes in different areas of the country that have teachers that are actually quite wonderful. I'm thinking of Professor Bill Streib, one of our alumni, a gifted writing professor at the University of Wyoming; Deme Chapman at Northwestern; David Thomas at Ohio University; Andy Horton in New Orleans; Francisco Menendez at UNLV; Robert Powell in Scottsdale; Jeff Bens at North Carolina; Paul Lazuras at Miami U; Rick Blum in Orlando, Florida. Then, of course, the three biggest education pillars, UCLA, NYU, and USC."

Is there anything else on script flaws?

"With the basic flaw being trying out the marketplace before being ready, the subsequent flaw lies in bad structure. Bill Goldman's admonition, 'screenwriting is structure, structure, structure,' is exactly right. It's entirely what Aristotle talked about. He did talk, very slightly, about character. On the other hand, Egri talks predominately about character and less on structure and plot, so I'd say weak characterization would be the next flaw in descending order.

"Then, boring or on-the-nose or obtuse dialogue. But people are fairly good at dialogue, fairly good at character, and really need a lot of attention paid to story structure. I can tell you, in my forty years as a professional in Hollywood, darn near every writer will say in his or her privacy, 'Structure's my weakest point.' Is it going to get better? I suspect that it will get better as each individual writes more and more scripts to get himself or herself better, then best.

"The most common dialogue flaw is that people have people talk *too* much dialogue. Too many 'talking heads' scenes. Predominately, with dialogue, less is more, a phrase I champion. The second is that good dialogue is dialogue that illuminates what people are *not* saying, Harold Pinter being the most classic example of this precept.

"An example I like to use is Billy Wilder writing a scene for Sam Goldwyn. Bill Wilder was a new writer for Goldwyn studios. A script needed a scene dramatizing a man and a woman divorcing. They went to the most famous Broadway playwright at the time, possibly Maxwell Anderson or Eugene O'Neill. The man wrote a brilliant ten pages of dialogue going back and forth between man and woman . . . a *Who's Afraid of Virginia Woolf* sort of thing. Sam Goldwyn said, 'Let's give this to Mr. Wilder. He's under contract. Let's see what he would do.' Billy Wilder wrote a half a page.

"His scene consisted of a man and a woman, well dressed—the man wearing a hat, the woman wearing a daytime suit—getting into an elevator. The doors closed. Cut to another floor, the doors open and stepping into the elevator, nodding acknowledgment to the well-coifed woman and the man with the hat, is a beautiful woman. The doors close. Four floors later, the doors open, out walks the beautiful woman and there stands the well-coifed wife and man, but the man now has his hat in his hands.

"They used Mr. Wilder's version.

"Mr. Wilder was a guest speaker in my class and said that one of the people he admired most was Ernst Lubitsch. And, that sort of thing was the Lubitsch touch.

"To give you another specific example, there was a movie in which a wife is cheating on her husband. Her husband is a general in the army and the miscreant male person is his lieutenant. We see the lieutenant climbing stairs, going into a bedroom, tearing off his clothes, piling them on a chair, then leaping in bed with the wife. Cut outside where up strides the portly general/husband. The general's footsteps are heard inside, so it's scramble, scramble, scramble! The lieutenant hides in the closet and the general, ready for amoré, also rips off his clothes and also leaps into the bed with his wife as an air raid siren sounds. 'Oh, my god.' He's got to go be a general! He leaps back out of bed, grabs his clothes, and rushes out the door. As he races down the steps, he buttons his shirt up, then draws his pants on at the bottom of the stairs where he then discovers the belt and waist of the pants *do not fit*. Cut to his face. *He knows*. He's being cuckolded.

"There was basically no dialogue. But that was the Lubitsch touch. That is what so many new screenwriters don't quite get early on. Sometimes they never get it and go into real estate. It's the sense of the eyes that most impact. So very often, new writers fill their script with blah, blah, blah, blah, blah, and ungodly exposition scenes.

"Humphrey Bogart one time said, 'If I have to read exposition, I hope the director puts camels, fucking, behind me so the audience will have something interesting to look at.' Generally, such talking scenes are bald and boring exposition.

"Oh, ingestation scenes! Drinks, coffee, food or whatever. New writers play scenes around dinner tables, breakfast tables, supper tables, bars, and 'Oh, let's have a cup of coffee' places. The characters have to listen to talk, talk, talk. ZZZZZZZZ. Usually and aurally, it's just boring. The only time it can be interesting is if you're going to do a movie where that's the crux. *Like Water for Chocolate, Babette's Feast, My Dinner with André*, or in *Tom Jones*—the seduction scene where they are both eating turkey legs with very fellatio-simulating lip gestures. Or, there's a scene where Julie Andrews's mother, in *The Americanization of Emily*, is teetering on madness because her husband, her brothers, and her sons have been killed in World War II. The author, William Bradford Huie, or the screenwriter, Paddy Chayefsky, wanted Jim Garner's character to come home and meet Emily's mother. The fragility of the woman's madness is placed in a fragile garden tea scene. An interesting thing of it is the tea doesn't drop on the ground. The scene simply goes against the grain. Yet, they're picking up the teacups with the delicacy of their fingers, then placing them down as they're having this brilliant, hard dialogue about the horrors of war. A stunning, riveting juxtaposition. All talking heads, but the violence in the verbosity of the scene serves as counterpoint to the static bodies and sedentary locale.

"So I think those are the most common flaws. Getting out too early, weak structure, and characters without character. Villains like Whipley Snidelash hiding behind bushes twirling their mustaches, and heroes like Dudley Dorights without flaws to identify them for an audience who screams for identification with the characters up on the screen. Aristotle wisely said that superior drama and comedy is drama and comedy that allows us to discover ourselves.

"You see yourself in Larry Gelbert's *Tootsie* (with additional help from five other writers that went before Larry). You see yourself in the *M*A*S*H* characters. You see yourself in *Citizen Kane*. You see yourself as Rick Blaine in *Casablanca*. Scarlett O'Hara in *Gone with the Wind*. We want to identify with those romantic and even miserable characters in *Midnight Cowboy*. We want to have an identification with all so we can learn more about ourselves when we leave these darkened caves after staring at those moving petroglyphs on the silver-screened wall.

"We want something to take with us. A piece of a memory. A piece of a dream. A piece of a thought. And, perhaps, we will engage in 'icebox talk.' Alfred Hitchcock said when I asked him about something that seemed ambiguous in one of his movies, 'Oh, Lewis, that's for icebox talk.' He felt that people, when they get home and go to the icebox to get sandwich makings, wanted their talking to be about his movie with many 'What did he mean by that?' questions as opposed to talk conjured from their own, probably banal lives. How exciting when we talk about movies after we walk out of the theater, instead of saying, 'Oh, let's go to Starbucks.' 'No, No, Let's do McDonald's!' The movie just dismissed, and that's the end of that. Two hours of your life blown away!"

What are the advantages of film school?

"The advantages have the same parallel as going to law school or medical school. The education gives you a foundation upon which to learn the craft of screenwriting and develop your talent simultaneously. Also, today, literary agents scout film schools for emerging writing talent in the same fashion that professional sports agents scout college varsity athletic programs.

"People say to me, 'You cannot teach writing.' And I say, probably more tactfully than what I'm about to say, 'Bullshit. I can teach screenwriting. I can't teach talent. That's your gig.' This was a posture I faced last spring at the Sorbonne. With arms tightly crossed, people said, 'You can't teach screenwriting.' I unfolded their arms by illustrating the mentors of Shakespeare, Molière, Pirandello, Monet, Tallchief, Caruso, and Ballanchine. At one point, someone said, 'Oh, you use the classics for your instruction,' and I said, 'Absolutely. The classics.' As much as I respect George Lucas, Spielberg, and Scorsese, these people don't have the classical stance of the aforementioned.

"I could add Tennessee Williams, Eugene O'Neill, Paddy Chayefsky, and Ingmar Bergman, during their artistic gestation. Coppola, myself and the UCLA 1960s gang grew up running down to the Laemmie Theater in Hillhurst in Los Feliz to see what Bergman is doing this year. Fellini, 'Oh god.' Antonioni, 'Fabulous.' 'Oh, gee, look what Godard did. I can't believe *Four Hundred Blows*.' Truffaut! 'Where in God's name was he born? On what planet? How can he be so wonderful?' I'm even chilling mentioning these giants to you right now. Of course, we felt in some ways that film was invented in the fifties and sixties, but, of course, it was invented at the turn of the century and started talking in the late thirties, when *The Jazz Singer* hit.

"Oh, yes, the concept of coming to film school and learning about these celluloid gods and getting smarter and smarter is going to be of tremendous value in building your creative base of operations with classmates and, hopefully, professors that have a right to their own opinion. Professors who have a professional cachet. At NYU, Venable Herndon and Janet Neipris are two wonderful professors. Oh, D. B. Gillis and Steve Jimenez are also very, very special teachers. All writers who happen to be screenwriting professors. At USC, John Furia is heading up the program. In addition to being a wonderful human being, he is also a superb writer, and I know he did have Frank Pierson down there and Ron Austin (UCLA alum) and other professional writers.

"At UCLA, we not only have our MFA graduate program, we have our sensational extension curriculum, and we have what we call our Professional Program, which also comes out of the School of Theater, Film and Television. This year [1996] we have eighty people marching through this [Professional Program in Screenwriting] meadow. From a normal of fifty (for reasons that are good and not good, or we just didn't pay attention) we're up to seventy in the graduate program. A total of 150 people. Talk about screenwriting hotbeds!

"What I'm getting to is, when you go to film school, it's the synergy of all these people coming together, all dedicated to learning about the craft and developing their talent in screenwriting, get to blend with professors who are or have been professional screenwriters. Starting with Richard Walter and myself, the two chairs, and Hal Ackerman and Dee Caruso. Hal's got a good number of plays in his background. Dee was an icon of comedy writing for *That Was the Week That Was, Get Smart,* and a number of the Jerry Lewis movies. Velina Houston is a renowned playwright who has done a number of wonderful film/tape pieces for PBS. Then we have our guest-star people who come in once a quarter, such as Michael Werb (*The Mask*), Dan Pyne (*Pacific Heights* and ran *Miami Vice*), Frank Deese is teaching for us this year (the principal in *Josh and Sam*), Greg Widen (*Backdraft, Highlander*), Debby Amelon has a number of movie-of-the-week credits and *Exit to Eden*; and Robin Russin, Loraine Despres, Linda Voorhees, Valerie West, Neil Landau, Judy Burns, Bob Poole, Corey Mandell, Rich Eustic, Michael Colleary, Ed Solomon, Ann Gills, and on and on and on. So, if you are developing your ability as a writer, in addition to getting the books and your writing, go to school. It allows you to connect a variety of terminals that may be dangling a bit or a lot.

"John Sweet won two awards last year and just sold a wonderful screenplay for a good bunch of money—a love story set in France in the revolutionary period. He submitted fourteen feature-length scripts to get into the MFA program.

"We went around the table last week asking people how they felt about themselves as writers—we do that at the end of every 434 session. John replied, "Oh, I think I'm so much better.' I said, 'Now, John, how can you say that when you've already written fourteen scripts?' He said, 'Oh, I now realize those scripts were pond scum. I hadn't really learned what the craft is about. I was kind of like the blind leading the blind.'

"I, Lewis Ray Hunter, strongly say that, when you get in harmony with fine professors and fine fellow students, some of the best teaching can go on at class mid-breaks or going to and from the parking lot, when you and your peers talk to each other. I.e., 'You know your script? What if you did so-and-so, or, have you thought about so-and-so and such-and-such?' Also, I will very often, in the context of my own class, say, 'Oh, my God. Rich Whiteside has a much better idea for your story. Forget what I said . . . use Rich's idea.'

"I was being interviewed in Heidelberg on German television and

I said exactly that. At the conclusion of the show, a young man rolling up camera cables came up to me and half whispered, 'In Germany, no professor would ever say a student had a better idea.' Sigh and such a pity.

"Every one of the people I've mentioned at NYU, USC and UCLA would in a flash say, 'Oh, my God, the sun broke through! An epiphany! He or she had the best idea of all. Go with it.' That energetic, empowering, encouraging atmosphere gives you, the writer, an opportunity to bud, grow, and flower. When you just jump in and write without guidance or nurturing, you are very, very, very, very much in danger of that hauteur theory which is almost totally going down the toilet in Europe, which is why I've been asked to help create the new European Conservatory for Screenwriting, which is disarmingly very similar to UCLA's. They are now realizing that nobody has ever done anything of quality making it up as they go along. We have structure, we have form, we have training.

"Another metaphor is Kerouac. Somebody asked Truman Capote what he thought of Jack Kerouac's writing, and Capote said, 'That's not writing. That's typing.' I think he really did use butcher paper. Got a roll of it and put it in his typewriter and just go, go, go, go. He would get on some form of inspiration, assisted by some ingestation substance, go for twenty-four hours and vomit out three hundred–plus pages. 'That's not writing. That's typing.'

"So, John Sweet might well say, without film school, he wasn't really writing, he was typing scripts.

"Ergo, you can well use film school for your own foundation. A structured foundation. You can well use the feedback from professors and students. You can also use film school for your own self-confidence, the learning curve, and for the lifetime associations you'll establish.

"Somebody asked Jon Peters in a UCLA producing program class, 'How do I get a script to you?' He said, 'Well, you can't. Oh, I guess if I accept a script, I'd have a reader cover it. I'd send you some form letter. You're way better off getting a script to him or her.' And he started pointing at students around the questioner. And what that means at UCLA specifically is, out of twenty people admitted to the program, twelve become professional screenwriters. And the professors are also substantially helpful in careers, both in getting an agent and getting material exposed. You also get an opportunity to win a variety of twenty-two awards the department gives out. That's also true of our extension and professional programs and at USC and NYU. Those awards and industry awards like the Nicholl Award, the Austin Film Festival awards, the Sundance awards and Chesterfield and Disney can be beneficial both to your pocketbook and your— well, I wouldn't quite say ego—let's say to your writers' confidence level. And that's even way, way, way beyond any financial remuneration.

"Finally, I mentioned lifetime associations. Michael Werb tells me that he and Christine Rohm, and others who graduated from film school nine years ago, once a month get together and encourage each other about their various projects. They share scripts, bitch about executives, even name children after each other. Michael Werb, Christine A. Roum, Don Mancini, and, I believe, Neil Landau is in that group. They all came out of film school like a pack of animals that leave a watering hole, and up come another pack of animals. Then they leave. One time the zebras, the next watering group, the giraffes. These people/animals group together, bond, and keep on going throughout life. They get to know other people, but their most substantive relationship is the one they have in film school. Of course, they're writers, and writers help each other.

"You see, I think three areas in the creative process of film and television are feminine: writing, cinematography, and editing. These areas are maternal. Accepting and giving, for as a woman accepts, she also gives. The male basically, and often, plunges forward, one might say. But in screenwriting, people help each other. They also encourage each other to become producers because, as I mentioned earlier, the show-running producers in television are all writers. They run television. I think motion pictures are very close to this reality.

Stone, Scorsese, Spielberg, Coppola all used the writing door for their entry. That is the older generation. Now, we've got the newer who overtly write and direct. Writing is not a passive-aggressive way to become a director. Lee, Figgis, Branagh, et cetera, want it all. Now and simultaneously.

"So, as I stand here in December of 1996, by the year 2000, I loudly predict . . . writers will be in total creative control of film and television, in my more than humble view. As they are in control of theater. As they are in control of books.

"The past is prologue. There you are. Wise words to the wise? People who are not availing themselves of all the learning resources of writing are going to be basically asking, whoever their boss is, who happens to primarily be a writer, 'What else can I do for you?' If you wish to be that boss, know what it is like to have that blank screen or piece of paper in front of you. Putting things on that empty expanse may, at first, be less than inspiring, but, I think, as time goes on, you, if you want to, can be as good as almost all the people involved. The players.

"I think we are all born with a striking similar amount of talent, sensitivity and insight. It's not the talent that distinguishes us from our fellow men and women, it's the energy and perseverance that distinguishes us, or lack of the same. How much we have or get the burn to write is almost totally equated to significant success.

"People tell me they can't write. I say, 'Would you please write me a letter telling me you can't write?' Over forty years, I have had many people who, at first, did not feel they were probably able to be wonderful writers who, later, turned out to be, if not wonderful, at least good writers, surprising themselves. Many are also able to take that ability and apply it to other areas of creativity in motion pictures and television. In gratitude, I've had thousands of people thanking me profusely. Two children have been named after me. So, I'll lay that accomplishment at the feet of my Writers Write concept. That's as good as it gets. I'm ready for the Guide Rock, Nebraska, Cemetery.

"L'chaim."

Professor Richard Walter (chair)

As I entered his office, Richard was on the phone, mid-conversation with an agent. He waved me into his office, a small, full space, and I couldn't help but overhear the conversation. The agent on the other end was picking Richard's brains for the most savvy new screenwriters in the MFA program. The agent was looking for both people and scripts—this instantly confirmed that I was in the right place.

He concluded his conversation, and we jumped right into the interview.

How long have you been with the MFA program?

"This is my twentieth year at UCLA."

What is your writing background?

"I came out to California thirty years ago for three weeks, I thought, and here we are. I fell into film school at USC. In those days, it was very easy to get into film school; there was no tradition of moving on into the professional community as there is today. Now, it's *the* number one way of getting into the professional community. Back then it was a real anomaly."

Why did you go into film school if it wasn't an entrée into the professional community?

"A man my age might have been dodging the draft, and to another extent dodging life—not wanting to be out in real life. Rather than dodge the draft, I wish I had turned in my draft card and gone to jail to protest the war. Instead, I collaborated and played ball with Lyndon Johnson. Imagine, I was awarded a student deferment because I was going to the USC film school! Absurd. Ridiculous at both ends.

"In any event, there I was. The truth is, had there been no war, had there been no draft, I probably would have done that anyway just to avoid life. I was pretty young and afraid, as people ought to be, to venture out. I've mentioned this many times to our own students because they too don't want to graduate; they want to stay. We'd love to keep them, but the regents insist that we move everybody along. It's much easier to call yourself a film student than an unemployed writer—which is what you become the minute you leave film school. So I probably would have stayed anyway. That's an answer to 'Why I was in film school?'

"I had already gotten a masters at the Newhouse School of Public Communications at Syracuse University in television broadcasting. I was going to continue there for a possible Ph.D. in instructional communications or something like that, but found that USC has a really great film program. Indeed, my classmates were Lucas and all those people who went on to own Hollywood, except for George, who owns Marin County. Instead of going back to New York as I always intended to do, I found myself after a year or so in film school starting to get assignments. I found myself making a regular living as a writer, supporting a family exclusively from income derived from writing.

"I'm also a novelist. I sold a novel, *Barry and the Persuasions*, which was later sold to Hollywood, and I wrote the adaptation. I have now published two more books. I published a how-to book (*Screenwriting: The Art, Craft and Business of Film and Television Writing*), and I have another one coming out next year [1997]. But most of my experience as a writer is in film and it always has been. I've worked for all of the studios. Did development deals. Had a few movies made. Even had some work in television, sold material to all of the networks, studios and so on. I'm a working-stiff writer and continue to be. But most of my work is in film."

Tell me about your screenwriting book coming out next year.

"It's from Dutton Signet called *The Whole Picture*. It's about film writing—film and television and life."

What events led to you coming to the MFA program?

"In the summer of 1977, I was invited to a party that I went to out of a sense of guilt. I say guilt because I'm not a big party type.

I don't party much. A big night at our house is pizza and *The Simpsons*. Like myself, my wife is not a big fan of huge gatherings, but it was she who said, 'We really ought to go to this party.' It was at the house of somebody who had been very supportive of my career, who had invited us to several big parties in Hollywood, and we had simply declined to go because we just don't like huge gatherings. We were afraid he might feel snubbed, so we went.

"When we got there, as we walked in the door, the host of the party pointed at me and said to the guy next to him (who was then the head of the UCLA MFA program), 'This is the guy I was telling you about.' So now I was being asked to come and teach.

"Now, I didn't need the job. Through the current era, my main sustenance is derived from income off-campus: my writing, consulting, and other activities that I'm involved in. I do a lot of public speaking now. Though I travel around the world, the first thing I am is a writer, and I still make money as a writer. I make royalties on my books, I get residuals on things that I have written in the past, and I continue to stay active writing. I'm in the market with a new novel, and I also have a screenplay.

"So that's pretty much what I've been up to all of these years. I'm going to stay another thirty years in California, and if it still hasn't worked out for me, then it's back to New York. 2026, I'm outta here! Watch my smoke!"

You have obviously read thousands and thousands of scripts to date. What are the common flaws you see in unschooled writers?

"Well, even in schooled writers, the major mistake is they write too much. They're not economical. They're not efficient. They fail to integrate their material. There are two kinds of material in a movie: there's visual material, and there's aural material. Things you can see and things you can hear. A movie script is nothing more than an elaborate list of those kinds of information. You will succeed if you will use each piece of information in such a way as to accomplish two tasks—and it's really only one task, but it describes better as two tasks—and that is: advance the story and expand the character. It really doesn't matter what the script is about. It doesn't matter what the scene is about. People will respond to material that is integrated, in which every sight and every sound moves the story forward, expands the character, giving you new information.

"As an example, I'm giving notes on a script right now, and at one point in the script—and this is otherwise a pretty good script—it reads:

Helen chooses her words carefully before she speaks.

Helen
This marriage is over.

Albert stops eating the cookie and shoots Helen an inquisitive look.

"Here is a writer with a pretty good story, pretty good characters, and the whole thing is drowning in unnecessary directions to the actors that intrude upon their territory and turn them into robots, and directions that intrude upon the territory of the director that get in the way of the tale. Excessive directions make the script harder to read and if excised, if deleted from the script, would absolutely make no difference. Nothing would be lost that's needed, and it would read more effectively. It would exploit the relationship, and 'exploit' is not a pejorative word; it means to make the most of the relation of the screenwriter and the other artists.

"It seems to me, too many writers are adversarial; they're too afraid the director will screw it up. That the actors won't get the lines right and so on. They don't understand the upside of collaboration. They're too caught up in their own egos and not enough in the collective ego of the collective enterprise.

"If you absolutely want to control everything, then write a novel. I've written novels, and it's a wonderful, elegant art. Write poems. Paint paintings. These are venerable, honorable media of creative

234

expression. Nothing wrong with them, and there you get to be the complete and total boss of everything. But if being the boss of everything is what appeals to you by way of creative expression, then don't go into film. If you go into film, rejoice in being part of a creative family of artists and craftspeople. That's what's good about film. That's what's fun about film.

"I'll tell you another common mistake writers make—they try to second-guess the trends. They outsmart themselves. They read the trades. They want to know what kinds of pictures are being looked for. I heard that a major agent said the other day that she can't sell anything that's not an event picture. Writers would be foolish to listen to that.

"First, what's an event picture? I guess she means *Volcano,* or *Twister* or something like that, *Independence Day.* Anything that's human and has a good story is an event. You just can't pay attention to that kind of stuff. You've got to write your own personal story and not obsess about the sale but think more broadly about establishing a career, a reputation. Relationships with other people in the profession, for example, a representative, an agent.

"The careers that have longevity are those in which the writers are working not just for this particular project but are thinking more broadly. They're crafty and savvy entrepreneurs.

"The biggest mistake you can make is to try and get in on this week's hot trend because it's too late. I have no idea what the trend is this week, and I'm here in the middle of it—I'm *in* Hollywood, here at UCLA, in the film school, and I speak to many professional people every day and I can't tell you what the trend is today. Even if you know what the trend is, it would be too late to get in on it because it is the trend."

True. If you sit down and write for the current trend, by the time you finish there will be a new trend.

"Exactly. You'll only be following, and you'll always be in back.

So if you want to lead, forget about that and follow your heart. That's what you ought to follow.

"I was just at a conference, and I go to a lot of conferences, and they're all fun. This one was the best fun of all; it was the Maui conference. How could you miss in Maui? But there I was listening to a panel of people in the movie business. Smart, good people. And they were advising writers on what to write in terms of achieving professional success. They said that one smart thing to do is write good roles that actors will want to play. Write lead roles that the bankable actors would want to play.

"Well, just think about that advice. That's just like saying 'Write good scripts.' Why would those be characters that the actors would want to play? Obviously, because they're good roles. Shouldn't everybody write scripts with good roles in them? Doesn't every good script have to have good roles in it?"

We got into a side discussion that led to Richard mentioning Ricky Black-wood, a former student he sees as a terrific writer but who had some writing hang-ups to get over.

"I have to tell you really quickly, in the beginning, he would write vastly overwritten material. Wonderful stuff, very passionate. He would write these incredible, touching love stories, but he was always underscoring the speeches for emphasis. And in the early pages, I would write gentle commentary like: 'You know, you probably don't need to underscore it.' And then as I read on, he'd be underscoring so much that I'd say: 'You know, you kind of debauch the currency of the underscoring by using it this much.' But by page seventeen or page nineteen, I'd be writing, 'TEN HUT, BLACKWOOD! ON YOUR FEET!' Actually writing this in the margins, 'Enough with the underscoring!' I was that forceful only because Ricky could take it."

Good point. I've read scripts where the writer used exclamation marks for periods throughout the script. Literally, hundreds of exclamation marks. What are your thoughts on this kind of stylizing?

"If you want your script to look like a comic strip, do that. Have funny punctuation. Worse than exclamation points is combinations. Double exclamation points. Sometimes throw in !?!? or !!??, throw in a # and an *—kiss my *. It is just like red neon flashing *amateur*, *amateur* if you do that.

"By the way, I will say to a writer, 'you shouldn't put exclamation points in or have funny punctuation,' and 999 out of 1,000 will immediately agree and drop that. But every once in a while, I'll meet someone who'll say, 'Well, I'm trying . . . ' and as soon as they say that, I back away. 'OK. Whatever you like.' "

Ultimately it's their script.

"It's up to them. If they want to look like an amateur, that's up to them."

Let's get into "Why film school?" Some people say, "Screw film school. Just get out there and learn from the seat of your pants." Others swear by film school. So, why go to film school? What are the advantages?

"Statistics are clear on this subject. Today, the major source of new artists is the film schools. Most of our screenwriting majors will get into the Guild. Over the past ten years, we have compared lists. We were able to determine that the overwhelming majority of our students in screenwriting, *the majority*, get into the Writers Guild. That means they've attained professional, bona fide writing employment for bona fide, real companies—real Hollywood companies that are signatory to the Writers Guild agreements.

"I know of some people who have succeeded by doing it all themselves; they needed nobody, they needed nothing. It just seems a pity going into a collaborative enterprise where you do need the support of other artists. What's wrong with collaboration? That's what's special about film.

"Beyond that, I guess I'm a little leery of people saying you can't really teach this. How come you can teach music? How come you can teach painting? How come you can teach literature? What writer of novels hasn't studied literature, hasn't read widely? Maybe one's study of film is more informal, and they succeeded anyway. But clearly, the best way to succeed is to come to a good, solid film school.

"We can't give you any talent; you gotta bring your own. What we can do is create an atmosphere, an environment where you don't have to work in isolation. Where you have the support of faculty and also your colleagues and classmates and cohorts who sit right around the table in your courses. Here, you're not working in a vacuum. Here, you have a safe place to try out stuff and get reactions and fall on your face and even to fail again and again. In film school, you can do what you need to do as an artist: find your voice, select your point of view, determine what it is that is your personality and your profile, and discover what's special about you that people will respond to."

Another advantage for students seems to be that you and Lew are besieged by agents and agencies looking for new writing talent and good scripts.

The Wall Street Journal profiled me, calls me—I've memorized this now, I realize—'The prime broker for Hollywood's hottest commodity, new writing talent.' Now I didn't say that. *The Wall Street Journal* said that, and let me tell you, they, unlike a lot of journalism sources I deal with, they are pretty rigorous. Also the press will print whatever I tell them [he laughs]. And it scares me about what I read that I don't know about.

"People say, 'There isn't much reporting that's terribly conscientious.' But I will tell you that the guy who wrote *The Wall Street Journal* profile was very rigorous and called people and checked everything out. They love to report a scandal, but they couldn't. They said that this is it, this is the place, the UCLA MFA screenwriting program. The *LA Times* recently surveyed the film schools and said that UCLA was the best in writing; that there are three great film schools: NYU, USC (my own alma mater), and UCLA. But they singled out UCLA for having a great writing program.

"I don't think you'd go wrong at USC or NYU, mind you. And those are not the only fine film schools, but those are clearly the glamour schools with the best and the biggest and the longest tradition at it. But there are other good film schools. Long Beach has a good department. San Francisco State. In the California State system, there are good film schools—San Diego State. I think Northridge has a uniquely good program. Loyola, an independent college, has a wonderful program. There are other programs back east, and maybe there are some programs that aren't very good, but certainly the leading film schools are the best way to get into the movie business. They're not the only way, but they're *clearly* the best way."

Is there a lot of networking with graduates who are in the business, looking for the new talent?

"Absolutely, and I'm still networking with my classmates from USC film school. Still active with them socially, and I'm still working with them professionally. The most important people you'll meet will be your classmates. That's another good reason to be in film school.

"I'll tell you a funny story. Jon Peters, of all people, lectured here to a group of production and writing students. Somebody asked, 'How can I get a script to you?' and he said, 'You can't. Well, OK, you can, but all you'll get is a mercy read, a courtesy read, and you'll get a letter back. The letter's already been written. It reads, "Thanks. There's so much that's appealing about this script, and we salute your talent and your discipline, but, alas, it doesn't fit our current production schedule." '

"That's not the way. A producer is not going to make a project from a script that somebody gave them in class. He said, 'The most important contacts that you can make here at UCLA are not with superstars who visit, but with the people around you. The people sitting next to you. They're next week's superstar producer, writer, and so on.'

"We've had great success placing people on TV shows. For example, our students dominate sitcoms. As much attention as we get for our successful features, and we have had a lot of successful features, we're getting bigger and bigger in sitcoms. The students hire each other. They're friends. They've worked together in classes.

"Kathy Stumpe has become a major figure in television. She created *Grace Under Fire*, but her real start came when we were able to place her as a staff writer at *Cheers* in its last couple of years. And it did not hurt us a bit that Rob Long, a former student here, was the executive producer of the show at that time. She then rose to be the head of the staff. Lately she broke all of the rules and has sold a new series for a fortune in money. Created a new series that she speculated called *The Brand New Me*. Unheard of. They're just not done that way. It's a real rule breaker. So, YES! Networking. Absolutely."

How many people apply for the MFA program each year?
"About 300."

How many do you accept?
"We admit about twenty."

So you have a total of forty to fifty students at any one time?
"Yes. It's a two-year program. We'll let people stay three years. If half of the people stay a third year, we have about fifty people."

What do they go through in those two to three years?
"They go through the hell that writers go through trying to write scripts and just trying to integrate with the professional community. They're in a wonderfully creative community. And, indeed, they avail themselves of the resources the whole campus has to offer, cultural and otherwise. Our program is centered around the feature movie, the feature-length film. That is the model that we use. We do have a point of view here. We're largely Aristotelian, which simply is to say we are story hard-liners. We think story is the most important thing of all. We don't think there's any such thing as character or setting or scene outside of the context of the story. Story represents

the integration of all of those elements. A story is much more important than the idea for a story. We think that story is the most important thing."

So you consider character part of the story?

"Yeah. We agree with Aristotle, who says, 'Character's extremely important, but it only exists in the context of a story.' The single most important thing is not character, but story. I would say, 'Story is character, character is story.' What is a story except what the characters do and say? What is a character but what he does and says inside the context of a story?

"The most widely discussed character in all of English language dramatic literature is without question Hamlet. Don't you agree? What is Shakespeare's description of Hamlet? I'll tell you what it is: it's three words, it's 'Prince of Denmark.' That's Hamlet. So where does this Hamlet character come from about whom libraries full of books exist? And the answer is from what he does and what he says in that play. That's where character comes from.

"In other words, character comes from story, not the other way around. But in any event, when people talk about the character-centered story, they're just talking about good writing. Because at the center of story is character. But one creates the other. They don't exist independently, that's the most important point. We believe it's much more convenient for amateurs and dilettantes to think about a wacky uncle they knew who worked on the Alaska pipeline than it is to come up with the incidents and anecdotes that will sustain an hour and forty minutes (the ideal movie length) that's a story. This happens, that happens, the next thing happens. If it's a good story, it will define, it will create characters worth spending some time with. So character is very important, so is dialogue. But story, story, story. We're story hard-liners.

"We also believe that the public and popular expression is for the public and populace. We don't think it's a sin to reach an audience or make a bunch of money. That's something we happen to believe in. That doesn't mean you have to have a blockbuster, but you do have to reach more than the immediate friends and family of the people who made the movie.

"Now that might sound like a given and not terribly controversial, but there's a lot of people who regard what I just said as very controversial. 'You're worrying what audiences think? A true artist really just makes it up as he or she goes along and doesn't worry about commercial considerations.' We reject that in public and popular expression, in audience-oriented expression like theater, film, and television.

"All of the great classics in theater were popular in their own time. Poets and painters get discovered after their times, sometimes, but not people who work for mass audiences, like playwrights and so on. All of the great Greek tragedies that we cherish today were big commercial successes in their own day. So was Shakespeare. Those were blockbuster, high-concept projects for their era. What about a guy who's married to and sleeping with his mother? This young guy who's married to a woman who's about eighteen years older than he, and it turns out it's his mother? That's *Oedipus Rex*. That's a high concept.

"We believe in story-oriented expression. We think we're all storytellers; we see ourselves first as storytellers. And, yes, we believe that you do need to succeed. If you are going to succeed at all, among the things you have to do is reach a bunch of people. It doesn't have to be trillions of people, but it's not a sin if it is. But it does have to be some substantial audience that will at least support that enterprise."

Tell me more about what the master's students go through in the program.

"We go through the drill in the first ten-week quarter. A typical student spends a minimum of six quarters (two academic years), but many people will spend three academic years. What they'll be doing in the rest of those academic quarters is getting a good background in critical studies: history, criticism, theory, animation, producing, film craft, film production, directing, sound, camera, and so on. All of which, I think, is enormously valuable. As a writer at USC, it was a very useful part of my own education to learn about editing, to learn about sound. It presses upon you the collaborative nature of the enterprise, and it also helps writers stand against those technocrats who might intimidate them with technical stuff—'You can't do that.' You know what I mean?

"Orson Welles was told, 'You can't do certain things.' Well, sure you can. My old classmate from USC, George Lucas, was told by the SC film lab, 'Well, you can't do this, that, and the other thing.' Lucas replied, 'Oh, yes. Why don't you try it this way? Bipack it, make it pass tail out, then make an interpositive high-grain dupe. Use that as a matte . . . ' and I remember the lab technician pulling out a clipboard and taking notes on what this student was telling him. Of course, George is unusual.

"If a writer will study the technical side, if he or she will not be afraid of it, realize that it's a tool that can be exploited and is part of his or her arsenal the same way a painter can use different kinds of brushes and different kinds of techniques, then that will really expand the writer's horizons. You will get that in our program. But the main thing that you get, quarter after quarter, is an advanced feature-writing workshop in which you'll write script after script. The least you'll write will be four scripts. The more industrious and ambitious, disciplined students will write perhaps as many as twice that number while they're here. They might get seven, eight, or nine scripts out of here, and they will come out of here with an arsenal.

"After graduation, in answer to the question, 'Can you write?', here's the answer: 'Read these.' And if somebody says, 'This one's pretty good. It's not quite right for us, but, boy, we really like your voice. We really like your handle on character. We really think you've got a nifty, crafty sense of story. Do you have anything else we can read?' You can say: 'Yes. I have this. I have that.' "

I understand that students have sold scripts while they are in the program.

"Indeed they have. *River's Edge* was written in my class. Right now we have Frank Deese teaching here. Frank wrote *The Principal* as an independent study project. Greg Widen wrote *Highlander* in class. He also wrote *Backdraft* in class. *Outbreak* actually started as a class assignment almost twenty years ago, according to Robert Roy Poole, who collaborated with Laurence Dworet and who shared credit with him on *Outbreak*.

"Our students do succeed. Some write material in class that sells, but the vast majority of those succeed after they leave here. And we try to dissuade them from thinking about selling scripts they write in the classes—not that we're ashamed if they do that, but it can limit them. If they concentrate too narrowly upon the sale, if they become married in advance to the expected outcome of some particular action that they take, they're just going to fail. And if you write a screenplay for the express purpose of trying to sell it, you're not going to sell it. You can't hit a target by aiming at it, they say in Zen Buddhist philosophy. You kind of have to feel your way there, you have to get a kind of sense of it."

Do you get a lot of students in their late thirties or forties?

"Definitely. We have a pro-age bias. We are first of all a graduate program; we give a master's degree. Our students are going to be older anyway. Here today you might find somebody in his early twenties, but, for the most part the typical student is thirty-five years old, a single mother. She's lived some life. She's had some experiences worth writing about other than the funniest thing that happened to her in the dormitory. She works in an ad agency writing copy or researching, something like that.

"We're much more interested in the person who's making the career change, as you described. We've had lawyers, many lawyers, and we have lawyers in the program right now who are trying to make the transition. We have doctors, we have physicians. One was Larry

Dworet, who supported his writing habit by working freelance in emergency rooms and writing a script that is yet to be made but won the Goldwyn prize and got him a lot of money; it's called *Code Blue*. Kind of a *China Syndrome* of emergency room medicine. And Lauri, as his friends call him, has a credit on *Outbreak*, which is a medical story. He's a seven-figure screenwriter now. And he was a doctor."

Going back a bit. Are you saying it's mostly single women with children?

"I don't know about single women, but we have a slight majority of women. But it's pretty close to fifty-fifty. Slightly more women than men, I think, just now. We don't want to keep it more one or the other. We want a diverse program. On the other hand, we want to evaluate everybody on his or her merits. We're proud to have diversified the program without ever having to condescend to patronize anybody or maintain lower standards for anybody. When I was here, and Lew Hunter as well, nearly twenty years ago, it was a white boys' preserve. And now it is a diverse group. And that's good. We think that's good because we think diversity is good. We think that the different colors and tones and accents and aromas in the human community are not evidence of some mistake that God made, but testimony to Her grand glory. That's our view.

"Not everybody feels that way, but that's why I loved growing up in New York City. That's why I love living here. Being on a campus and being in a community where there are all kinds of people is an asset. I loathe and fear the apparent balkanization of our society where people seem to want to retreat. It's one thing to get to know your roots; it's another to replace your relationships with other people who are somewhat different from you with your roots and only deal with your own kind of people. I see all kinds of people doing that, and it's deplorable. I'm hopeful, though, that that's just a passing fad. You can't really stop integration in a huge multicultural community as we have here."

There's probably a lot of people who fear becoming this one homogeneous mixture.

"Well, that's a real possibility in the global village. But there's no stopping that. We don't have control over that. I do predict that there will be only one language. There will only be one race. And I think it will be just like it was when humans first arose in the Great Rift Valley in East Africa when the creatures who are us first arose, if you can believe the anthropologists, and I do. Everybody was the same, spoke the same language, was the same color, lived in the same village, had the same experiences. Then everything diversified with migration. People moved up to Asia and through Asia across the Bering Strait over into what they now call the Americas.

"Eventually Europeans went around the other way across the ocean and met the ancestors of the other people. Since that time, there has been an inevitable, predictably tremendous amount of intermarriage. Put people together, they'll marry each other. And I predict eventually, less diversity. But I don't think anybody plans it. It's a natural force.

"If you think of it, the broader universe is the same way, if you can believe the cosmologists. The phrase 'the Big Bang' was first created by people who were trying to denegrate the notion of the Big Bang. But it's become accepted as the canon in cosmology. Not that I'm an expert in it. Nevertheless, I believe in the Big Bang, this week anyway.

"The reason I mention it to you is that at the moment of the Big Bang, everything was the same. For one negative exponential, one tiny little moment, there was this one item that everybody is trying to find now. Maybe it's Higg's boson—one of the last six particles, they think. Of course this changes every week. But let's say that is what it was. Then the very next moment, I mean the very next micromoment, those started to marry each other, and they were some other kind of particle, some other kind of element. And eventually over the billions of years, they say about thirteen billion years, Earth years anyway, we ended up with the universe we're living in right now, which is a very diverse universe. It's vast spaces of nothingness. Then there's clumpy, clumpy stuff—rocks and planets—there's gases. There's plasma that's red hot. You have a very diverse universe, exclusive of people, just the stuff that's out there.

"Hot stuff. Cold stuff. Hard stuff. Soft stuff. Dense stuff. Sparse stuff. It's diverse. But what's happening, according to cosmologists, and again there's a lot of controversy over this, but I'm not a cosmologist—I've read enough to have opinions about stuff—and I do agree with those who say that eventually the universe will stop expanding and then it will start to contract again. And when that happens, then eventually there's going to be an end to diversity. Eventually it's all going to meet together in another Big Bang. I believe that this goes on all the time, which is a great big expansion and coalescence over and over again.

"My point is, if I'm right about that, and a lot of scientists say that is the case, at least about the return, then everything will be returned to Higg's boson. Everything will crash into everything else. Get real hot and will be the same. So there'll be the end to diversity, and there'll be just sameness again. But then there'll be an expansion and diversity again. I think that's the nature of the universe. It seems to me that it's mirrored on the planet again in the way I just described.

"It started with the Big Bang in human evolution, Australopithecus Man, whatever they called that, in the Rift Valley. That led from sameness to diversity, and I think that the global village that [Marshall] MacLuhan talked about—we all live in one world now—it's already happening. I'm predicting, for example, that in another twenty years, another quarter of a century tops, there won't be any more Chinese characters. They won't write anymore in Chinese characters and Japanese characters, too. And the reason is computers can't handle them. They can print them, but you can't have them on keyboards. So they're already coalescing Chinese characters, of which you need to learn 3,000 if you just want to be marginally literate as a Chinese. If you want to be a Chinese writer or intellectual or artist, you must learn 30,000 of these characters. This compares to our twenty-six letters. Instead of twenty-six, you have to learn 30,000. That's going to stop because of computers and the need to get everything down onto the computer board.

"One more point about this, because it is pertinent, it's not just a lot of far-flung stuff. Film, to me, is very hopeful in this regard because it represents the ultimate in the history of the universe. At least in the history of our experience here as humans on this planet, in this corner of the universe. Nothing represents more effectively and more perfectly and more wholly the coalescence of everything, the creative and the affirmative and nourishing and the healing co-operation of different enterprises as a movie does. You've got science, you've got art, you've got hardware, you've got software, you've got everybody working together commonly in a common enterprise that will produce a result that will be a surprise, to some extent, to all of them. And I think it's wonderful.

"I think that's why it's especially exciting to be in film at this moment in the coming new millennium."

Conclusion

In this final section, I was asked to pull together my thoughts on this book as a whole—what I learned. To begin with, of the volume of excellent advice on writing I will leave it to you to decide what is most relevant to you. After conducting these interviews and then going through the extensive editing process, I got to know them intimately. Yet, as I reviewed the manuscript one last time prior to turning it in, I still found the interviews fresh, fascinating, informative, and timely. I realize that I will continue to refer to this book myself to keep my thinking on track.

By Lew Hunter's standards, I haven't earned the right to an opinion yet. I haven't been down the screenwriting road long enough to truly have a completely informed opinion, I would agree. Nevertheless, after completing this book, I have come to a few conclusions. Skipping the overwhelming amount of wonderful scriptwriting notes, what shines through most clearly in these interviews is that film and television is a business first and foremost and art second—a very distant second. It makes sense because being artistic means taking a risk, and the money backers want what my father humorously told me he always sought in business. In fact, he had a plaque made with the quote. It reads, "All I want is an honest advantage." The system wants security and so the decision makers judge a script in front of them by looking to the past for what has succeeded. That's why we seem to have films that are cut from the same mold as other successful films—*Die Hard* on a boat, *Die Hard* on a train, etc. They trust that formula to return a profit and they will stay with it until it fails to perform.

That doesn't mean that art doesn't exist in Hollywood, because clearly it does. However, the system is unmistakably driven by the need for profit. "A show can actually be marginal in households but do very, very well demographically in the eighteen- to thirty-four-year-old female/male demographics. So that becomes a show you can sell on Madison Avenue for more money."—Stephen J. Cannell. "Studios generally make genre films, and that's because they know how to sell them to people. Rarely do you see studios sell mixed-genre films."—Sandy Weinberg. It's the bottom line first. And the considerations that go into those decisions usually are a complicated mix of Who is going to star in it?, What has been popular lately (what do the backers trust that they can sell and make a profit on)?, and so on.

Pretty Woman is a perfect example of Hollywood avoiding a risky script and instead having the original script rewritten to conform to a standard, happy ending/fairy tale format. You see, the original script (titled *$3,000*) is an anti–fairy tale. It's a very dark piece in which the Julia Roberts character is a hooker with something like eight years' experience walking the streets, and who is a habitual drug user. The Jason Alexander character (the Richard Gere character's lawyer) runs a high-class prostitution business on the side, and the Gere character picks up the hooker from the street to save on the money he'd otherwise pay his attorney friend. When the week is up, the Gere character drives the Roberts character back to her low-income neighborhood. Along the way they get into a huge fight, and he kicks her out of the car, throws the three thousand dollars at her, and drives off. In the script's final scene, she's on a bus taking her roommate, who is dying of drug use, to Disneyland knowing she's going to die soon and there is nothing she can do to stop it.

A studio bought the script and then hired the original writer and others to deliver the fairy tale they wanted. To the studio's credit, they hired the original writer to begin the rewrite—very unusual in Hollywood. What came out of that process is *Pretty Woman*, and it did great at the box office. This is a case where the studio execs felt more secure with what they believed would *sell* best—going with their instincts. The original script, well worth reading, is a writer being artistic, taking a chance, and exploring a dark subject. I guess there are two lessons here: one, you can be artistic and win, and two, Hollywood prefers to go with what is already proven to succeed.

But there is another truth in Hollywood. While on the one hand, Hollywood strives to be safe, on the other hand, Hollywood loves and highly respects risk takers. For example, early in David Koepp's career, he turned down his first potential script sale to a major studio because the studio wanted to change it: "I originally was going to sell [*Bad Influence*] to Universal, but they wanted a bunch of changes that I just didn't feel good about. So, we went elsewhere and made it as a lower-budget independent film. . . . Casey Silver here at Universal was impressed that I went elsewhere with [it] rather than just take the deal and make the changes and try to live with it [that] he offered me an overall writing deal here, which I took." "In this business, people pay homage to somebody with a vision who sticks to that vision—not letting anyone corrupt it."—Ian Gurvitz. So, without a doubt, being a maverick can pay dividends.

The next lesson I learned is that contacts and perception are critical. "The industry goes much more on reputation and spin and perception and personality and contacts than it does on genuine talent."—Carelton Eastlake. That sentiment has come out in most of the interviews I have done in the last four years, whether they were for this book or for my newsletter. Talent is important, but how you get along with others and other political factors can outweigh the need for a high level of talent. "Because this is so collaborative [a business], among the people you work with on staff, the actors, the director, the studio, the network—you really have to learn to listen. That's one of the most important skills you can pick up from being in a room."—Ian Gurvitz. So, if you are one who shies away from politics, you are potentially ruining any chance at building a career in Hollywood. There are just too many talented people fighting to break in to ignore this truth. You need to network and be a team player.

Concerning story development, nearly all agree that the three-act structure is key. Only a couple of writers I've talked over the years refused to acknowledge this concept; however, I believe that their stories do conform to a three-act structure, whether they accept it or not. Certainly the most highly successful writers feel strongly that the three-act structure is critical.

As a screenwriter, understand that great screenwriting is structure and conflict. "Bill Goldman is so right when he says, 'Screenplays are three things: structure, structure, structure!' . . . 'Bill,' [I asked], 'could they also be three other things: conflict, conflict, conflict?' He agreed."—Lew Hunter. Lew put this out casually; however, he couldn't feel stronger about this. There is a lot of depth in his understanding of what structure and conflict mean. It's not the seemingly simple statement it appears to be.

Contained within Lew's understanding of conflict and structure are the complicated elements of character and plot. At UCLA they stress strongly that you need to know the teachings of Aristotle and Lajos Egri. *"There are no secrets [to writing].* They're all clearly illuminated by Aristotle two thousand years ago, and most recently in 1946 by Lajos Egri in *The Art of Dramatic Writing.* Those, in my opinion, are the two bibles of performance drama/comedy."—Lew Hunter. Aristotle teaches that story is plot. Egri teaches that story comes from character. I suggest that you read Aristotle's *Poetics* and Egri's book. If you haven't, it will be eye-opening and exciting.

The UCLA philosophy is that if you have a story that pays as much attention to plot as it does to character, you will have a strong story that will hold up over a standard 110-page script. It will have the potential for strong drama and unexpected twists and turns that will thrill readers and audiences.

Finally, the most important lesson I learned about what it takes to be a good writer is to write in a regimented and consistent manner. You learn this craft by doing. All the great writers here expressed this one thought: writers write all the time. Go back through the interviews; you'll find it. All of them wrote constantly and consistently; they made a habit of writing regularly. And they keep to that regimen to this day. That is a key to developing your craft.

It is my sincere hope that you got as much out of this book as I did putting it together. See you on the front lines of the screenwriting life.

Appendix: Screenwriting Software Programs

As *the editor* of the newsletter for the UCLA Writer's Block I get *a lot of questions from newcomers to our monthly social. The most common question, outside of UCLA class stuff, is about what scriptwriting software program I use. The answer is not a specific program because what I use may not be the best program for somebody else. I feel this is an important subject to address, so I added this chapter.*

The layout in this chapter is different from that of the rest of the book. It's not set out as question and answer. Instead, I asked the companies to write four to five pages on their program. I asked them to tell me in those pages why they first developed the program, how the market has changed, what were the problems along the way, and where are they heading in the future. In addition, each company has provided contact information at the end of their section.

I have not singled out any one program as being the best. All these pro-grams are high quality. Also, not all the programs on the market are covered. These are the ones I am most familiar with and are the most commonly used programs (in my opinion). There are programs for writers who want stand-alone systems, and there are programs for those who want templates or "add-ons" (programs that work over existing word processing programs such as WordPerfect or Microsoft Word).

Most writers' concerns, after money, fall into one of three categories. First, there are writers who want maximum control; they want to be able to tweak everything. Second, there are writers who want ease of operation; they don't need all the subtle controls, they want it simple—to be freed from having to deal with script format. Third, there are those who are expert with WordPerfect or Microsoft Word and who want to work with an add-on so they can stick with their favorite word processing program.

Before getting into the interviews, here are some basic screenwriting formatting terms as well as thoughts on what a scriptwriting program needs to do and to accomplish.

Script Elements

To begin with, a script is a technical document, and software companies often refer to "script elements," which are the technical, formatting requirements for scripts. A script serves two primary functions: it tells a story, and it contains key information that a production company's department heads need to know to prepare and budget for a shoot. The following page is a sample script page set up like a shooting script. It contains only the very basic script elements, enough to make my point and set up the interviews. If you want to know more, there are books on the market that get into greater detail.

ACTION/DESCRIPTION paragraph: This is, in essence, the prose writing, nondialogue text. "Action/ description" paragraph formatting is basically standard paragraph writing.

BASIC SCRIPT ELEMENTS

Scene #

30 EXT. ISLAND BEACH—NIGHT ◄——— Slug Line

Scene #

30

Action/
Description

The SEALs have linked up. Trent pulls alongside one of the
two swimmer scouts and speaks in quiet, low tones.

                    TRENT ◄——————— Character Name
          Anything?

                    LINDSAY
          No, Boss. No movement. No sound.

Trent checks the homing device then gives the MOVE OUT
signal. They silently and alertly patrol down the beach,
staying in the shadows.

They find THE ADMIRAL'S CLOTHES with the homing device in a
knotted-up pile, washed ashore with other debris. Lindsay
bags it and the unit patrols inland.
                          Transition ————► CUT TO:

30A INT. SEAL DEBRIEFING ROOM—DAY   30A

The SEAL squad stands casually around LCDR PARKER (mid 30's,
tall, and slim) as he takes down notes.

                    TRENT
                    (wryly) ◄——— Parenthetical
          We found this.

Trent dumps the contents of the bag on the table.

                    TRENT (CONT'D) ◄——— Dialogue continued
          The Island was clean. We found no
          sign of any activity at all.

Something in the debris catches Parker's eye, and he picks
at it.

                    PARKER
          What's your opinion?

                    TRENT
          The Chief thinks it's debris from a
          diesel sub.

                    PARKER
          A Diesel sub?

*CHARACTER NAMES: are set out in capital letters and placed on the
page near the center, a tab, if you will, in the middle area of the page. This
way all the names start at the same spot in the middle of the page.
DIALOGUE: is about 3.5 inches in width and is, in effect, set up by moving
the left and right margins in by an inch or so.*

PAGINATION: As a script is written, the way that a page breaks is important. If a character is in mid-dialogue, that character's name has to reappear on the next page and usually there is an indication that the dialogue is continuing from the previous page. When a scene continues from one page to the next, that, too, is indicated in some scripts.

PARENTHETICALS: The writer can define a character's line delivery using a parenthetical. This will appear on the line below the character's name and, like the character name, is nearly centered on the page.

SLUG LINE: a single line of text set out in all capital letters with at least one line space before and after. The slug line is the first line in a scene; it defines three things: whether the scene is an interior location (INT.) or an exterior location (EXT.), the name of the location, and the time of day (DAY, NIGHT, EVENING, etc.).

TRANSITIONS: define how the scene changes from one scene to the next. For example: CUT TO, DISSOLVE, FADE OUT, *etc.—all technical terms for the editing people, and it may help the director decide on how to shoot a scene. Some writers feel that it gives a stronger visualization to the reading.*

Now, a shooting script is different from a spec script. A spec script is formatted using the above basic script elements. When a production company makes plans to shoot a script, it has to be analyzed by the various departments: props, makeup, wardrobe, sets, location, etc. This is the stage where script formatting becomes a necessity. A script, as I said, is a technical document; it helps the departments break down or determine what they need to provide for the shoot and what it will cost. Location people can quickly look at the locations they need to find. The director can see how many day or night scenes he or she has to plan for. Set designers can quickly list the interior and exterior sets they need to build, and so on.

Once a production company is ready to shoot a script, the script will be "locked," which means that scenes are numbered and the number of the page that the scenes are on is fixed. After that, if there are any more script changes, the changes cannot *change the page number that the scenes are on or change* any of the *"fixed"* scene numbers. Yes, it is more than a little confusing, especially to the uninitiated. At this point, if a new scene is added, then you have to define it without renumbering the whole script. This is called creating *"A"* and *"B"* scenes and, similarly, *"A"* and *"B"* pages. Simply put, if I add a scene after scene 30, it becomes scene 30A. If those changes force a new page to the script, the additional page become an *"A"* page. In the sample page I have included above, if a scene was added on, say, page 17, after scene 30, and the changes forced a new page to the script, then the new pages would be numbered 17A, 17B, etc. Page 18 will start exactly where it started before the additions or deletions. This may mean that page 17A has only one word on it, if that one word forced a new page.

This is all the further I am going to take this. Hopefully, this is enough to get this one basic point across: a script is a technical document that has to be laid out in a specific format.

I have just touched on the very basics here. There is a lot more to formatting, and this is where the scriptwriting software companies come into play. They have taken all these formatting requirements and automated them. A writer no longer has to dwell on spacing, scene numbering, page numbering, pagination, centering character names, etc. He or she can focus on the story and let the program make the correct formatting decisions.

As the formatting rules have changed slightly over the years, and as thousands of people have used them and provided feedback to the companies, the software providers have modified their programs. These companies have put a lot of hard work into each program or the generation of a new program. Each company was started by one person, and his or her program has become something personal, something they are extremely proud to market and defend. I asked each person to tell me in a personal way why they got into this business and what problems they were striving to solve. I was fascinated by all the personal accounts. Here are their stories.

MOVIE MASTER
(IBM Windows and Macintosh)

'We're here to help'

Jules Leni

Background

In 1984, I hired a computer programmer who had graduated a few years earlier from NYU's Film and Television Department. Computer programming was his livelihood; his passion was writing screenplays. Although my company had nothing to do with the film business, he persuaded me to allow him devote a portion of his time to a product that would combine his two skills. Two years later, Movie Master was born, a state-of-the-art stand-alone word processing program that automated the tedious (and time-consuming) tasks of formatting screenplays and sitcom scripts.

In those days, most writers were still using typewriters. The latest Intel processor was a 286 with a clock speed of 8mHz (as compared to today's blazing 200mHz 586s). PCs were limited to 640K of RAM, and a 10mB hard drive cost $500. The Macintosh was found almost exclusively in schools and art studios.

Not surprisingly, Movie Master took the Hollywood script factories by storm. For the first time, writers could concentrate on their scripts without the distraction of setting tabs, typing MORE and CONTINUED, or counting pages. Movie Master gave the Hollywood studios and their writers what they wanted—ease of use, flexibility, speed, and lots of hand-holding.

In the early days, Hollywood writers were generally paranoid about computers. Movie Master's technical support staff gained an early and much-appreciated reputation for providing extended and toll-free phone support. It is this commitment to helping writers that motivates our efforts today as much as it did in the early years, and that may well explain the enduring loyalty of Movie Master users. Since its introduction, Movie Master has been used by most of the television sitcom shows.

In 1991, the programmer who had written the program left my company to pursue other interests. Because I was engaged in other activities myself, program development (a never-ending aspect of the software business) languished until 1995 when, in response to persistent pleas from an increasing number of Movie Master users, I searched for and found a top-notch programmer to write a new version of Movie Master for the Windows and Macintosh environments. The initial release of the Windows version occurred in October 1996.

The New Environment

In some ways, screenwriters have not changed over the years—particularly in their aversion to computer technology. 'I'm a writer, not a computer person,' is the common introduction of writers calling our support line. Yet, more and more writers are moving with the flow, as evidenced by the growing use of e-mail and the channel for sales and technical inquiries.

While there are still a surprising number of writers who stubbornly defy the "DOS is dead" maxim, the IBM-compatible universe has become a Windows universe. Twenty-five percent of the writers who upgraded from Movie Master DOS in the first three months use Windows 95; similarly, 25 percent of our sales inquiries come from Mac users.

The biggest challenge in writing the Windows version was matching the simplicity and speed of the DOS program. Our goal in the Windows version was twofold: I wanted the new Movie Master to be state of the art in its programming, in keeping with its ancestry, and to accommodate the thousands of DOS Movie Master users who are accustomed to the speed, flexibility, and keyboard convenience of the old program. Furthermore, many of the Movie Master faithful are still laboring on 386 computers, a requirement which added to the already harsh demands on our programmers.

In order to encourage Macintosh programmers to work in the Windows environment, Microsoft has created programming tools that facilitate the conversion of Windows code to the Macintosh environment. Thus the Macintosh version of Movie Master is essentially an image of the Windows programs, with modifications to reflect the keyboard as well as the 'look and feel' to which Macintosh users are accustomed.

The Strengths of Movie Master

Movie Master pioneered the Easytype™ script entry system, which automates all basic scriptwriting and formatting without repetitive tabbing and typing. Pressing the Enter key when you finish an element moves the cursor directly to the start of the next logical script element. (Page numbers and scene numbers are inserted automatically.) You interrupt the flow with a single keystroke to start a new scene or to insert a special element (e.g., Action between Characters). Either way, Movie Master reduces formatting to a one-key process.

The Windows and Macintosh versions of Movie Master provide writers with additional convenience features, such as:

* multiple undos (up to 20 levels), complete font, margin and line-height control, including font selection, size, and color (either selected globally or for elements or selected text), plus a format editor that allows additional lines (up to 75 per page) to fit onto a page.
* an index card/scene shuffler, which allows scripts to be viewed in outline form, scene order to be rearranged, and scene headings and descriptions to be printed.
* the ability to copy and paste formatted files from any Windows word processor.
* the ability to write script notes (as well as to import graphics, text,

spreadsheets, sound files, etc. via the OLE function) that can be displayed or hidden at will.
• a 4-color highlighter which doubles as a color-coded bookmark.

What has made Movie Master a favorite among the production companies is its powerful handling of revisions (A and B pages and scenes) as well as an assortment of breakdown reports for production planning. The latter include separate reports breaking out interior and exterior scene slug lines, listings of characters in each scene, slug lines with the first action in the scene, and the dialogue for each character by scene.

Because a script processing program, by its very nature, is a complex piece of software, we have taken great pains to make Movie Master easy to learn and use, and we also provide a level of technical assistance that is unique to our industry.

Built into the program is a help system which combines drag-and-drop inquiries with easy access tools for exploring the program's manual on-screen. Clicking on the context help icon on the toolbar displays a pointer which you can drag onto any menu or toolbar item. Then click again to display the help topic for the desired item. The manual navigation tools include a "hyperviewer" which allows you to cruise through the help file and navigate through the many available topics with ease. The Find+™ feature scans the entire contents of each topic for a desired word or phrase.

Our Changing Focus

The number of movies produced by the Hollywood studios each year represent fewer than 1 percent of the screenplays submitted. Many of these submissions are discarded without being read because the writers did not take the trouble to format them correctly.

Most aspiring writers may well find it difficult to justify spending $249 (the current street price) for a specialized program containing features that they will not need until they sell a screenplay (at which time the issue of affordability becomes a moot point). For that reason, we now offer Movie Master in two editions: The Production Edition includes both submission and production tools for screenplays, sitcoms, and stage plays, and allows format customization. The Freelance Edition, which sells for $129, includes the submission formats only. An upgrade from the Freelance Edition to the Production Edition is also available.

Making screenplays easier to write by eliminating the distracting hassle of formatting will hopefully encourage talented writers to realize their dream of creating the Great American Screenplay. Who knows whether the outcome of these efforts might just be the next *Star Wars* or *Jaws* or *Raiders of the Lost Ark?*

Movie Master is the only script processing program to offer toll-free phone support, and Movie Master offers technical support via e-mail and its web site (www.scriptwriting.com). Upgrades can be downloaded directly from the web site.

ScriptThing
(DOS and Windows/Macintosh available summer of 1997)

ScriptThing is a stand-alone word processor designed specifically for film, television, theater, and multimedia scriptwriting. Script-Perfection [Schafer's company name and the name of his original DOS scriptwriting program] has been creating scriptwriting software since 1991; the first version of ScriptThing was released in 1994. Writing faster and more efficiently is ScriptThing's goal. ScriptThing automatically handles all the hassles of industry standard formatting, letting you focus on writing your story as fast as you can get your thoughts onto the [computer] screen.

Ken Schafer

I'm a writer myself, and I also spent several years as a script co-ordinator on a number of TV shows. None of the existing programs really did everything I wanted, in the way I wanted them to. They either didn't do all the page breaks automatically, or they didn't have the power inputting options I wanted, or they were limited or, I felt, poorly designed in some other way.

By doing my own program, I could make it my wish list and simply put in any formatting feature I ever wanted as a writer (or as a script coordinator in production). Having worked with a lot of other writers, I knew that I wanted to create a program that almost anyone could work with at whatever level he or she felt comfortable.

So, if you're one of those writers who ranks learning how to use new software only slightly above being audited, then ScriptThing lets you write and edit your script knowing only about two or three key-strokes, using pull-down menus, a mouse, and so on. However, if you don't *mind* learning more, there are all sorts of quick keys that you can use to make it go even faster. The program lets you put in char-acter names with one keystroke, or build entire scene headings with as few as five or six keystrokes, and so on. I figure that most people use only about 20 to 30 percent of the program's capabilities, and that's fine, but for most people, like me, it's all there under the hood in you want to go search it out.

The first thing on my wish list was to have all the page breaks with (MORE)s, (CONT'D)s, and so on done automatically. Why couldn't a scriptwriting program act like any other normal word pro-cessor and automatically put in the page breaks as you write? The only difference would be that it would have to follow all the arcane page breaking rules of the particular script format that you're working in, whether that is television sitcom, feature film, a CD-ROM script, whatever format. This is exactly what ScriptThing does.

I'm also a very lazy typist and I hate typing anything that I don't have to. Most script formats have inherent in them a LOT of repetitive text: character names, INT./EXT., locations, times of day, and what-not, and, although other programs at the time dealt with page breaking in one way or another, none of them really dealt with the problem of repetitive text much beyond the input of character names.

After the page breaks and the repetitive typing, to me, it was also very important to be able to keep an entire script in one file, and to have the whole file loaded in RAM on an average user's machine. I think these fast, high-powered computers that are available nowadays have made a lot of programmers very lazy—and I'm not talking specifically about programmers for the film industry, either—they rely too heavily on the computer's speed and resources to take up the slack for inefficient programming.

"My own laptop computer at the time was a 286, and so I can tell you I spent a LOT of time fine-tuning ScriptThing to make it fast and memory efficient so that it would run on some pretty basic systems. Our DOS versions of ScriptThing run quite happily on the average 286 machine; they can keep about 150 pages of a script in memory and still paginate real-time! [On the screen as you work.]

Another thing that I always wanted from a scriptwriting program was the flexibility to adjust margins individually, and cheat stuff around. Speaking as a writer, I know that if I'm locked into the word processor's margins, I too often find myself editing to make the format look pretty, rather than editing for the best needs of the script. It's not uncommon to have a line of dialogue that's word-wrapping badly, pushing one word over to the next line. That makes the speech one line longer and can screw up your page break. With other programs you could only set the margins globally, you couldn't adjust just one margin line without affecting the whole script. It drove me crazy. So, this is the sort of flexibility that I made sure I put into ScriptThing.

Also, as a script coordinator, I was working with a lot of freelancers. This meant dealing with scripts coming from and going to a lot of different word processors, which is why ScriptThing has the ability to export a working version of the script as a fully qualified Word-Perfect file, Microsoft Word file, RFT file (which you can take over to virtually any Windows or Mac word processor), or formatted ASCII file. Therefore, you can get a script from ScriptThing into most any other program, and the import on ScriptThing for Windows is even better. You can directly open scripts written in MS Word (including Word 7.0), WordPerfect (5.1 and above), those saved in RFT format (which most Mac and Windows word processors support), formatted ASCII, and several other specialized formats.

I was recently snowed in over Christmas at my parents' house in Massachusetts with only their Mac to write on. I had to work on some outlines, so I did them in MS Word on the Mac, then I e-mailed them without any conversion to my home in San Diego. Once I got home, I downloaded them onto my PC, and ScriptThing for Windows opened the Mac Word files without a hitch.

It's funny, I never wanted to develop ScriptThing for Windows, and now I can't even imagine going back to the DOS version. I was basically dragged into developing the Windows version kicking and screaming. As I saw it, at the time, the big advantages of Windows over DOS were the WYSIWYG (what you see is what you get) display and fonts . . . neither of which seemed particularly useful for scriptwriting. I mean, since a script doesn't use anything other than courier 10cpi, and that already is basically WYSIWYG in DOS, what's the point? The speed of any Windows program will plummet in comparison to its DOS version. What will run on a 286 in DOS needs a 486DX in Windows with at least four to five times the RAM. But *people wanted Windows.*

What I found out, however, is although the Windows environment doesn't necessarily offer the user a lot, it *does* offer a lot of things to the programmer. Such as handling all the printers. That gave me access to line control in hundredths of an inch, regardless of what printer is used; and that opened up a whole new range of ways to cheat the length of the script. That gave the program a flexibility I couldn't even *consider* implementing in the DOS program.

Also, in the process of moving the program to Windows, I had to recode a lot of the functions of the DOS program, and I suddenly found myself improving features that I had thought already were perfect. I'd suddenly see new and better ways of doing things. Such as, easier editing using Drag'n'Drop, changing fonts, rewriting in color, alias substitution text, unprecedented control over the layout of individual pages, and more.

For example, the DOS version lets you view your script as if it were on index cards. ScriptThing for Windows allows you to actually write and edit on the cards themselves, letting you write whole outlines for new scripts on index cards.

Since Windows shares the clipboard with any application that cares to use it, cut-and-paste importing/exporting to and from other Windows programs was suddenly an option, as was a graphic WYSIWYG print preview, and a lot of other nifty things I don't have space to tell you about it.

But I'm never satisfied. I'm constantly working on ScriptThing... either I'll come up with a new need in my own writing, or a user or production company will call up with some ideas for a great new feature that no one's ever wanted before, or someone will e-mail me a suggestion for how I could improve an existing one. I'm constantly adding new stuff and giving the user even more control. People want to know how long it took me to write the program, and I never have a good answer. It's a continually evolving process; it'll probably never be done.

Direct contact can be made at: ScriptPerfection Enterprises, 4901 Morena Blvd., Suite 105, San Diego, CA 92117-3424, (800) 450-9450, http://www.ScriptPerfection.com

SCRIPTWARE
(Windows and DOS)

Steve Sashen

While getting my master's degree in screenwriting from Columbia University, I tried every program available to help get the stories out of my head and onto the page. With everything I used—from WordPerfect with a bunch of macros to the stand-alone programs—I felt frustrated. Macros and key commands got in the way of my creative flow. After-the-fact pagination and formatting took just as long to double-check as doing it all by hand. I knew there had to be a better and easier way to write scripts; a way that let my creative juices flow and let me forget about formatting.

"Using my background in cognitive psychology, I analyzed how scripts are put together and how we naturally think when we write and type. I realized that script elements have simple physical relationships to each other: one script element is under another or to the right of another (or to the right or the left margin). When you're typing, "under" equals "Enter" and "to the right" equals "Tab." I also thought, "Different script elements—like Action, Scene Headings, etc.—have different formatting rules . . . so why couldn't a program determine the element and then format automatically, on the fly, as I'm writing?" By putting all that together, I had designed a way to type a script with the fewest possible keystrokes, where all the formatting and pagination and numbering happened in real time, on the screen. That way, all I would need to do is type and print!

I called the scriptwriting software companies at that time and offered them these ideas. I didn't want any money, I just wanted a word processor that handled scripts the way I thought they should be handled. But each company turned me down, saying that their products were fine and if I didn't like them, I didn't need to buy them. With that lucky rejection, I asked myself the five most dangerous words for someone with entrepreneurial spirit, "How hard could this be?" and I decided to make my own program.

Luckily, I was incredibly naive. I knew nothing about writing a software program, or running a company, or what programming languages could or couldn't do. All I knew was how my idea should look and feel. Had I known any of the things I didn't know, I would have never gotten into this business and risked every penny I ever earned plus another $200,000! But I was sure that my ideas were sound and that enough other people wanted what I wanted, and I ignored all my "advisors" and friends and started searching for a programmer.

At that time, my day job was stand-up comedy and acting—that's what was paying my way through film school. Then one evening, at a comedy club, I was toting around my laptop case (I did most of my writing in comedy club green rooms while waiting to go on stage) and a guy with a *PC* magazine T-shirt asked what kind of computer I had. His name was Stuart Greenberg, and he was the senior programmer at *PC* magazine's labs. I told him about my scriptwriting word processor idea and he said, "I know how to make that happen. It's an idea that's never been done before, but I'm sure I can do it."

The next day over lunch we formed Cinovation and started creating Scriptware. Between Stu's ideas about code and mine about design, we totally reinvented what a word processor was and what it could do. Stu had access to a new programming language that wouldn't be for sale for almost a year; that gave us the technology to do everything we needed. The only thing it didn't give us was more of his time.

After a year, it became clear that we needed more programmers to work on this project. It was much bigger than we had imagined. After much searching, hiring, and firing, we found Larry Houbre. Larry took over the day-to-day creating of the program while Stu managed and designed the architecture of the code. Meanwhile, I was convincing lawyers, accountants, graphic designers, and manufacturers to work for free until we had a product to ship.

We showed an early version of Scriptware at the ShowBiz Expo in

Los Angeles in 1991. People went nuts! When I showed them that typing 'int.' [lower case or uppercase] created a Scene Heading—uppercase, proper spacing and margins, proper numbering (if they wanted it)—they were stunned and ecstatic. One women burst into tears as she was typing and just kept saying, over and over, "This is just what I've been dreaming of." She later became one of our best salespeople!

Unfortunately, computer software being what it is, it took us another year to finish the program. I had hundreds of orders that I couldn't process and I was losing money like crazy trying to keep the project afloat. I had thirty-three credit cards, each one maxed out, and I was paying off one with the other (someday I'll write a book about how to do that). My hair fell out, literally! A three-inch patch of hair was just gone one day. After a few months, it still hadn't grown back and my doctor said, "Stress induced. You can wait about two years and it'll grow back or with some hydrocortisone it will take two months." I knew the longer I had my bald patch, the more likely it would be that I'd shave my head to match, so I got the shots.

In the months before Scriptware was ready to ship, I was trying to get on welfare and collect food stamps. I was hundreds of thousands of dollars in debt, and my programmers couldn't tell me when Scriptware would be ready. To say that this was one of the unhappiest times of my life would be an understatement. I couldn't imagine bailing on the project and leaving my friends, family, and investors (mostly friends and family) in the dirt. But I also couldn't imagine how I was going to make this all work.

On November 11, 1992, my one-bedroom apartment/office was filled with friends who duplicated disks, stuffed boxes, and addressed packages. My sister (mistress of the blow-dryer) operated the shrink-wrap heat gun like a pro. The next day, much to the chagrin of my UPS driver, we shipped 200 copies of Scriptware.

Almost instantly my hopes and ideas proved themselves. Within six months, Scriptware became the best-selling scriptwriting word processor. We got rave reviews in the *New York Times* and the *Journal* (of the Writer's Guild of America, west). We got phone calls and letters from writers, thanking us for giving them more than they had ever imagined. Script typists at studios let us know they were more productive with Scriptware than they had ever been in their twenty-year careers.

Then the work began! Improving the product, growing the company, supporting our customers. I was doing it all (except for the programming, which was still Larry and Stu). Once it was clear that I was a full-time software person, and not a full-time performer, I moved Cinovation out of my Manhattan apartment and out to Boulder, Colorado (post-earthquake beachfront property). Scriptware keeps growing. We've added hundreds of features to the program. We created the first Windows-compatible program. All the reviews still rank Scriptware at the top. The company has doubled in size every year. We now have over sixty television shows and dozens of movies using Scriptware. We have over 10,000 customers, a full-time support staff, sales staff, and programming staff in a beautiful downtown Boulder office. Scriptware can be found in stores and catalogs around the world, and increasing competition has only seen an even larger increase in Scriptware's sales. Each new competitor has un-successfully tried to take Scriptware's ideas (we've seen that anything someone else does, we can do, but there are many things Scriptware does that others will never be able to accomplish).

Now we're looking at the future. We're constantly improving Scriptware—adding features, speedups and improvements. Our Mac version will be shipping in the second quarter of 1997. Our interactive version around the same time. We're looking to expand Scriptware's power so that the script file can actually become the blueprint for a production—producers, department heads, accountants, directors, editors, and others using the same program and file to do their jobs. We're making strides to increase distribution domestically and internationally. Cinovation has grown well beyond what I envisioned in the shower in 1989 and we're positioning the company to do tens of millions of dollars in sales while helping writers in the creative arts around the world!

Scriptware is the best overall program for scriptwriters on the market today.
—*Journal (of the Writer's Guild of America, west)*

For more info: http://www.scriptware.com or 303/786-7899

SCRIPT WIZARD
Scriptwriting software for
Microsoft Word For Windows

Stefani Warren

A Little History

In 1984, personal computers were still new, and you could list the number of scriptwriters using them on the back of a couple of napkins. I was one of them, and through the coincidence of background and a chance encounter, I became a consultant for The Writers Computer Store—the now-famous California retail venture catering exclusively to writers in Hollywood and elsewhere. Among other things, I taught screenwriters, playwrights, and production typists how to use the then-preferred combination of programs (Microsoft Word with Prokey or Smartkey, and Scriptor) to write and print scripts.

Three years and over nine hundred clients later, it was clear to me, as it was to a number of other people, that there had to be a better and simpler way. So, in the fall of 1987, when Microsoft released the first version of Word to include a programming language, I began to develop the first full-service script processing add-on.

The first edition of the Warren Script Applications (WSA) was released in January of 1988, and we have been upgrading and enhancing our applications in lockstep with Microsoft ever since. Our current product, Script Wizard, is a Word for Windows add-on. We have two current versions of the basic program, one for Word 6.0/7.0 and another for the new Word for Windows 8.0. Script Wizard turns Word into a full-service script processor and supports a wide variety of professional script formats, including screenplay, stage play, sitcom, soap, 2-column A/V, 3-column, and Interactive.

Why Word?

Back at the dawn of the PC revolution, Word was not the most popular word processor—WordPerfect had the lion's share of the market. When it came to typing scripts, however, there was nothing that could come close to Word's style sheet for speed and ease of use.

Encouraged by the success of our program and Movie Master (the first successful stand-alone program), other developers began to get into the act. By the end of 1991, script processing programs had become a software niche and a clear division in the marketplace had materialized—especially Word; and there were those who *hated* the full-service word processing environment—especially Word. Today, almost ten years later, that distinction still applies, although many more people like and use Word now.

Off and on over the years, I have been asked, "Why has Warren & Associates never developed a stand-alone program?" One reason was that I saw no need for it—the stand-alone camp has been admirably represented—in fact, overrepresented—from the get-go. Then too, like the writers who fill the ranks of Script Wizard users, I *prefer* using a full-service word processor and believe it to be the best working environment for the independent scriptwriter.

No specialty product can provide a writer with the wealth of features that the major software developers provide. The much-hyped freedom to create was given to us, not by any one program, but by

Microsoft when it developed the innovative technology of paragraph styles and allowed users to assign their key combinations to them. The rest—in every scriptwriting product to come onto the market since—has been bells and whistles.

Word always gives writers the most versatile writing, editing, and proofing tools and the biggest collection of reference utilities. Only one program, such as Word, can provide the tools a writer needs to customize the way the program looks and feels and works, to his or her own satisfaction. Word provides all kinds of help to writers who are translating work between languages or trying to write scripts in English for the first time, and the list of benefits goes on and on.

Recently I have been asked if I plan to incorporate the Tab/Backspace convention into Script Wizard. In that convention (developed by Steve Sashen for his stand-alone program), writers are prompted, at every touch of the Tab or Enter key, for a formatting choice (character lists, transitions, etc.). This gives a novice a certain amount of security, and all of us in the script processing software arena have incorporated similar features in our latest releases. Nevertheless, Script Wizard is a tool developed originally for use by working professional writers who do not need to be prompted at every change of element, and I do not ever intend to alter that design premise. Writers do not write 'elements'—they write *scenes*. Hunt-and-peck drafting techniques are OK when you're stumbling around trying to get a scene going, but a killer if you've got the thing wired and are chasing inspiration. The goal is to be able to keep up with the scene unfolding in the mind's eye, and nothing can match our Alt- or Ctrl-key combinations for speed and fluidity when you're on a roll.

Despite my focus on the needs of the working writer, I am attentive to the fact that newcomers to scriptwriting are looking increasingly to this category of software for help and guidance in mastering the form. We have always included a glossary and other special information in our documentation to help the novice where we can. In Script Wizard 8.0, we have developed "A Primer on Script Writing," which includes instruction on the basic parts of a script and other writing requirements, some fundamental Do's and Don'ts, and a handful of produced scripts on disk for study and review.

While I'm on this subject, it's important to remember that there is a clear distinction between the process of writing a script and the process of *formatting* one for professional purposes. There seems to be an implicit promise (in advertising campaigns and elsewhere) that using a script processing program will actually help someone write a sellable script. Scriptwriting software, however, is a typing tool, *period*, and any suggestion to the contrary is terribly misleading.

If we include the cost of Word, the person who purchases Script Wizard has paid the same amount of money as they would have for a stand-alone program. Script Wizard is a deal only if someone already owns Word. But the real deal in using an add-on is its cost-*effectiveness*. For writers who spend most of their working hours at a typewriter, the value of having one program do it all, and having the time spent mastering that typewriter pay off in every literary endeavor, cannot be estimated. For those who want to keep up with the state of the art, the upgrades are as much a blessing as they are a hassle.

What's Next at Warren & Associates?

At the outset, my goal was to make it possible for working writers to invest in and learn one program instead of three (and to cut down on some of the hours I spent driving around LA every week). As time went on, and I began to develop custom applications for production companies, it became clear that Word could also be the nexus of a full-service production office application.

Word for Windows 8.0 has outstanding new features to appeal to the scriptwriting and producing community and, true to its advertising, is one of the most compelling upgrades in the product's history. Document maps, Hyperlinks, on-line editing, improved revision tracking, the corkboard-like Notes utility in Outlook and other new and improved features make Word a program of choice for interactive script writers as well as those working in the standard formats.

But it is Visual Basic for Apps, the new Office programming language, that makes a fully integrated production office suite a viable proposition. With Word 8.0, we were able to simplify and streamline our shooting draft tools and eliminate most of the opportunities for user error. Our goal is to make Script Wizard the centerpiece of a reasonably priced production office package, with budgeting, scheduling and a raft of predefined report and business forms geared to meeting the day-to-day needs of the smaller independent companies.

I suppose that one of these years, I will install a new version of Word and be disappointed, but it hasn't happened yet, and I don't expect it will until well into the next century.

FINAL DRAFT
(IBM Windows and Macintosh)

Lynn Hacking

In 1990, Ben Cahan and Marc Madnick decided the world needed an easier and faster way to get the idea for a screenplay, sitcom, or stage play out of one's head and onto paper. Ben is a software engineer, and Marc is a numbers guy. Both were bitten by the bug which dictates that one must create an idea for a film—the Hollywood bug. They immediately recognized the need for an industry-specific set of screenwriting tools. Together, they created Final Draft, a program that has evolved into the preferred screenwriting software of Hollywood, and therefore of the entertainment industry worldwide.

Todd Holland is the multiple Emmy recipient who writes, directs and produces such shows as *The Larry Sanders Show*. What he expressed is exactly what we at B.C. Software set out to achieve: Final Draft is the Swiss Army knife of script software: the original, bona fide, ask-for-it-by-name, accept-no-substitution solution to the mundane terrors of the blank page. Final Draft has many, many features that make creating screenplays, television scripts and stage plays easier and faster than ever before.

We are not in the software business as much as in the entertainment industry. We are not selling our features as much as helping people realize their dreams. Like a character in a well-written script, one will slowly unravel Final Draft's character. This sleek little program is packed with features such as automatic industry-standard formatting and pagination as well as character and scene heading storage, to merely scratch the surface of its abilities. It has satisfied the most demanding professionals, on an interface that is simple enough for the computer novice to begin writing with immediately, whether they own a Windows machine or a Macintosh.

Forget having to learn the business of script formatting; Final Draft does it for you. Our goal is to get the writer writing, and it is reflected in everything we do in our Los Angeles offices. Need help and can't find it in the manual? Our technical support team is there to help with human voices that understand the creative mentality. Many on our team were recruited from the ranks of working Hollywood professionals.

Without question, our user base is composed of the most popular actors, directors, producers and writers in the business. Many of them, including Robert Altman, John Badham, Steven Bochco, Terry Gilliam, Tom Hanks, Lawrence Kasdan, Paul Mazursky, Anthony Minghella, Christopher McQuarrie and Sydney Pollack have graciously given us incredible quoted testimonials to use in our promotions. Why? Because Final Draft is the set of drums that Hollywood beats out screenplays on, and when these important people speak, everyone listens. Including us. Especially us, for when a seasoned professional makes valid suggestions for improving the program, our in-house engineering staff gets to work immediately, incorporating those improvements into Final Draft. It is simply common sense.

But don't take our word for it, take theirs ... Lawrence Kasdan, who wrote *Raiders of the Lost Ark* and *The Empire Strikes Back*, says,

"Final Draft is the only program that works for me. The basic concepts, combined with the relentless improvements and innovations, have made me a believer for life. Long live Final Draft!" Anthony Minghella won an academy award for Best Director for *The English Patient* (which also won Best Picture) using Final Draft. This is what he has to say: "Final Draft is the writer's secret weapon. It works, it's simple, it evolves, and it's supported. It belongs, with the pen, in the list of essentials." Christopher McQuarrie won an academy award for Best Original Screenplay for *The Usual Suspects*, written on Final Draft. He says, "Final Draft is what allows me to do a six-week rewrite in twelve hours . . . but don't tell Disney." Tom Hanks has successfully made the leap from actor to writer-director using Final Draft. He states that "Final Draft makes it possible to simply imagine the movie in script form. If you can think in cinematic terms, you can write in the terms of cinema." Sydney Pollack has made numerous suggestions to Final Draft and is one of our staunchest supporters. *Out of Africa*, *The Firm*, and *Sabrina* were all brought to the screen via our software. He has said, "I found the Final Draft program facilitated the work enormously, worked flawlessly, and was a pleasure to use. Final Draft has become the standard by which all other programs are measured. If you went to the movies, saw a hit television show or a stage play recently, chances are that it was created with Final Draft.

For more information call (310) 636-4711 in LA or (800) 231-4055 outside of LA, or you can visit our web site at http://www. bcsoftware.com